MURDER AT NO.4 EUSTON SQUARE

'Gripping, Gothic and deeply poignant.' *Mail on Sunday*

'A meticulously researched book.' **Brian Viner,** *Daily Mail*

'Sinclair McKay is an accomplished and talented author with a rare skill... True crime fans and history buffs will enjoy this book, coming away with an enthralling true crime story and a new knowledge and understanding of Victorian London.' *Crime Traveller*

THE MILE END MURDER

'McKay is excellent at evoking the flavour of the area. He combines social history… keen sleuthing and a pleasing flourish of conjecture. It's a winning combination.' *The Spectator*

'A fascinating book, by turns riveting and unsettling, and wonderfully rich in period detail.' **Craig Brown,** *Mail on Sunday*

'Tale of crime and police incompetence… told in lurid detail.'
James Marriot, *The Times*

THE SECRET LIFE

'I found this a truly breath-takin

'McKay has succeeded in honouring a genuinely remarkable group of people in a solid, often entertaining, and above all warm-hearted way.'
Daily Mail

THE SECRET LISTENERS

'Painstakingly researched and fascinating as his bestselling *The Secret Life of Bletchley Park*, and an essential companion to it.' *Daily Mail*

THE SPIES OF WINTER

'As he has proved before, Sinclair McKay has no peers when it comes to the history of Bletchley Park – and its aftermath. Lucid, well-researched and rich in detail, *The Spies of Winter* is a valuable addition to the genre.' *Daily Mail*

'Recreates the unique atmosphere of this extraordinary place… remarkable.' *The Daily Telegraph*

'A portrait of one of the most remarkable brain factories the world has ever seen.' Max Hastings

'This very readable and competent book captures well the extraordinary atmosphere of eccentrics working hard together in almost complete secrecy.' *The Guardian*

MURDER
AT No. 4
EUSTON SQUARE

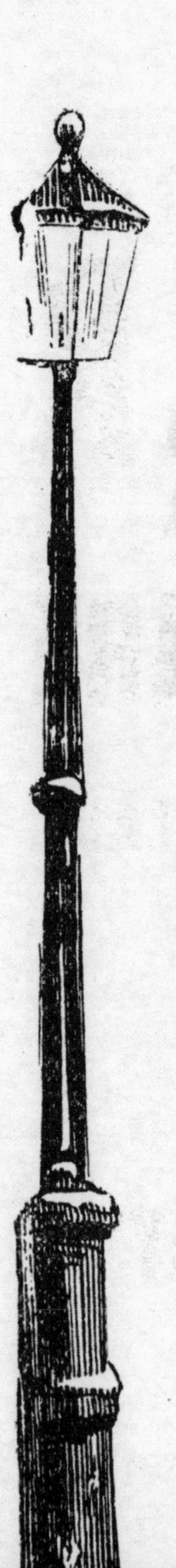

MURDER AT No. 4 EUSTON SQUARE

THE MYSTERY OF THE LADY IN THE CELLAR

SINCLAIR McKAY

Aurum

First published in hardback as *The Lady in the Cellar: Murder, Scandal and Insanity in Victorian Bloomsbury* in 2018 by White Lion Publishing, an imprint of The Quarto Group.
The Old Brewery, 6 Blundell Street
London, N7 9BH,
United Kingdom
T (0)20 7700 6700
www.QuartoKnows.com

This paperback edition first published in 2021 by Aurum

A catalogue record for this book is available from the British Library.

ISBN 978-0-7112-5583-8
Ebook ISBN 978-1-78131-799-0

10 9 8 7 6 5 4 3 2 1

Cover design by Paileen Currie and Maisy Ruffels
Typeset in Caslon by SX Composing DTP, Rayleigh, Essex, SS6 7EF
Printed by CPI Group (UK) Ltd, Croydon, CR0 4YY

Contents

'I had walled the monster up within the tomb!'

– *The Black Cat* by Edgar Allan Poe

Preface – The Dislocation of the Dead

Before its notoriety, the house presented an impeccable and genteel face to the city.

It stood four storeys tall, in the middle of a long, elegant Georgian terrace. The cream stucco frontage, the large French windows overlooking the leafy garden square, the covered, tiled porch before the front door and the first-floor balcony with decorative canopy above for shelter, spoke of some refinement. There were handsomely wrought, black ironwork railings, in front of steps that led down to a basement.

In that basement area, there was a door to the scullery and kitchen, and also a door to cellars that ran beneath the pavement above. These cellars were expressly intended – as stated in the leases for the houses in this terrace – for both coal and wine.[1] The house changed in different lights; if the spring evening burned with a crimson sunset, for instance, the stucco would glow a reflected pink, then a mesmerising lavender, against the darkening eastern sky.

So any prospective tenant approaching the smart black-painted front door of 4, Euston Square, in 1879, might – without any difficulty

– have imagined themselves a person of some distinction. And any servant coming to work here might lose themselves in daydreams of ownership. Within these walls were people who – both knowingly and otherwise – took on new identities.

Yet this prosperous-looking home stood just on the border of quite another kind of world. At the back of the house, at the very northern tip of Bloomsbury, and in the mews and the dusty streets and alleys of Somers Town beyond, the refined air gave way sharply to the heavy iron percussion of the railways. There was the grand classical terminus of Euston, its passenger locomotives pointing to the northern night; the goods trains feeding the sooty coal depots; towering cylindrical gas holders standing by the slick, thick oily canal; terraces of more ramshackle properties stained a permanent charcoal by the smoke. This district was a portal: into the great terminals – including nearby St Pancras and King's Cross – came countless newcomers to the city, from around the country, and from lands beyond.

London was seething with reinvention; and in order that its new, modern identity become fixed, the past was being exhumed.

Quite close by to the house in Euston Square, the ancient churchyard of St Pancras Old Church had, just a few years previously, been dug up to make way for train platforms and marshalling yards; centuries-old gravestones were extracted like old teeth, carried to the other end of the remaining graveyard and then rammed back into the earth, clustered tightly against each other around an old ash tree in an extraordinary circular pattern of pagan supplication. In charge of this melancholic operation was the poet and novelist-to-be Thomas Hardy. There were many bones pulled from the soil too, which had suddenly protruded, yellow, under the digging works; bodies that had lain at peace in that earth for decades were now obliged to find a new home: a pit was shovelled out for their new communal resting place. There had been terrific public disquiet about disturbing the remains for such nakedly material reasons. Even in an age of enterprise and velocity, there were still strong superstitions concerning the disposition and the displeasure of the dead.

The horse-drawn traffic to Euston station was continuous. The hansom cabs would turn off the Euston Road – which had been widened to allow cattle-driving from the Caledonian Market a mile away, and which also had embedded rails for horse-drawn trams – and drive along the thoroughfare that divided the square. In 1879, one tram company was trying an experiment: some vehicles were drawn by mules especially imported from Spain. Large wheels whirred and crunched on the frequently moist, gravelly road. Yet the ceaseless movement did not affect the charm of Euston Square.

It had been built in the earlier part of the nineteenth century, some time before the first railways had been laid. At that time, the square formed part of a nexus with other Bloomsbury streets; the building of these houses had been a speculative venture and it had paid off. Here were to be found wealthy residents: distinguished gentlemen; ladies with titles from old families.

By 1879, the social composition had altered a little. Ladies and gentlemen of quality still abided there, among them doctors and retired military men and clerics; but now there were also what the newspapers were beginning to refer to as the 'bourgeoisie': writers, artists, skilled craftsmen. The brother of Pre-Raphaelite painter Dante Gabriel Rossetti had recently settled on the south side of the Square. Euston Square had its reputation, and there was a distinct community that kept a watchful eye on its newer neighbours.

Unlike nearby Torrington Square – which was gated and bordered with rails to discourage non-residents – Euston Square was open to all. But its smarter residents were continually vigilant for any tokens of transgression. Young, unaccompanied ladies who seemed to linger too long in the shades of night were scrutinised carefully from windows.

The district had a youthful feel and, on warm spring evenings, there were young promenaders, some returning from nearby Regent's Park: women dressed in the brightest of the colours that chemists were now able to manufacture – mauves, hypnotically deep blues, startling yellows. Their young gentlemen companions, sporting smart brocade waistcoats and silk ties, might have had in mind a popular music hall song from the comic artiste William 'Billy Beau' Bint:

'I tell them my father's a Marquis
But wouldn't society frown
If they knew that he shaved for a penny a time
In a little shop down Somers-Town.'

Yet this was also the intellectual centre of London. Euston Square lay just a few streets to the north of London's university, plus the Reading Room of the British Museum. In 1879, Karl Marx was in there almost every day. He travelled down from his house in the northern suburb of Haverstock Hill, but he was always more associated with Bloomsbury. Continental socialists, who had yet to use his name to define their beliefs. were to be found in the pubs in the streets around Euston Square. In the 1870s, one policeman was asked by a young French man the directions to a particular pub. The constable told the young man exactly where it was, adding drily that all the anarchists went there. Among these young Europeans were those who went beyond fiery rhetoric: the German exile Johann Most was preaching in nearby Charrington Street pub back rooms, about the use of dynamite and bullets. 'No great movement has ever been inaugurated without bloodshed,' Karl Marx told the editor of the *Chicago Tribune* in 1879.[2] Yet many of Marx's fellow immigrants to London felt uncomfortable about such sentiments; they had left tumult on the continent and had come to this city precisely to find peace.

Euston Square, and others like it nearby, had for some time proved particularly attractive to recent immigrants. London was rich in opportunity and offered the stability in which skilled businessmen and tradesmen and artisans could flourish and build their fortunes.

Their domestic point of entry was most frequently the boarding house. Boarding or lodging houses had been a feature of London life for a long time, satirised by Charles Dickens and William Makepeace Thackery; but now their popularity was spreading and, indeed, as the capital grew richer, so the number of upmarket establishments proliferated. The better sort of house would provide certain services: maids, laundry, food cooked on the premises.

This was a new way of life for so many Londoners too. Previously lodging houses had been associated with more precarious incomes; now, establishments such as number 4, Euston Square offered a much smarter proposition.

Such living arrangements, although used by all sorts of people and families, generally tended to be more favoured by women and men who were single; those who were quite young and embarking upon their lives. They were also the province of the more eccentric; men and women of a certain age who had never married or who stood at a noticeable angle to conventional society in other ways.

The boarding houses in the centre of the town answered other needs, both economic and sometimes emotional too. If one was new to the city, this was the sort of establishment in which one might make new and valuable acquaintances.

Yet there was another side to these homes that would become apparent deep into the night – and that was the wakeful sense of living among strangers. Once doors were closed and lights extinguished, houses could sometimes still be filled with their own curious noises: unfamiliar footsteps on landings, restless movement from rooms above. Even with a locked door, there might not always be a sense of perfect security.

Number 4, Euston Square, seemingly so prosperous, well-run and attractive, was a boarding house filled with unease; a house that was restless at night; a house with secrets.

Soon it would seem like some gigantic doll's house, open to examination by the entire nation.

And the mystery of what happened within would persist for many decades afterwards; a byword for the darkest subterranean impulses of a violent city, and the cruel anonymity that could sometimes be forced on its victims.

1
The Day Before

On 8 May 1879, there was welcome news for Mary Bastendorff. A new lodger, a businessman, had confirmed that he was preparing to move his effects into 4, Euston Square. He would be taking the rooms on the first floor: an elegant apartment with high ceilings and two large windows, with a balcony, that faced out on to the garden square. This was the apartment that generated the most income and went a long way towards the upkeep of her house.

There had been, of late, a dearth of paying guests. This was not wholly surprising in a city which, by 1879, had 14,000 houses licensed to take in lodgers. The population of the city was expanding dizzyingly and was now close to four million; and, while in some districts, notably to the east, this was resulting in overcrowding and squalor, in many others there were vast improvements in terms of comfort and hygiene.

A rising middle class was developing ever more refined tastes; and in boarding houses such as 4, Euston Square, it was possible to give an appearance, or simulacrum, of gracious living. In addition to this, there was the tremendous – and modern – convenience of the nearby Metropolitan Railway underground station at Gower Street. Steam trains, adapted to minimise the smoke vented into stations, ran every five minutes into the heart of the City, terminating at Moorgate Street. The difficulty for the Bastendorffs was that so many other establishments around the immediate area offered similarly fine accommodation.

Mary Bastendorff, dark-haired, 32-years old, generally tried to keep herself aloof from the day-to-day running of the house. She wanted to concentrate on her four young children. But on 8 May, she would have roamed from room to room, shadowing her young maidservant, checking that the establishment was in a suitable state to receive Mr Brooks the following day.

On the ground floor, apart from the high-ceilinged entrance hall, light angling through the fanlight above the door, the floor muffled with linoleum, oilcloth and with rugs and carpets, there was a fine drawing room. Here was a table at which meals might be taken; tightly upholstered sofas and chairs were gathered around the large marble mantelpiece, the fireplace and the piano.

Mrs Bastendorff was strongly fixated with her children; but she also appeared to some to be an abstracted figure, the reason most likely grief. Mary and her husband had lost three young babies; and the house surely contained many sharp reminders of their short lives.

But Mary was not unsociable. In the evenings, the ground floor drawing room was generally her domain; any particularly valued tenants would be invited to take some brandy and lemonade with her.

Up the stairs, on the first floor, were the rooms that the new guest would be taking, moving his own furniture in. There was a water closet on this floor too, although it was not for the sole use of the first-floor tenants. Climbing further, on the second floor, were two principle bedrooms – the larger facing out on to Euston Square, and a smaller bedroom at the back, which faced out over the yard and the mews beyond. All were lit with gas: the lady of the house had procured ornamental glass globes to frame the wall-mounted gas jets. The carpets were thick and green; they had been a relatively expensive purchase, and she was alert to any stains or danger of mess.

The windows of the first- and second-floor bedrooms had blinds in addition to curtains. So even though the horses and cabs below were constantly churning up dust, their noise was muffled and the rooms were broadly insulated against the irritating particles that would infiltrate in the summer. And at the top of the house, there were three more bedrooms, one used by Mary and her husband, and the others for their children.

Her husband, Severin, aged 32, had been born in the Grand Duchy of Luxembourg. He was one of sixteen children and had been brought up in an intensely rural world. His transformation from a boy of the deep European forests into an urbane Londoner – not merely acquiring the language, but also the tastes and habits of the English middle classes – seemed complete. The previous year, he had been naturalised as a British subject, a move that none of his brothers – who had also immigrated to London – seemed to be tempted by.[1]

However, Bastendorff continued to identify very strongly with German culture; and indeed in the district of St Pancras, there was much to be enjoyed, especially at an institution, recently founded, called the German Gymnasium. This hall, near the railway marshalling yards of Battle Bridge Road, not only provided facilities for gymnastics – suspended ropes, vaulting horses – but also lively concerts of German classical and popular music, and German-themed banquets; with an estimated 30,000 Germans in London, there was great variety there and elsewhere of continental art and culture. Added to this, a few streets away, was the Bavarian Church, at which German Catholics attended Mass.

Severin Bastendorff, who was a little on the short side, had thick, dark red hair; and whiskers which he had cut into the most fashionable style. He was always proud of his facial hair. He had deep-set eyes of pale blue; and his manner could tend towards swaggering. Yet in one sense this was justified. He had achieved a very great deal in the space of eight years.

His business – and his skill – was furniture making. He employed ten people. At the back of the house, across its yard, reached via the basement kitchen, and in the shadow of the houses that stood on the next street, was a large workshop. This had once been an artist's studio, where young women had posed for life portraits. Now there was the constant rasp and buzz of intricate woodworking; Bastendorff's bamboo furniture was becoming ever more popular. This studio, in turn, backed on to a stabling mews; this enabled Bastendorff to keep a horse and cart, for the purposes of deliveries, and also for the occasional family treat.

A couple of years earlier, Bastendorff had gone into business with several of his brothers; they shared and acquired the necessary skills. Joseph and Anton, like Severin, had found themselves London-born wives.

Unusually for a self-employed man, Bastendorff was not especially particular or urgent about making an early start to the working day. This might have been because he frequently spent evenings out with business associates at public houses such as The Euston Tavern, the Sol's Arms and The Orange Tree. It is reasonable to assume that on the morning of 8 May, he had had the newspaper taken up to his bedroom so that he might contemplate the world as he waited for his own to come into full focus.

He would have been most interested that day in news of a European conference called by German manufacturers. This was a time of intense industrial expansion and businessmen in Westphalia were calling for a widening of free trade and an end to all tariffs. Since the 1830s, the pre- and post-unified states of Germany had belonged to a customs union which allowed free trade within that region; some wondered if there was a way to expand that principle throughout continental Europe, perhaps even including Britain?

That day, there were also bulletins from ongoing wars: the curious, unwanted British conflict with the Zulus in southern Africa, and the seemingly endless instability in Afghanistan. To a man born in Luxembourg – which had been the subject of constant predations from neighbouring France and Germany – there might have been a blend of admiration and discomfort about Britain's colonial affairs. Bastendorff's family had known what it was like to be pulled back and forth by different administrators from different countries; the requirement to speak this language or that, the demands for taxes or preferential exports. Equally, though, Bastendorff would have been wholly at ease as a foreign national in this ever-brightening and ever-accommodating city; there was a growing appetite in London for Germanic culture. Publishing houses such as Chatto & Windus were that year issuing volumes of *German Stories*, translated into English.

Throughout the day, there was constant movement in the yard workshop at the back of the house in Euston Square, and high-spirited noise and joking. Severin's brothers, Joseph and Anton, went in and out of the main house, through the back door which led to the kitchen and through to the scullery, which in turn looked out to the front of the house, light spilling down from the street above. Immediately outside this downstairs scullery was a small paved area, with some steps leading up to the pavement; and then, in the area beneath the pavement itself, was a door leading to two large cellars. In the main, these were used for coal; the delivery men would open a manhole in the paving stones and throw the order down into the sooty darkness. The Bastendorffs kept timber and bamboo there, as well as imported wine.

The kitchen and the scullery were largely the domain of the Bastendorff's young maidservant, Sarah Carpenter, who was 13-years old. At that point, she would have been responsible for all the cleaning and the cooking; she would also have been required at certain times to help with the young Bastendorff children. But in some ways, Sarah's Euston Square situation might have been more congenial than many of her peers; at present, without lodgers, the workload of the house was not heavy, and the pay, while not lavish, was also far from miserly. Added to this, Sarah was the only servant, which actually gave her a certain amount of flexibility that would not have been allowed in grander Belgravia establishments. There was no hierarchy of servants for her to fit into at 4, Euston Square; just the instructions she received from Mary Bastendorff. And Mary's diffidence meant that Sarah Carpenter was able to use her initiative more than many young servants in her position.

In the three years since Severin and Mary had taken on the lease of the house, they had had a wide variety of paying guests and servants; some regular lodgers who came and went, men and women alike. Perhaps when they had first arrived in 1876, their noticeably smart neighbours on the Square might have been a little alarmed at the prospect of a house filled with transient people. There may have been a fear that such tenants might give the Square a louring appearance. Yet the Bastendorffs had never received complaints from other residents. The house was always known as respectable.

For all the difficulties that Mary and Severin had faced – the aching sadness from the loss of their children – there was more family support than simply from Bastendorff's jocular brothers. Mary's mother, Elizabeth Pearce, lived around the corner in her own lodging house in Charrington Street, a rather dowdier area, which lay close to the busy canal abutting the good yards and the old graveyard and was an easy ten-minute walk for her daughter. Elizabeth was a frequent and welcome visitor to number 4, Euston Square as well. Severin Bastendorff seemed rather fond of his mother-in-law, and she was certainly rather fond of him. The warmth, from her point of view, might have been partly generated by contemplation of his secure prospects. Added to this, perhaps as a foreign national, he was difficult to pinpoint in terms of class; and that might have been a terrific advantage in a city where anyone English-born was instantly betrayed by speech and manners. If Severin Bastendorff chose to dress as a swell gentleman, who was to say that he had no claim to such a station?

There was only one sense in which 4, Euston Square might have been seen as a less than proper house; and that was on those Sunday evenings when Severin Bastendorff would gather friends together for card games, played for money. Throughout those contests, alcohol was drunk; Severin, in particular, had a lively appetite for it, especially the imported wine which he kept in his cellar. But even in such instances, when the Bastendorff's immediate neighbours might have been able to hear through the walls any unusual high-spiritedness, they would have seen nothing that would have brought disgrace to the square.

In all, Mr and Mrs Bastendorff, their children and the respectable men and women who formed their ever-changing roster of paying guests, were a testament to the city's atmosphere of social mobility and unselfconscious diversity: from wildly differing and modest backgrounds, this young couple had made an enviable home, only a little apart from London's more fashionable streets.

By the following morning, however, that secure home – and the lives of all within it – would be under the most macabre and terrible of shadows.

2

'There Is Something in the Cellar'

The weather was wet and disagreeably chilly on 9 May 1879. Mary Bastendorff was making sure all was in final readiness for the new tenant Mr Brooks, even as her young children were having their breakfast in the downstairs parlour. Severin Bastendorff was not in evidence.

Sarah Carpenter had already been out to procure milk and bread and any viands that the landlady had ordered. They were curiously spoiled for choice for milk-sellers; large numbers of Welsh dairies had set up business along the Euston Road, sometimes having the milk sent from Wales on the overnight train or indeed keeping a few cattle on their London premises, occasionally in the basements.

To make the best impression upon Mr Brooks, fresh supplies of groceries were necessary. There were boarding houses that had a reputation for rather indifferent food and even more indifferent cooking; but 4, Euston Square was slightly more sensitive to its residents' needs. In general terms, their paying guests tended to be men of business; merchants who were often away attending to deals in other parts of the country, or ensuring that goods imported from Europe were fetching the best prices from wholesalers.

Mr Brooks' first-floor rooms had been prepared: the bed freshly changed and aired, surfaces dusted and cleaned, a cupboard cleared in the kitchen specifically for his own non-perishable food. All that was left now was to make space in the cellar for his fuel. That was quite the usual arrangement at the time: the cost of the rooms did not include food, drink or coal for the resident's fire. And so it was that Mary Bastendorff needed a portion of the coal cellar that lay at the front of the house to be cleared to make way for Mr Brooks' supplies.

The family's 15-year-old errand boy, William Strohman, who lived some three miles away in Providence Street, Whitechapel, had arrived for work that grey morning; and Mary directed him immediately to the cellar.

Coal deliveries were made via a coal-hole: that is, a small, round iron manhole in the pavement. When opened, the requested weight of fuel would be dropped down there as if through a chute. It was important that the area beneath was sufficiently cleared so that there would be room for a delivery of some two tons. Even in the warmer summer months, coke and coal were indispensable for the heating of water and for cooking three main meals a day.

The sky was heavy that morning, and in the scullery, the light was subdued. William Strohman went out into that basement area, opened the cellar door, and manoeuvred his way through the increasingly thick darkness of the coke and coal stores. His eyes adjusted. With the door open, and the angled grey daylight from above, the boy did not require a lamp, although there was one permanently kept there.

The coal cellar was a cramped place: five-feet high and ten-feet by eight-feet wide and deep. The grey suffused light would have made the great mounds of coal glitter a little. The boy had with him a basket and a small shovel; the coal delivery man was due to arrive shortly. As well as the mounds of coal, there were some very old broken bottles and other small items of rubbish.

Strohmann had dug his way through some of the black pile, and he abandoned the shovel, finding it quicker to work by hand, the basket filling steadily. With each load, he moved the coals across through the dusty gloom to the other cellar section. Returning to the coal pile with his empty basket, he started in on the greater pile again, using the shovel once more. And as he did so, the implement pulled out something from beneath the coal. It was 'a large bone'.[1]

Even in the dim light, and even though it was part smothered with coal dust, it was quite clear that the bone was that of a human foot.

The boy, in his shock, thought quickly; and his first impulse appeared to have been not to disturb the lady of the house. Instead, with some speed, he backed out of the cellar, briefly back into the open air, and then crossed through to the scullery. From there he ran out of the back of the house, across the rear yard to the furniture-making studio. There, Strohmann anxiously caught the attention of one of Bastendorff's employees, Joseph Savage, bidding him to come and see what he had found. Savage, a 'fancy cabinet maker', thought the boy was imagining things.

Savage's brother, Albert, was in the workshop too: and unsettled by the boy's obvious urgency, Joseph told Albert to go with him to have a look.

They tracked back through the scullery, through to the cellars, and the boy pointed to where he had struck the bone. Albert leaned forward and received the same shock as the boy. They returned through the scullery to the workshop and Joseph, hearing confirmation from his brother, came back with them to investigate further.

In the cellar, Joseph now took the lead, observing what seemed to him to be a 'black mound'. There was fabric of some kind, darkened by the coal. Savage pulled at it a little, gingerly at first and then more adamantly. As the coal fell away, more of this mound was disclosed and the fabric gave way too. Savage found that he had been pulling at the legs of an almost completely decomposed body.

The decay was so very advanced, it appeared, that there was no noticeable smell; whatever odour there might have been was masked by the coal dust. Perhaps that is what enabled a fascinated Joseph Savage to go further: he pulled at the leg bones until, at last, from beneath the dust and the tattered clothing and the scraps of skin, a skull became visible. Some 'pieces'[2] of the skeletal structure had come loose. Its limbs were hardly attached at all. Now, Joseph, his brother and William the errand boy could see, without any ambiguity, they were staring at a human body.

The symptoms of shock or fright can produce curious effects on people. In the case of Joseph Savage, he suddenly became most concerned that the revelation of this corpse would now cause the cellar to become suffused with its foul stench. So, while William Strohmann was sent up the basement steps into the street at the front to try and find a policeman, Joseph went back through the scullery, found Mrs Bastendorff and told her what they had found. His next immediate concern – almost unheeding of her blankly disbelieving reaction to the news – was to ask her for some 'chloride of lime';[3] it was his intention to sprinkle it around the cellar to mask any offensive smell.

There might have been a mistaken element of hygiene in Joseph's actions; despite all the scientific advances of the previous two decades, there were still many who believed that the very scent or 'miasma' of the dead carried the power to kill those overcome by its fumes.

Joseph Savage found what he wanted in the scullery; he returned to the coal cellar and began, with a small implement, to throw powder around liberally on the floor, although not, as he was to emphasise later, anywhere near the body. Joseph's first instincts had an almost neurotically domestic aspect to them: to preserve the peace of those upstairs from the reality of the rotting horror below. But he also knew that the body could not be disturbed further.

As all of this was unfolding below stairs, the coal delivery man, George Fulcher, who worked for Mssrs Woods, had pulled up at the property with his horse and cart, containing a ton of coals. Fulcher had gone up the steps to the front door to announce his arrival; he had forgotten the name of the customer at number 4, but he had a 'ticket' confirming the order of the coal.

The door was opened by Sarah Carpenter. When apprised of his business, Sarah confirmed that Fulcher was 'quite right' and then added that the cellar was not quite ready for him. It is not clear whether she was fully aware of what was happening in the cellar. By that point, Mary Bastendorff had gone downstairs, still incredulous at the news, and the coal delivery man was left waiting on the front doorstep.

Fulcher was impatient to get on, however; all he required was the opening of the pavement cover to tip the order down into the property's coal-hole. And since he was being paid by delivery, he could not afford to be left hanging around. Perceiving that there was some activity in the cellar, he made his way down the basement steps and saw figures moving lumps of coal by hand. Exclaiming that it would be quicker to use a shovel, he joined the Savage brothers there.

As Fulcher leaned forward, he too quite clearly saw the shape of the skull, with some auburn hair still attached to the scalp. It is not certain, but it seems that Mary Bastendorff may have already swiftly withdrawn from the scene of horror. The coal delivery man's reaction was swifter than the brothers had been; he immediately decided to run up the stairs and find a police constable.

Fulcher ran out on to the square; then across it and, as he was looking about, in nearby Drummond Street, he happened across a police constable, Thomas Holman. Fulcher's account of what he had seen, as they strode back across Euston Square, through the unheeding traffic, must have been daunting for the policeman: PC Holman wondered aloud if perhaps this was going to require someone more senior than himself.

On reaching the cellar of number 4, PC Holman asked Joseph Savage if he was 'the governor'; before Savage could put him right, Fulcher pulled the policeman towards the remains with the words 'look here'.[4] PC Holman gazed upon the putrefied skeletal remains which he observed appeared to be partially covered up in some kind of domestic oilcloth, of the type used in flooring.

Yet as all of this had unfolded, no-one – not Joseph Savage, Mary Bastendorff or Sarah Carpenter – had tried to find or summon 'the governor', Severin Bastendorff. PC Holman now wanted to know where he might find him. The policeman was told, possibly to his surprise, given that it was now 9.30a.m., that Mr Bastendorff was still in bed. But his wife, Mary, galvanised out of her initial stupor, ran upstairs to fetch him, rousing him from his bed by informing him that 'a human being has been found in the cellar'.[5]

Very shortly afterwards, Bastendorff came downstairs to find PC Holman, the Savage brothers and Fulcher standing over the hideous discovery. He seemed as bewildered as everyone else. Certainly, in the confusion, he made no effort to establish what was happening under his own roof. Instead, he stood on the sidelines, saying and doing nothing. By this time, the errand boy, William Strohman, had also found a policeman in the vicinity – a constable, Isaac Dowling – and he, too, came down the steps to the cellar. Together, the men stooped under the low ceiling, their boots crunching in the coal dust, as above their heads, the hiss and clatter of passing traffic continued.

It was PC Dowling who went out to search for the nearest doctor: Henry Davis lived several doors along the road at number 1. Duly summoned, Dr Davis hurried to join everyone in the cellar. His first impression was that the body might have been burned; but then he realised he was simply looking at the cumulative effect of coal dust. He also swiftly ascertained, beneath the remaining clothes, that the body was not whole; the bones of the arms had become dislocated from the trunk, as had the legs. One of the feet was missing.

There was a rope tied around what had been the neck of the corpse. Indeed, it had been tied around twice. It seemed all too clearly to confirm that this was foul play. Dr Davis was reluctant to carry out further detailed examination in the cramped, dim cellar. He sent instructions, via the police, that the remains should be gathered up with the utmost care and removed to the nearby St Pancras mortuary.

Before this could be done, however, word was also sent to the Albany Road police station. This station then sent a communication to Scotland Yard. The body would not be moved until seen by a senior detective.

Several hours later, Inspector Charles Hagen arrived at number 4, Euston Square. By the time he came, the men in the cellar had long dispersed and the general area had also cleared, the better for the Inspector to take a preliminary look at it. He, too, stooped under that low cellar ceiling. He observed the 'small quantity of coals' and assorted 'rubbish'.[6] Moving close to the body, he saw the scraps of clothes adhering to it. Among them were the tattered remains of an elegant black silk dress.

There was more too, obscured by the coal: the 'remains of a large circular cloak' which had a 'hood lined with silk and ribands'. There were also fragments of a 'quilted silk petticoat' and a 'large quantity of black lace'.[7] There appeared to be no linen or crinoline. But there was a decorative brooch with a 'red stone in the centre and white stones around it'.[8]

Swiftly, the constables had fetched a 'shell' (in essence, a wooden casket) and manoeuvred it into the cellar; with enormous care, the remains – some in a near liquid state – were lifted by means of the oilcloth, and placed within. Despite all efforts, no-one was able to find the missing foot.

They then carried the casket out through the scullery and to a cart; this would most likely have been via the back of the house, where the property opened up on to Seymour Mews. For by this time, a crowd of curious onlookers had begun to gather outside the front door of Euston Square.

St Pancras mortuary lay half a mile to the north-east; a brick construction favoured with large gothic windows, which helped with the light. It stood near the edge of the churchyard of the ancient St

Pancras Old Church. As soon as the remains were carried within, Inspector Hagen continued his initial examination. There did not appear to be marks of violence to the skull; but the remains of the rope twisted around the neck seemed to tell their own violent story. Where the rope was touched, it disintegrated.

Dr Davis summoned his sons, also medical practitioners, to set to work immediately under the flames of the gaslights. It was as if the body had been partially mummified. There was very little flesh left anywhere, except on the legs. The patches of hair that remained on the head were of a brown/auburn colour. The doctor found no 'marks of violence' on the head.[9] Whoever the woman was, she had lost the greater number of her teeth. There were four centre teeth remaining in the upper jaw, seven in the lower. And it was from these remaining teeth that the doctor made an estimate of this woman's age: she had been somewhere between 55- and 60-years old.

The arms and legs were 'dissevered',[10] but not through violence; more simply the result of decay. How long had this corpse been in that cellar? The doctor investigated what remained of the viscera. Of the brain, there was nothing left but a 'soft semi fluid'.[11] The eyes were no longer there. The cartilage of the nose had also disappeared. Dr Davis and his sons wondered if it was possible that the body had been partly consumed by rats; but there was no obvious sign of this. And then the fragments of rope that were left twined around the neck; on further investigation of this extremely delicate twine, there were small patches of flesh left beneath it that seemed indented by the pressure.

This was a new age of forensics; and the little that remained of the flesh and internal organs would be subjected to much more detailed tests. Was there, for instance, any trace of a poison such as arsenic to be found in the system? It was too early to presume that strangulation had been the cause of death. None the less, even before the closer examinations could be carried out, the doctor knew that he was looking at a victim of murder. This was not some well-dressed lady who had somehow found her way into a coal cellar and expired of natural causes.

Under the flickering yellow of the gas, with the grey spring sky outside the gothic window, Dr Davis made his further preliminary guesses: this was a body of a woman who had been around five feet tall, with the possibility of a slight curvature to the spine. That, together with the earlier estimated age added to the mystery.

It wasn't just the evidence of violence; it was the fact that, judging by the very advanced state of decay, the murdered body of a finely dressed lady had lain in that particular coal cellar for what could have been several years.

3
The Man from X Division

The Scotland Yard detective assigned to this macabre case was German-born, fluent in several European languages and had had some extraordinary experience across a wide range of cases, some of which involved a degree of espionage.

It was clearly felt within the Metropolitan Police that another dimension of expertise would be invaluable here: the name 'Bastendorff' might have suggested that a detective with a European family background would be ideal for examining the household at number 4, Euston Square.

Inspector Charles Hagen was a rising star. He was one of the pioneers of the recently formed Criminal Investigation Department (CID).

The new CID itself was the result of a dramatic modernisation programme within the Metropolitan Police. This was partly a swift means of distancing itself from the former detective department, which had been undermined by several scandalous cases of corruption. But it was also a response to a fast-growing, thickly populated, increasingly cosmopolitan city.

In previous years, detection had been largely instinct combined with circumstantial evidence; by the late 1870s, such techniques as fingerprinting and the photographing of convicted criminals were being introduced and used with growing confidence. The art of detection was becoming a science.

Among those thriving in this new department were Inspector Abberline (who ten-years later would find himself confronted with the 'Jack The Ripper' murders). Meanwhile, Inspector Hagen, it was declared in *The Times*, would also form part of this 'X Division'. (The 'X' had no special significance except to differentiate the new CID from the other alphabetically coded policing districts of London.)

Hagen was already a familiar name to newspaper readers; a few years earlier, he had spent some time 'in attendance' to the Prince of Wales as a form of police bodyguard. In 1873, he accompanied the Prince on a state visit to Austria; and there was a comical moment one evening as the Prince, who had been attending a dinner at the Vienna Exhibition, left the restaurant, followed closely by the detective. The Austrian police, with no idea who he was, swooped in and arrested Hagen. He was 'conveyed to prison by the Austrian police for pressing too closely upon their Royal Highnesses footsteps.'[1] He was released very soon after as the mistake became plain. Even though the incident was treated light-heartedly, it spoke of a certain official nervousness: this was a febrile time in Europe; an era of terrorism and assassination.

Following on from his royal duties, Inspector Hagen set to work on a wide variety of cases in London; and these cases reflected the city's increasingly continental nature. A striking example was when Hagen was called upon to investigate an ugly case of extortion in Bloomsbury. The victim, Herr Sigmund Diespeker, president of the German Benevolent Society, was entrapped by a young woman called Elise Arnold. Miss Arnold claimed that she was leaving London and wanted him to look after her dog. He was lured to her room in a lodging house, whereupon he was ambushed by German thugs, who roughed him up, accused him of sinister sexual intent towards Miss Arnold and demanded money to prevent further violence. When the case was brought before the court, Hagen was required to act as an interpreter for the defendants and the witness.

A rather more ambitious crime involving Count Schuvaloff, the Russian Ambassador to London, required Hagen's expertise in 1877. The Count had been approached by a gentleman called Janacek Williams, claiming to be an inventor who had perfected two new super-weapons: 'three cannon of an extraordinary character for destructive purposes' and 'a contrivance for infallibly picking up torpedoes and so completely neutralising their effect'.[2]

Count Schuvaloff was sceptical – quite wisely as it happens: Williams was a serial swindler, his targets frequently German. Less baroque than the top secret weapons fraud, but slightly more cruel were his attempts, via advertisements placed in German newspapers, to entice men to come to London on the pretence of securing (non-existent) jobs for them for a fee. Inspector Hagen moved in for the arrest. The con man was sentenced to six-months hard labour and was led from the dock 'crying piteously and wringing his hands'.[3]

By 1878, X Division of Scotland Yard had developed intriguingly close ties with police forces across Europe; the efficiency of telegraphy among other elements made such co-operation possible. But it was also indicative of the porous nature of many national borders at the time. Unlike in countries in continental Europe, new arrivals to Britain were not required to register with the police, and there were no limits placed on the amount of time they might spend here. This meant that as well as an increasingly thriving number of different nationalities in London in the 1870s, there were fugitives, too.

Just a few weeks before the events at 4, Euston Square, Hagen found himself in pursuit of a French man called Monthaye, a forger who had fled Paris. In his absence, Monthaye had been sentenced by the French courts to ten-years' hard labour. Hagen and a colleague tracked the man down to a tavern in the heart of the City. A 'desperate struggle' broke out and Monthaye managed to escape from the inn. The detectives gave chase through the narrow, twisting streets, for some distance. The felon was caught and brought before Bow Street to face extradition.

So, by the time the public were learning of the grisly find in Euston Square, Inspector Hagen of X Division was a regular figure in the 'Police Intelligence' columns read all over the country. There was now some glamour attached to his job; a coalescing sense (after earlier decades of mistrust) that the detectives of Scotland Yard had unusual powers of perception. Not only could they detect guilt, but they could also somehow see within men's hearts and divine motivations.

Yet the Euston Square case was to take the Inspector into darker, and very much more complex, territory. There was a sense here that Scotland Yard was approaching the affair with a proper sympathy and sensitivity, as well as rigour, by appointing a policeman of German heritage to a case involving a German household. This seemed an acknowledgement that a household called Bastendorff might otherwise be vulnerable.

His initial task was to question Severin and Mary Bastendorff. It is difficult to know whether he spoke to Bastendorff in German; that was certainly his approach in other cases. Both husband and wife appeared genuinely mystified by the discovery of the corpse. They could not tell the Inspector whose body it might have been. Bastendorff gave voice to his own theory: that one night, some time ago, he had been alerted to a noise outside the scullery of the house next door, in the basement area just by the cellar. It was a lady, in a state of advanced inebriation. The gate to the steps down from the street had not been locked that evening. The lady in question was drunk and lost. So was it possible that the body in the cellar was another such unfortunate who had made her way down there by mistake?

Nothing at that stage could be wholly discounted, but Inspector Hagen's next task was to carry out a thorough examination of the house: every floor, every room.

The Bastendorffs had little choice but to look on as Hagen went about his minute exploration of all the cupboards, the drawers, the wardrobes, all their own possessions, as well as the furniture in the empty tenants' rooms. Every corner of their house, from the water closet to the kitchen, was subject to his scrutiny. Hagen spent a great deal of time in the coal cellar, examining the floor, the brickwork, for any traces of marks. When he was back in the house and climbing the stairs to the top floor, he asked Bastendorff how best he might gain entry to the attic.

It is easy to envisage the two men on that shadowy third-floor landing, Bastendorff having procured the wooden steps, and informing the detective that the attic was always open; Hagen climbing those steps, pushing against the attic door – and finding resistance.

There are no notes to suggest that he enlisted Bastendorff's help; but it initially seemed that the door was jammed. Hagen examined it further; contrary to what Bastendorff had said, it had been tightly bolted.

After some further effort with the stiff bolt, Hagen forced the attic door open, and climbed up into the darkness. There was little up there to detain him save one incongruous item: a wickerwork tray of a type that belonged to a basket trunk, which held a few miscellaneous items, including an eyeglass. The tray was passed down and Hagen had it taken to the police station for further examination.

More questioning: this time directed at Bastendorff's brothers, Joseph and Anton, in the bamboo workshop and the young men they employed. And then, after all that, there was little more at that stage to be done: Inspector Hagen had taken in the initial measure of this couple, their young children, the house they ran. He was not yet to know just how deep this mystery would become.

4

A City of Disappearances

The ghoulish sightseers had arrived almost immediately; and by the time the sinister discovery in the cellar had been reported in the national and the local newspapers, the crowd outside number 4, Euston Square was almost a mob. It had to be held in check by policemen who were detailed to stand watch over the premises.

To the smarter neighbours, the horror would have assumed two forms: the first, most obviously, concerning the dark secrets that had been concealed in their midst; the second, the sense that the carefully maintained gentility of Euston Square might be ruined by an unwholesome reputation attached to one house. Such things had happened elsewhere.

And in the dazed hours following the removal of the body, there is little to suggest how the Bastendorffs dealt with the menacing presence of the onlookers outside their door; or, indeed, what sort of discussions they had between them concerning the hideous mystery.

They had moved into the house three years previously, in 1876; the state of the uncovered corpse suggested to one mortuary observer that its presence in the cellar might have pre-dated their arrival. All that is certain in those immediately adjacent hours is that the new lodger

Mr Brooks – for whom the coal cellar was being cleared – announced that in the circumstances, he and his family would not be moving into 4, Euston Square.

It was not just the idea of murder; it was the additional tragedy that the corpse could not be identified. Here was a body of a finely dressed, clearly refined lady to whom no-one could lay any claim. This, it seemed, was a grim parable of a modern city filled with almost four million souls: the realisation that some of these souls might vanish and not be missed by anyone.

This was one of the reasons why the case was so fascinating for the newspaper and periodical reading public, both in Britain and across the Atlantic: this sense of London having become so vast and so amoral that even a fine lady could be murdered in circumstances of gothic anonymity.

The authorities let it be known in the local newspapers that the remains of the body, which had been conveyed to St Pancras mortuary, would be available to view. There was the hope – despite the decay – that someone might be able to make an identification. The slightly rounded shoulders, the shade of the clumps of remaining hair, the golden brooch which had been made in Birmingham, they hoped that these fragments might prove some sort of memory spur.

It is possible that the authorities anticipated a few members of the public making a visit; they would certainly have been ready for possible charlatans ready to lay claim to any potential riches that the well-dressed lady might have had.

What the authorities had somehow not anticipated was London's appetite for necrotic spectacle. By the second day, there were queues of people outside the mortuary.

The appalled officials tried to initiate some close questioning of all these potential viewers to establish that their interest was quite genuine, and not simply voyeuristic.

In the early fog of speculation, the one thing that could be said with certainty was that Severin Bastendorff and his wife gave every appearance of being unfailingly helpful, polite and attentive when dealing with the police; there was no sense at any time that they were withholding information. And so, as Inspector Hagen assessed the household, and began to piece together its recent history – not merely the paying guests who had come and gone, but the staff as well – he was already quietly pursuing two shrewd theories about the identity of the body, and about how the poor woman might have met her death.

His first step, a precautionary one, was to reach a little further into the past; and to try and contact the house's previous owner, a Mr Milnes. He had been the sculptor who had built the studio in the backyard, and who worked with life models.

This had been the subject of local lascivious speculation. While other men earned their livings through honest toil, there was clearly a sense among some that this was not quite a proper calling; that a man so raffish and bohemian might be tempted by his nubile life models into immorality and, in turn, perhaps into darker depravity.

Yet Mr Milnes was still pursuing his artistic career quite openly; he had simply moved to the exquisitely beautiful Forest of Dean, near Gloucester and the Welsh border. He was very quick to talk to the police; and they were equally quick to dismiss any idea that he might have a connection. They were satisfied that the body was not that of an artist's life model.

As this was unfolding, the national news coverage had inadvertently brought a potential lead out into the open. Down in Bideford, north Devon, the news story in the local journal concerning the discovery of the body was met with horror by two middle-aged parents, William and Susan Dobbs.

They had not heard from their daughter, Hannah, for an unusually long time; it was as though she had vanished. Hannah Dobbs had been working in London as a maid.

And the house in which she had lived and worked was 4, Euston Square.

5

'I Am Not a Judge of Human Bones'

Hannah Dobbs' parents ran The Blacksmith's Arms public house by the river in Bideford. The last time they had seen their 24-year-old daughter was about six months previously when she had come down from London by train on a visit.

On that occasion, Hannah 'came . . . with two children', ran one local news report, 'and then stated that she was married to a Mr Bastendorff, of 4, Euston Square, but the children she said were not hers'.[1]

William and Susan Dobbs had appeared to accept their daughter's sudden manifestation as a married woman. There had been one more flying visit: from Hannah, and from the man who claimed to be her husband. 'In November last,' reported the Press Association, 'a man, who gave the name of Bastendorff, came to Bideford, and stayed several days, and passed as the husband of Hannah Dobbs.

'A photographic likeness of this man is in the possession of Mrs Dobbs,' continued the report. 'Hannah Dobbs did not return to London in company with her supposed husband.

'And after her supposed return to Euston Square, a telegram was sent back (to her parents) by Bastendorff saying she was safe.

'From that day to this,' the report stated, 'no tidings whatever have been received of Hannah Dobbs by her parents, though repeated letters have been sent through to 4, Euston Square they have invariably been returned through the Dead Letter Office.'[2]

The *Western Morning News* added: 'Hannah Dobbs was a fine built woman, with fair complexion, light hair worn in curls (and) had lost a front tooth.'[3]

So why did Hannah Dobbs' parents not make more strenuous efforts during that time to get to the bottom of their daughter's mysterious and uncharacteristic silence? At first there seemed to be a good reason. 'While home at Bideford,' the Press Association reported, '(Hannah) stated that on her return to London, she was going abroad to Germany with Dr Bastendorff, R.A., brother of her husband, and her parents naturally supposed she had so gone abroad.'

But then there had been the first uncanny inkling of discomfort and anxiety. 'They received a letter some little time after she had returned to London from a person (at another address) in Euston Square, asking what they should do with some boxes belonging to Hannah Dobbs, who had gone away.'[4]

Quite why Hannah Dobbs' personal effects should have been in a house owned by someone she had never before mentioned was puzzling; yet it was still Euston Square, and here was mention of Mr Bastendorff. Perhaps Mr and Mrs Dobbs assumed that there had been some mix-up; that upon emigrating to Germany, Hannah had been required to leave some surplus effects behind.

Her mother had written back swiftly, as suggested, asking that 'the boxes had better not be removed, as her daughter might call for them' upon her return.

But now came these news reports of the discovery of an unidentifiable corpse. The Dobbs contacted the police, who tried to sound reassuring; then the couple engaged a solicitor and sent the following panicked communication – in the name of Mr Dobbs – to Inspector Hagen at the CID:

'From reports published of the Euston Square mystery, I am led to believe it is my daughter Hannah Dobbs, alias Hassard. I have telegraphed Scotland Yard, and the answer received is not at all satisfactory, as everything corresponds so minutely.'[5]

In this period of hideous suspense, the Devon police communicated as much as they could, via telegraph, with Scotland Yard; and the local press darkly averred that in the midst of the uncertainty, it could be said that 'one thing was clear, that the man accompanying the woman to Bideford was not her husband at all'.

Indeed, journalists were sent to north Devon to discover more particulars about the background of the missing maid. 'The quiet town of Bideford . . . has been in a great state of excitement,' ran one report.[6] Local inquiries yielded old local scandals from when Hannah had started working with one of the grander families in the area: tales of theft and sexual promiscuity. That assumed name of hers was noted, 'Hannah Hassard' – comparisons were made with Daniel Defoe's extraordinary heroine Moll Flanders.

The agonised grief and anxiety of Hannah's parents was clearly acute; the reply they soon received from the CID was extraordinary and wholly unexpected.

The news was conveyed to the Dobbs by a Bideford policeman, who had received the telegram from Scotland Yard.

Hannah Dobbs, they were told, was actually very much alive.

Clearly it had taken the police a few days of checking.

The reason nothing had been heard from Hannah for so long was that she was in prison in London. Hannah had been convicted for petty theft; continuing the theme that had begun in her youth in Bideford. She had not wished her parents to know anything of her disgrace.

This development provided Inspector Hagen with new problems to unravel. There was so much in Hannah Dobbs' return visits to Bideford that seemed irregular: a maid-of-all-work for the Bastendorff household, who returned home, dressed notably finely, claiming marriage to a man she called Mr Bastendorff. What were these domestic arrangements in number 4, Euston Square?

Meanwhile, in the mortuary of the St Pancras coroner lay the pitiful remains of a woman whose identity seemed ever more elusive. Someone in that household surely knew who this woman was?

As was the legal custom then, the inquest on the body was convened long before any suggestion of arrests; the aim simply was to try and ascertain the cause of death.

And so, just several days after the discovery, Dr Hardwicke gathered jurists – local businessmen, in the main – and witnesses at the St Pancras Coroners Court. 'The proceedings excited great interest and the court was densely crowded,' reported *The Times*.[7] Severin Bastendorff's solicitor, Mr F. Jones of Freston and Co., was there watching the proceedings carefully. The coroner opened by explaining to the court that the jurists had already visited number 4, Euston Square. They had, one by one, ducked their heads to enter the coal cellar, but they had also examined the rest of the property, the positions of all the rooms and the stairs and the passages.

The errand boy, William Strohman, was the first witness to be called; he told the court how he had found 'a large bone and foot' and had run 'into the shop' (the workshop) to tell Albert Savage. In turn, Joseph Savage relayed how he 'at first did not believe' the boy.[8]

Joseph informed the court that he was a japanner. Jappaning was the art of lacquering wooden cabinets in the Eastern style: layers of elaborate varnish inlaid with gold paint or other decorative materials, forming elaborate and delicate patterns on the jet-black surface. It was a skill much in demand in 1879; and it also conveyed to the jury something of the flavour of Bastendorff's business concerns.

The coal delivery man, George Fulcher, swiftly confused the court with his testimony; he said that as soon as he went down to the cellar, and picked up a shovel to help move the coals, 'a man came in and sprinkled a lot of white stuff over the cellar'. The next witness, Thomas

Holman, PC178 of S Division, deepened that confusion by telling the jurists that 'he did not see any white powder about' when he at last reached the scene.[9]

This disputed scattering of powder suggested a deliberate effort to mask or alter the remains by means of quicklime; and Joseph had to be recalled. He told the court that he had gone to Mrs Bastendorff who had given him the chloride of lime; that he 'fancied there was a bad smell'.[10]

Now, for the first time, Severin Bastendorff's own account of that morning was to be heard. He took the stand and described his occupation as 'fancy cabinet and bamboo worker'. He told the court he had 'eight or ten men in his employ'. He explained how somewhere between 9 and 10 o'clock that Thursday morning, his wife had come up to their bedroom and told him there was 'something in the cellar'.[11] Bastendorff explained how he had then gone downstairs to find the police in attendance.

The coroner wanted to know a little of the house's recent history. How long had Mr Bastendorff been there as landlord? 'I have been in the house about three years, and let the upper part of the house furnished and the drawing rooms unfurnished,' said Bastendorff. He described how there had been numerous lodgers. 'I think I could tell who they were,' he said. 'They were a genteel lot of people.'

What were the terms on which they stayed? 'I had eighteen shillings for the second-floor front and seven shillings for the second-floor back per week,' said Bastendorff. 'The attics I have let, the front for eight shillings, and two little rooms at five shillings a week. I may have had about twenty different lodgers. I have let the drawing room floor, but until lately it has been vacant seven months.'

Could Mr Bastendorff put a name to some of these previous tenants? 'A Mr Hickinbotham had (the drawing room floor) rooms for eighteen months,' recalled Mr Bastendorff, 'and a Mr Brooks before him.' This was a different Mr Brooks to the man who had lately sought accommodation elsewhere. 'I have also let the parlours occasionally furnished,' he continued. 'My wife mostly took the money.'

The coroner was anxious to know more about the cellars and about the frequency of their use. Mr Bastendorff explained that the former lodger Mr Brooks 'had a coal cellar next to this one', and that it is 'approached through the scullery, and I have used that myself for coals'.

And who else had the use of these cellars? Were they kept locked? 'There was a place for a padlock,' said Mr Bastendorff, 'but there has never been one on it. It was always open.' And did these cellars see frequent use? 'I had coals in about six weeks or two months ago,' said Bastendorff. But, he added, 'no lodger in the house had a cellar except Brooks. He left about two and a half years ago.'

As the court absorbed this, the coroner was still clearly puzzled as to how a dead body could remain undiscovered for so long; especially in a house that was continually busy and thriving.

'I do not recollect the cellar being cleared out before this,' said Bastendorff. 'It was (being) cleared out for the newcomers also of the name of Brooks, who required a coal cellar, and I gave up my own cellar, as I had some wood in the other cellar.'[12]

Was it really possible, given all that was kept in his cellar, that Mr Bastendorff had noticed nothing at all in the last few months? The coroner pushed this a little further; and now the iron certainties began to melt a little.

Bastendorff was now at last seemingly moved to recall a most singular occasion some six months previously. Indeed, his story was to elicit an involuntary shocked laugh from among the onlookers.

'I went into the cellar about Christmas,' he told the court, 'and picked up a bone, which I thought was a sheep's bone, and it had some flesh on it.

'I took it into the kitchen and showed it to my wife, saying "what a wasteful girl that servant must be, throwing away half legs of mutton". That is what I took it for.'

This drew a further laugh from the spectators; the pitch-blackest of comedy. The court officials brought hush. Bastendorff continued: 'I went and threw this particular bone back again into the cellar. I am not a judge of human bones.'

Nor, he added, did he 'detect at that time any unpleasant smell in the cellar'.[13]

One jury member, having absorbed this, had a question of his own about the running of the house, and how the Bastendorffs selected their lodgers. 'My wife has usually gone after references when lodgers have come in,' said Bastendorff, 'but sometimes we had no references. When lodgers went away, I did not know where they went to.'

Bastendorff explained further about having had the house for three years. 'I took the house from Mr Kemp, the house agent,' he said. He explained further about his first sight of the property, and added one faint possibility about the identity of the body: 'There was a woman in the house as housekeeper when I went there. I do not know when she went away or where she went to. So (as) soon as I got the keys from Mr Kemp, I gave orders to take in my furniture. But five or six days elapsed before my furniture was taken into the house.'

Who else would have had access to the house (and by extension, its residents)? 'One of the workmen, Harry, and my brother used to come through the area (downstairs) door to go and open the back shop, which opens into the mews,' Bastendorff said.[14] In conclusion, he was asked about how secure the house was, and what possibility there might be of people effecting entry? He insisted that usually, the downstairs 'area' gate was kept locked, and that there were horizontal bars over this area. This precluded his own initial theory about the identity of the body: that this was a passing woman, perhaps drunk, who had crept down to that 'area', got into the coal cellar and somehow met her death down there.

Bastendorff's next-door neighbour, Dr Davis, was called to take the stand. Having led the coroner and the jury through the gruesome details of decomposition, and confirmed the presence of some kind of clothes line around the neck of the corpse, he allowed himself to speculate on the amount of time the body might have been there. 'It was almost impossible to say how long the body had been where it was found,' Dr Davis said. 'It might have been three years or more than three years, or it might have been but one year.

'It depended mainly on the action with the atmosphere,' he explained, 'or what the remains were brought into contact with. There were,' he confirmed, 'plainly the indentations made in the neck by the cord.' That said, it was 'impossible to say what was the cause of death. She might have been poisoned and the rope put round her neck afterwards.'[15]

If it was poison, might there still be traces? 'If arsenic existed, it would be found there now,' the doctor told the coroner, who nodded towards another present, one Professor Pepper: he was intending to make a 'chemical analysis of the viscera'.

The next witness – the Bastendorffs' young current maidservant – was called. Sarah Carpenter told the court that she had been working for Mrs Bastendorff for nearly five months. She testified that she 'lived in the back kitchen'.

Just a fortnight previously in the cellar, she said, she 'picked up a bone and took it out into the scullery and looked at it'. Then she 'took it to her mistress', and declared to Mrs Bastendorff that it was 'part of a foot'. Mrs Bastendorff had replied, 'Oh nonsense!', and told the girl that it was 'a wild boar bone of one they once had'.

The jurists – once beyond the gruesome implications of her discovery – might have been a little astonished at the idea of a family dining on wild boar; but it would later be established that the Bastendorffs, as a family, did, indeed, sometimes favour game that had been shot in the Black Forest.

According to Sarah Carpenter, Mrs Bastendorff took the bone and 'threw it in the sink'. Then, having looked more closely at it, she picked it up and quite simply cast it out in the basement area in front of the coal cellar. This was not quite an end to the matter. A couple of days later, Sarah, again poking about in the cellar, found and picked up 'a little bone' about the length 'of her finger'. Rather than troubling her mistress with it, she threw it into the dust hole, which was where all the household rubbish was consigned.

And had the servant ever found anything else in that dark cellar? Yes, she said. She had 'picked up rags and things in the cellar and had burnt them'.

Prompted by the coroner, Sarah concluded by declaring: 'When I took the bone to show my mistress, I said I was sure it was the bone of a person's leg.'[16]

The last witness for the day was Inspector Charles Hagen, who gave the coroner and the jury an exact description of the dimensions of the cellar, plus a minutely detailed account of the clothes that the corpse had been wearing: the black silk, the ribands, the 'quilted silk petticoat', the 'steel busk of a pair of stays' and 'a large quantity of black lace'. The lady's linen was gone. The brooch, with its red and white stones, was common, and most probably 'of Birmingham manufacture'. He also produced what remained of the rope that had been tied around the neck. They were too fragile to touch. But they appeared like 'fragments of sash line'.

Indeed, despite the prompting from some in the jury, who had heard local gossip of a serving girl from Devon who had once been the Bastendorffs' maid-of-all-work, Inspector Hagen was not free to say any more for the moment. But he was, at least intuitively, a little ahead of both his colleagues and the press.

There was one more examination of the remains later that day at St Pancras mortuary, conducted by request of the coroner; the inquest's Dr Hardwicke called upon the services of Bastendorff's near neighbour, Dr Davis of 1, Euston Square. He, in turn, called upon his two sons – also doctors – to assist at the mortuary. They were joined by a police surgeon called Dr Jakins who belonged to S Division.

The subsequent report in *The Times* relayed their findings: 'The greyness of the hair, the state of the teeth, and other evidence showed that the deceased must have been a woman between 50 and 60 years of age,' the doctors declared. 'This entirely disposes of the statements in reference to a young woman who is said to have been long missing, and who was in the habit of sitting as a model for the sculptor who had occupied the house before its present tenant.

'Having placed the remains in proper position and taken the circumstance of the curvature of the spine into consideration, the medical men came to the conclusion that the deceased must have been 5ft 7 inches or 5ft 8 inches in height.'[17]

Here was a new medical confidence in the studying of cadavers; no matter how ghastly the details, there was also a curious fascination with the way that the state of a corpse might be read or interpreted to offer deductions or wider theories; a scientific séance, in which the doctors sought answers from dead matter.

'The flesh of the face was entirely gone,' the newspaper report continued, 'but the hair adhered to the scalp in patches. The limbs were dissevered from the trunk, no doubt through the action of the quicklime which had been used; but in the former there was still a considerable portion of the internal viscera still remaining.

'Both hands and one of the feet were entirely gone, except a few fragments of the bones. That quicklime had been extensively used was beyond a doubt, as the sockets of the eyes were found to contain a large quantity. The body was placed where it was found fully dressed as, although in the first place the textile fabrics of what were her stays had been destroyed, there were the whalebones by which it was supported in their proper places.'

The reporter – relaying what he had been told by the doctors – was in macabrely intimate territory, further underlining not merely the horror of the crime but also the queasy incursion into domestic rectitude. 'The underclothing all fell to pieces as it was touched,' the reporter wrote of the body, 'as did the outer clothing, although sufficient remained to show that her dress was of black silk, with a jacket of corresponding material, over which were a black lace shawl and an outside wrapper with hood.'

Then there was the matter of the cause of death. There had been a length of what had been described as 'washing line' wrapped around the woman's throat. 'As the remains were lifted up from the cellar, not only was the rope discovered to have been twisted twice around the neck, but a brooch of extremely common metal dropped from the shawl.'

There was also a ring; and the 'remains of a bonnet'. This, according to the report, 'answers to the fashion of some three or four years since'.[18] Dr Davis was of the view that that was roughly how long the corpse had been in the cellar. The police surgeon Dr Jakins disagreed; he thought the remains were very much more recent.

There was more information gathered about the house's previous tenant. Mr Milnes was 'a very old inhabitant of the Euston Road, and was well-known as a sculptor', reported *Reynolds News*.

'In the rear of the house, he built a studio backing on to Seymour Mews, now occupied as a workshop by the present tenant Mr Bastendorff, who is a manufacturer of light cabinet work.

'Between the tenancies of Mr Milnes and Mr Bastendorff, the house was empty for half a year.'[19]

Was this then the key period for the police to examine? Dr Davis and his sons believed so. 'It is during that interval,' the report stated, 'should the medical theory that the body has been there so long prove correct, that it is believed the murder must have been committed.'[20]

There might have been an element here of subjectivity on the part of the doctor, possibly with an eye on maintaining the respectability of the Square: to have a murder committed in an empty house, though a bleak prospect, was not as horrible as the alternative. Clearly the murderer was not the elderly sculptor. But the alternative – that the murder had happened in the full and bustling household of Severin Bastendorff – might have been too much for his near neighbour at number 1, Euston Square, even subconsciously, to countenance.

Meanwhile, Bastendorff was interviewed by the police once more. They were learning a little more of his own background.

He re-iterated that he was baffled as to the identity of the corpse in his cellar, and the questioning pursued his first theory: was there the chance that the unfortunate woman could have got into the coal cellar without first passing through the house?

Bastendorff had to concede that this was in essence impossible; there were horizontal railings across the open basement area at the front of the house.

What, then, of the possibility that the woman had been an 'unfortunate' who had committed suicide? A lodger suffering acute depression? Could this have been even a faint possibility?

No: the Bastendorffs would obviously have missed such a person.

It emerged however that it wasn't completely impossible to infiltrate such basement areas; for the horizontal bars were always lifted to admit tradesmen during the day. Bastendorff told the police once more of a scene some two or three years back when he became alerted to a woman who had effected entry into the basement of the house next door.

She had 'apparently been drinking' and she 'took no notice' when Bastendorff went down the steps to tell her that she could not stop there.[21] Indeed, so impervious was this inebriated woman that he was impelled to ask his maid, Hannah Dobbs, to try speaking to her.

But this was not the case at number 4, Euston Square; he re-iterated to the police that the bars blocking entrance to the basement were firmly down.

Then there was the question of time: how was it possible for the corpse to have been in the cellar so long without Mr Bastendorff having had some sense of it?

What about the smell? Surely someone at some stage must have noticed? Bastendorff recalled that some time back, he and several others had noticed what seemed to be the pungent odour of rotten eggs; he said that it was assumed that this is exactly what it was, and that the eggs had been thrown away.

And what of the Bastendorffs' dealings with Hannah Dobbs? Mr Bastendorff recalled that the maid had 'left his service' on 17 September 1878.[22] And he appeared to be aware that she was now in prison for stealing from other furnished lodgings.

He concluded by repeating to Inspector Hagen that 'in his opinion', 'he did not think the lime' that had been thrown around the cellar 'had been used for the purpose of destroying the body'.[23]

In the meantime, public interest in the case had spread right the way across the country and, indeed, across to the United States.

How was it possible for a well-dressed woman to have been murdered and lain dead in such grotesque circumstances without being missed? There was a sense here not merely of the flinty anonymity of streets and crowds; but also the unsettling and unheimlich transience of boarding houses.

This growing fashion for sharing furnished lodgings with complete strangers still struck many as being an unnatural and potentially amoral way to live. In some ways, number 4, Euston Square was starting to represent a certain kind of city life.

6

Superior Apartments in a Quiet Home

As the Euston Square mystery was unfolding, readers of *The Times* were still running their fingers down the closely printed classified advertisements in search of lodgings close to the centre of town very similar to the establishment run by the Bastendorffs. 'Board and residence (first class) close to Kensington Gardens,' stated one such advertisement on 16 May 1879. 'A private sitting room with bedroom adjoining on the first floor is now vacant. Queen's Road, Bayswater.'

Meanwhile, in nearby Princes Square, lodgings were described as being two minutes from the Metropolitan Railway; there was also on offer an 'excellent table' (or food) and perhaps more valuably, 'select society'. References were naturally required.

For those with slightly more modest means, the attractions were framed slightly differently. In Westbourne Park, a mile or so away from Kensington Gardens, there was on offer 'a most comfortable home', perhaps suited to 'one or two ladies'. It boasted a 'large pleasant front room' and 'cheerful society', as opposed to 'select'. The terms were 'moderate'.

The increasingly cosmopolitan nature of the city was reflected through these advertisements as well. ''Board and residence wanted by a young foreigner,' declared one notice, 'with a superior English family, with young and cheerful society.' Elsewhere, a home was sought 'for a young French gentleman in a good English family where he can acquire the language'.

Some residences advertised '*table d'hote*'. Some made a feature of the fact they offered 'late dinner'. Some made mention of bathrooms; others cheerfully highlighted their pianos. There was a deliberate emphasis upon gentility; not least because across the years, such a way of living had gathered a reputation for racketiness and transgression.

Boarding houses had been the subjects of one of Charles Dickens' first satires written for the *Monthly Magazine* in 1834. 'Boz' took a sardonic look at the house run by Mrs Tibbs in Great Coram Street, in the east of Bloomsbury, and the class-conscious manoeuvring of the landlady, her daughters and their gentleman tenants.

Other writers for weekly journals enjoyed exploring the possibilities of social and sexual awkwardness that these houses offered. A frequently reported anecdote in gossip columns involved the arrival at a boarding house of a young gentleman, seeking lodgings as he established himself in the great city. The landlady of the house, in these stories, was swift to dance attendance and indulgence on such young men, making sure they had excellent food and good drink at the dinner table: the reason being that these landladies were determined to pair their daughters off with these eligible catches. And, indeed, in several such sketches, reported mirthfully in London papers as un-bylined urban news, the gentlemen concerned found themselves entrapped, being told by the landladies that their hands in marriage had been offered, and that if they attempted to withdraw, all sorts of horrid legal consequences would follow.

Yet sometimes it worked the other way around. In 1874, the young Vincent Van Gogh found a room in a lodging house in Lambeth run by the landlady Ursula Loyer. He was very happy there; working by day in the centre of the town, spending spare hours tending the back garden in Hackford Road. But Van Gogh fell for his landlady's daughter Eugenie: the young woman was already answered for, and Van Gogh took the news badly, suggesting in letters that he did not like living in houses with 'secrets'; only some time later was he able to restore his friendship with his erstwhile landlords.

Also prevalent in anecdotal accounts of boarding house life was the trope of the predatory widow; the lady of a certain age reduced after the death of a husband to taking furnished lodgings and then keeping a keen eye out for new arrivals such as prosperous and peripatetic salesmen who might serve as new husbands. Male widowers sometimes featured in such stories too.

And these sketches struck at the very heart of the nature of the boarding house; in the early and mid-Victorian years, with an expanding middle class, there was a concomitant rising sense that the ideal home should be a detached sanctuary: a place where one family dwelled under one roof, in domestic stability, sheltered in every sense from the chaos of the world. Rising middle-class affluence brought a rising taste for privacy. The boarding house, by contrast, introduced a measure of enforced proximity with strangers; total privacy was a practical impossibility.

This was also a distinctly continental way of living; in Paris, for example, apartments and shared stairwells were the norm; even by 1879, this still seemed something of a novelty in Britain. There were humorous essays concerning such modern nuisances as living in an apartment with a young family occupying the rooms above, the children stomping ceaselessly throughout the day.

'There is no way in the world,' wrote William Makepeace Thackery, 'by which a man . . . can be placed on family terms and sudden intimacy with those who up to yesterday were perfect strangers.' He also noted that 'there is a certain element of romance and history about a boarding house which is attractive in one way but ought to be suspicious in another'.[1]

But elsewhere, the author of *Three Men in a Boat*, Jerome K. Jerome, found rich inspiration in this particular style of domesticity. As a young man, he had sought to escape a career as a clerk by becoming a success in the theatre; and this necessitated living in a series of north London boarding houses. Because of the irregularity of his hours – and his frequent return home in the small hours – the landladies were required to be quite understanding.

And such homes clearly made a deep impression on him, for they became recurring leitmotifs in his fiction. In his turn-of-the-century novel *Paul Kelver*, Jerome's young protagonist recalled the delicate economics of these arrangements. 'My first lodging was an attic in a square the other side of Blackfriars Bridge. The rent of the room, if I remember rightly, was three shillings a week with cooking, half a crown without. I purchased a methylated spirit stove with kettle and frying pan, and took it without.'[2]

And it was in the nature of such houses that unexpected intimacy could be sparked; occasionally with the darkest consequences. In one house in fashionable Bayswater, in 1858, Dr Thomas Smethurst lodged with his wife. Dr Smethurst, 54, was a feted pioneer of hydrotherapy; he administered what became known as the water cure to various well-to-do patients in the Chilterns. Back in Bayswater, he enjoyed the sociability of this elegant and tasteful boarding house; the easy evening conversations with other residents in that drawing room before the landlady had the dinner served.

Into this house arrived a single woman called Isabella Banks, 43, who joined the other residents in that drawing room each evening. Isabella and Dr Smethurst fell for one another very swiftly. It is not difficult to envisage the furtive nights that followed; Mrs Smethurst perhaps feigning sleep as her husband crept from their rooms.

But the relationship was too intense to be sustained and the landlady of the house soon became aware of the affair. The landlady demanded that Isabella Banks leave; she did so and Dr Smethurst left with her. They set up home in Richmond upon Thames and might never have been heard of again were it not for Isabella Banks dying suddenly and Dr Smethurst standing accused of her murder.

He was accused of poisoning her to get rid of a baby; as it transpired, the evidence was tainted. His lover had died of an infection. But what gave the story extra resonance, on top of the tragedy of Isabella's death, was the way that it had begun in the better sort of boarding house; adultery and promiscuity were more usually associated with the lower sorts of establishments to be found in the poorer districts.

In George Gissing's *The Nether World,* published in 1889, but set ten years previously, there is a vivid account of a boarding house in Clerkenwell (not very far away from the more handsome houses of Euston Square). Here, the house is dilapidated; the landlady and her daughter confining themselves to the downstairs and their lodgers upstairs. At the start of the novel, we are led to believe that there is one female lodger in the first-floor front room; but finally, as we are led up the stairs, the door opens to reveal a harassed young mother with three young children, a teenaged daughter and a father who is out of work.

Food is taken in that one room; upon his return from job-hunting, the father is offered a piece of cold steak, some bread, and tea using the tea leaves from that morning.[3]

In the grander houses of Bloomsbury, the catering was daintier: at the same time, there was obviously no obligation to dine with one's fellow residents. You could arrange to have your supper brought to your room. In many houses, the residents would sometimes purchase their own ingredients – pies, chops, wine – and arrange for the maid-of-all-work to heat the food in the kitchen before bringing it all upstairs on a tray.

The other attraction of boarding houses – both to younger aspirant people, and also to those older residents who had known more affluent days – was that the better properties were furnished to give every impression of a fine middle-class home.

Even by the 1870s, the fashion for darker wallpaper was still prevalent: deep rich greens, lustrous dark reds. The reason was not just aesthetic. Gaslight and oil-light were, over time, injurious to such paper; their fumes would gradually stain any lighter shades. The greens and the reds masked the depredations.

The heavy furnishing and the heavy curtains and carpets also had the effect of insulation, both physical and psychological; a shield against the cold and the commotion from the outside world. In the centre of London, the horse-drawn traffic was now so dense that the streets seemed alive even into the depths of the night. But there was not only the sense in these houses of swaddling oneself from noise; there was also an element of feeling safe. The fullness of the furnished rooms – the padded leather of the seats, the deep velvets, the ironed linen of the sheets, the polished wood, the china ornaments, the glass of the gas lamps – conveyed a sense that its occupants were cosily hidden and protected from the world by many layers. But this idea of protection could be an illusion.

7

'A Mass of Light-Coloured Ringlets'

Suicide was still a distantly possible solution to the Bastendorff affair; a few weeks earlier, a woman called Emily Collett, who lived in Drummond Street, close to Euston Square, had been arrested and prosecuted for attempting to 'destroy' herself. It was a criminal offence. She had what would today be termed alcohol dependency and mental health problems. The authorities saw only moral weakness.

Such melancholic stories were increasingly prevalent in the ever-growing city. For all those who found the pace of life exhilarating, there were others who were overwhelmed, terrified of their insecure future.

Yet in this instance the idea of suicide still left too many questions unanswered and Inspector Hagen and his team were proceeding with another possibility. Perhaps it was something to do with his background in cases of fraud; but what Hagen was bringing to this case was a keen eye for its more material elements. To start with: a well-dressed woman such as this would have had jewellery and valuables; so what, he wondered, had become of them?

In addition, this elderly woman must surely have wanted to attend to her health; so, he wondered, what appointments might have been made with local practitioners that had not been kept? Ingeniously, Hagen also wondered if this woman had had dentures made to fit around her existing teeth: who would have attended to this?

Dentistry was a highly competitive trade in London at the time, jostling with innovations to make life easier, especially for the elderly. Having one's teeth removed and replaced with dentures was now a commonplace, if still deeply unpleasant, procedure. In 1879, 'surgeon dentists' such as 'Mr Eskell', based in the City, proclaimed in advertisements that he had 'introduced the only perfectly PAINLESS system of DENTISTRY. Artificial teeth secured to the mouth entirely by suction without fastenings of any kind. They defy detection, and are perfect for eating and speaking.' Another Mr Eskell (possibly this was a family business) in Mayfair wished it to be known that his false teeth 'are of such density as to admit of masticating the hardest substance without the least liability to fracture'.

Near Regent Street, Mr B.L. Moseley was advertising his use of nitrous oxide gas guaranteeing 'entire immunity from pain' and 'successful painless adaptation of artificial teeth'.

Hagen's dental inquiries were focused around St Pancras, Bloomsbury, Somers Town and Kentish Town. And remarkably, after a few days, they did yield an affirmative response; a local practitioner near Euston Square told the police that around two years ago, a female client had come in with the aim of being fitted for new dentures; and to this end the dentist had taken a cast of her mouth and remaining teeth. She had never returned. But he had held on to the cast.

This was relatively simple to check against the body in the St Pancras morgue. The dental match was exact.

At about the same time, Edward Hacker, an elderly gentleman, aged 67, presented himself at the offices of Scotland Yard.

Mr Hacker had been following the Euston Square mystery in the newspapers; and some instinct had made him fearful that the corpse was that of his sister, Matilda, from whom he had not heard for some two years.

There had been no estrangement, no cross words between them; simply the puzzling blankness of sibling neglect. It might seem extraordinary now to conceive of a brother having no curiosity about even the whereabouts of his sister; this might have been one of the atomising effects of city life. It transpired that Edward Hacker lived in Rochester Row, in Kentish Town, barely a mile north of Euston Square.

Inspector Hagen would have known and been familiar with families forced into silence by emigration, by voyages around the world; but a brother and sister living in the same city? How could there be so little care or heed?

It was immediately obvious that there was something abstracted about Hacker; and it was soon to become clear that his eccentricities were reflected many times over in his missing sister.

As Hagen's other enquiries around the pawn shops of the area – checking and rechecking valuables that might have belonged to the corpse – continued, Hacker was taken to the St Pancras morgue. It is not known with what degree of curiosity the detectives observed this old gentleman as he was required to make the most hideous of identifications; whether there was any flicker in his reaction that could not quite be read. But Hagen must have been watching him very closely.

First, Hacker was called upon to look at the clothing that had remained on the corpse; was this his sister's mode of dress? It was. Inspector Hagen then asked him if there might be any other distinguishing features with which they might be able to identify her.

There was the matter of her hair; despite her advancing years, the deceased was in the habit of wearing it in striking auburn ringlets. Hacker was adamant about the colour. The hair that remained on the skull was indeed dyed that shade.

Were there, he was asked, any items of valuable clothing or jewellery that would be particularly distinctive and recognisable? There was a gold watch; one that had come from the family's old home in Canterbury.

Edward Hacker was allowed to return home. There was, for a few hours more, some caution on the part of Inspector Hagen and his team; the newspapers were clamouring but the police did not want to make prematurely public the name of the woman. Hagen would also have been acutely conscious that identification of the body was merely one step; discovering how that body had come to have been found in the coal cellar was another.

None the less, some journalists had got hold of a name; and they were swift to arrive on the doorstep of 4, Euston Square. They wanted to put it directly to Severin Bastendorff that the murdered woman had been one of his lodgers.

Constables from the local station had just managed to reach Mr Bastendorff in time, however, and the journalists were thwarted, left merely to note that Bastendorff 'refuses to say' if the victim had lived under his roof 'or indeed to answer any inquiries on the subject, stating that he has been counselled by the police to withhold all information' pending the resumption of the inquest.[1]

The strain upon Bastendorff, his wife Mary, his young children and his brothers, was increasing by the hour. The publicity would surely only lead to any further possible tenants shunning the house. There were also crowds gathered at all hours of the day (and into the evening) just outside; gothically fascinated sightseers who wanted to take a long look at this landmark of murder.

'Euston Square continues to be of great interest to the public,' reported the *Morning Post* blithely, perhaps only half aware that its own detailed reporting of the grisly horror was half the reason. 'Two policemen are stationed at the corner of the thoroughfare for the purpose of restraining the exuberance of the sightseers.'[2]

The positive identification of a gold watch was the next step towards giving a definitive identity to the murdered woman. It had materialised in a pawn shop in St Pancras. On the back of it was the address of its maker – a Mr Warren, of Canterbury, Kent. Inspector Hagen, in the meantime, had been contacted by his colleagues in that town; there was indeed local talk of an eccentric lady who was known to have moved to London and subsequently vanished.

To be certain, Hagen took a train from London to Canterbury, bearing the gold watch and some of those ringlets of auburn hair. He presented himself to Superintendent Davies of the Canterbury police and laid the items before him. Davies had had some rueful dealings with the lady in question several years ago.

And now, as he looked at the items and affirmed that they were absolutely hers, Inspector Hagen knew for certain that the murdered woman was Matilda Hacker, described as an 'elderly maiden'.[3]

She was a renowned eccentric, in her mid-60s, who had been a colourful, aggravating and often madly impetuous figure. She was wealthy too. But in terms of finances, debts and obligations, she was curiously irresponsible and prone to quarrelsome chaos. Although a blithe spirit herself, Matilda Hacker, it seemed, had led a formidable dance of infuriated figures across the years.

But what sort of dance could have led to this ghastly end?

8
The Canterbury Dolls

The mummy in the cellar had at least her public identity restored. 'The body is . . . supposed to be that of an elderly maiden lady, named Hacker, a native of Canterbury, who removed from that city to London, on the death of her sister, between two and three years ago,' reported the *London Evening Standard*, '. . . and when last heard of was living in apartments at the (Euston Square) address in question.'[1]

Yet the revelation of her identity only added a further dimension of mystery to the case; for now, the authorities knew Matilda Hacker was also a woman of sizeable property and fortune; and how could such a lady have ended up hidden for months under a pile of coal in a London boarding house cellar?

Matilda Hacker had also, in her latter years, moved about under a variety of pseudonyms. The one name she had never used was her own. She had, for some reason, considered herself a fugitive. 'Miss Hacker and her sister were persons of very eccentric habits,' ran one newspaper report of the years before Matilda Hacker came to London. 'Though both upwards of sixty years of age, they were accustomed to dress in the style of girls of eighteen, and while owning, it is stated, a considerable amount of property in Canterbury, and being of comfortable circumstances, they yet lived in the most penurious circumstances, keeping no servant and resolutely refusing to pay their rates and taxes, or indeed any debts, until summoned.'[2]

Matilda Hacker's father had been a builder in Canterbury, and in the years immediately following the Napoleonic Wars, he had become very prosperous through the building and letting of housing. He had three daughters and one son. By 1879, the son Edward was the only one of them still alive.

It was through all the housing in Canterbury that the Hacker children derived their incomes; each of them benefited in the father's will. After the leanness of the war years, a rising population across the country brought, for some, terrific opportunities as landlords, even in a cathedral city that was more sedate than the fast-growing industrial metropolises.

Edward Hacker, the artist, had embarked upon the journey to London. Matilda and had her sister stayed with their mother until her death.

The two sisters inherited a large house in Wincheap Street, Canterbury. Their lives were, it seemed, a source of incessant material for local gossip. 'From their peculiar style of dress,' reported the local correspondent, 'they came to be known as "the Wincheap Dolls".' As well as the exaggerated youthfulness of their dress, another peculiarity about them was that 'they were always attired exactly alike; one never wore anything the other did not'.

On top of this, they were 'so much alike' in personal appearance 'that it was almost impossible to distinguish one from the other'.[3]

There must have been a time in their younger days when Matilda and her sisters were being viewed by others in Canterbury as being eminently eligible for marriage; yet each of the daughters somehow either avoided the attention of bright-eyed suitors or even deliberately set out to discourage them. Strikingly, Edward did not marry either. Who was this family, that acquired with such ease, ever increasing amounts of housing (and the constant flow of income from tenants), yet seemed to stand aside from the broader currents of social convention?

The deaths of their parents brought to the Hacker sisters a sort of freedom quite beyond the imaginations of the vast majority of women; even the vast majority of wealthy women. They were able to live blithely and quite independently on the rental money that continued to flow in. They were quite without any ties or obligations.

But did this somehow in turn influence their behaviour? Were the eccentricities pathological or in fact a form of defence against a world where women were expected to place all their financial considerations in the hands of their husbands?

'It was the custom of these ladies every summer to go to the seaside, Margate and Dover being their favourite resorts,' reported the local correspondent. 'And there they would be accompanied by a groom.' This seemed to be one of the Hacker sisters' very few servants or employees. 'They were also regular visitors to the cricket ground during the Canterbury week,' continued the correspondent, 'habituees of which will remember them as one day riding about the ground on anything but over-fed steeds, with their groom behind, and on another day promenading on foot, attired in costumes of extraordinary pattern and grotesque style. For years, these two maiden ladies passed their days in this manner.'[4]

They also received a great deal of jeering attention from local children, if not from local grown-ups; but even if their outlandish behaviour – bordering on a kind of whimsical anarchy – was not rooted in some psychological cause, it still demonstrated the insulating effect of money.

'They looked after their property themselves, and were their own rent gatherers,' observed the local journalist. 'They lived entirely to themselves, keeping no company, and in fact, having no personal acquaintances.' They also acquired a house in elegant Brighton, where they enjoyed promenading in ever more extravagant clothing and jewellery.

But then, in around 1871, Matilda Hacker suffered the trauma of losing the sister who had most clearly been her soulmate. For a while after this loss, she continued to occupy the Canterbury home: now the sole occupant (for neither sister ever felt inclined to take on a full time servant). Life went on 'in much the same way . . . except she became more and more eccentric', noted the local correspondent. 'She persistently refused to pay the rates and taxes for her property, and gave the collectors no little trouble. At last she was summoned for non-payment and after appearing in court and attempting to prove that there was some mistake in the matter, she would pay.'[5]

In other words, there was a streak of pure, almost reflexive irresponsibility in Matilda Hacker, which genuinely resembled that of a child. There seemed to be no doubts about her intelligence, and certainly not about her sanity; but this refusal to pay dues was vexing for the authorities.

By now, Matilda Hacker's position was singular to say the least; with her one remaining sibling Edward carving himself out a life of an artist in Camden, London, she was left to promenade alone. More than this: she had a portfolio of properties to look after. And it became plain that she was a bad landlady.

'She was called upon,' ran one report, in common with other owners of cottage property, to have certain sanitary works done in conjunction with her property, but she neglected to carry out the order served upon her and eventually the local authority did the work and in her absence, and charged her with the cost.

'Failing to pay the claim, she was summoned, but did not appear in court, and in her absence, an order was made upon her for payment, a distress to be put in if the amount was not paid within a given time.'[6]

It was at this point that Matilda Hacker appeared to buckle under the demands that were being placed upon her. The response that the authorities received sharpened her reputation for dottiness. 'Instead of attending to the order, she wrote libellous letters to the Mayor, the

Town Clerk, and other officials,' reported the local correspondent, 'but no notice was taken of them.'

And when she repaired to the Lansdowne Place property in Brighton, Miss Hacker's behaviour seemed to be becoming more volatile. 'Her attire usually consisted of a blue satin dress, looped up so as to show her high-heeled boots and silk stockings, while on her head she wore a brown straw hat with a large white feather,' noted the Brighton-based journalist. 'Her hair was worn in an abundance of small ringlets so that her appearance from the side or the back was that of a girl of eighteen. There was, however, a slight stoop in her gait.'[7]

And her vulnerabilities were beginning to show ever more clearly. 'When not crossed, she was lady-like in manner,' wrote the Brighton correspondent. 'But when she met any opposition, she gave way to violent abuse.'

This became increasingly noticeable; and Matilda became a well-known face to the local police in Hove, not least because she was frequently running into their station demanding that they take action against those whom she perceived to have wronged her. 'Once,' wrote the correspondent, 'she was ordered to leave Hove police office in consequence of abusing the officials.'

There was no suggestion from any report that there was drink involved; and her relationship with the world seemed not so much angry than simply bewildered that such continual demands be placed upon her.

But the court cases now started mounting up. In 1875, Matilda let the Brighton house, furnished, to one John Sanderson, who was living in Clapham, south London. The property was intended to be his for a month that summer so that he and his family could take the healthful sea airs. For one week, they lived in wonderful comfort. But then the bailiffs arrived and removed all the furniture. Matilda had lost another court case; this seemed the fastest means of recovering money for the complainant.

The Sandersons were obliged to move out; they could hardly stay in a house with no furniture. And so, with the month's sojourn ruined, Mr Sanderson decided that he too would seek some form of compensation.

Again, Matilda proved elusive; and the court in Brighton was forced to find against her in her absence. But she had certainly received the summons for, as the judge of the case pointed out drily in his summing up, the court and other authorities had been in receipt of letters from Miss Hacker touching upon the character of Sanderson her accuser. 'She described some of the parties concerned as Guy Fawkes,' reported the Brighton correspondent, 'and in addition cast other reflections upon them. Subsequent to this,' added the correspondent, 'other letters were received anonymously but supposed to be in Miss Hacker's handwriting in which the conduct of certain gentlemen was commented upon.'[8]

Even at a distance, her brother Edward seemed conscious of the effect that her capriciousness was having on the lives of others, and during that period he made occasional attempts to rectify wrongs, visiting the properties in Canterbury to arrange repairs and proper rent collection. In 1875, he 'was in the habit of seeing his sister every three or four months'; but he seemed not aware of her subsequent plans.

In the latter stages of 1875, Matilda Hacker was in the process of assuming the identity of quite a different woman.

She made her way to London; and she devised new ways of making it difficult for her enemies to follow her. Matilda Hacker moved into a boarding house in Russell Square, Bloomsbury. She introduced herself to Mrs Bridges, the landlady of the house, as 'Miss Bell'.

In normal circumstances, new tenants to lodging houses might be required to produce some references; but the manners of this Kentish lady, though eccentric, were also clearly engaging, and possibly also amusing, and her manner of speaking conveyed that she was a woman of quality. Single ladies of a certain age were not unusual in such establishments, and 'Miss Bell' must also have brought a certain quantity of money with her.

And the landlady Mrs Bridges was soon beguiled by her guest. 'Miss Bell''s 'disposition was exceedingly pleasant,' she later told journalists. And there were soon some extraordinary domestic diversions which only increased the landlady's fascination. 'Miss Bell' was by now receiving letters, that had been sent on from other offices, and under different initials. She was also receiving regular cheques: these were the sums collected in rent by a property manager that she had taken on called Mr Cozens. And 'Miss Bell' was frequently telling her landlady that where she could, she always preferred to use large sums of cash to buy gold; gold, it seemed, was more satisfactory to her than keeping her money in banks.

A few weeks into 'Miss Bell's' residency in Russell Square, Mrs Bridges answered the door to a man introducing himself as Superintendent Davies of the City of Canterbury police. The woman calling herself 'Miss Bell' was, the landlady learned for the first time, actually called Matilda Hacker.

Superintendent Davies had apparently cornered his quarry; he, like so many other enforcement officers in Kent and Sussex, had the task of recovering unpaid Canterbury rates from Miss Hacker.

Matilda's response to this intrusion was that of 'violent resistance' and hot words. By means of securing the payment, Superintendent Davies took from her one of her boxes of belongings, plus a gold watch and a chain. That watch was later to become a vital key to the entire mystery of how she had ended up in that coal cellar.

Matilda appeared outraged by what she considered the terrible injustice perpetrated against her. Determined to retrieve her jewellery, she caught the train to Canterbury and made her way to the accounting offices of the city council.

There, she paid in full the amount of rate money that had originally been demanded of her; and with this, the officials returned her confiscated property to her. This was the spark for another tirade from Miss Hacker, this time directed against Superintendent Davies of the City of Canterbury police. He had, she announced, 'stolen' these items from her. Indeed, she went further, marching into the County Court office and demanding to take out 'a summons against Mr Davies', claiming thirteen shillings for 'illegal detention of property and damage to a gold watch and chain'. A few days later, it was reported: 'the superintendent received a letter from her solicitor, Mr J.T. Moss of Gracechurch Street London, to the effect that she had abandoned the action and therefore he need not trouble himself any more about the matter.'[9]

But Matilda Hacker's materialisation in Canterbury alerted past creditors further afield. By the later stages of 1876, it seemed that it was time for her identity and address to change once more.

She took rooms in Chelsea, which by 1876 had pretty streets of terraced white stucco houses, and the nearby prospect of one of the cleaner stretches of the London Thames. And again, Matilda Hacker, under a new name, mesmerised her landlady and fellow tenants alike with her extravagant dress style and curious mannerisms.

There was another move; this time to Dorset Square, a smart tree-filled prospect near Baker Street. Her legal conflicts were now being handled by another solicitor in Lincolns Inn Fields and once more, there was an elaborate system devised by which she could receive post without anyone knowing her address.

She would have understood very well that this was a city in which one could be whatever one chose. Her self-assurance made her an attractive prospect to her new landlords. Added to this, she brought diversion to her fellow lodgers by way of her interest in astrology and dreams. She cultivated the manner of one who could see beyond the veil. In the London of 1870s, this was a talent that many had the most acute interest in.

Some compulsion led Matilda to move once more. And so it was that a 'Miss Sycamore' presented herself at a respectable house a little to the north of Euston station in a street called Mornington Crescent. With her came the minimalist luggage of the strong box, plus also her tarot cards and what she referred to as 'the dream book'.

Her new landlady, Mrs Nash, was greatly impressed and bemused by her new tenant, who had instantly conveyed to her the fact that she was enormously wealthy. And soon, Mrs Nash and her maid-of-all-work were engaging in lively debate as soon as 'Miss Sycamore' went out for one of her ostentatious silk-clad perambulations. That hair: was it dyed or not? Given the age of the lady, surely it must have been? And yet during the time she spent at Mornington Crescent, neither of the other women were aware of 'Miss Sycamore' keeping the lengthy appointments with the hairdressers that such a procedure would require.

And as at Dorset Square, landlady, servant and fellow residents in that stuccoed Georgian house came to relish the evenings in the downstairs drawing room when, after the dinner things were put away, 'Miss Sycamore' would entice her companions either into readings from her cards, or consultations with *The Book of Dreams*, delivering celestial prognostications.

It also seemed to be the case that 'Miss Sycamore', when she felt herself to be among friends and equals, was congenial and even kind company. But there was that consistent restlessness to her as well: she appeared to be a compulsive walker. And as Mrs Nash noted with some wonder, no day would pass when 'Miss Sycamore' would not dress in the 'fashion of a sixteen-year old' despite clearly being in her early sixties. Children would follow her and laugh. The clothes were a continual source of admiration: rich red silks, beautiful scarves. And 'Miss Sycamore' seemed for a time to have found some contentment in this simple life.

Yet for some reason the tranquility disturbed her; and in the summer of 1877, after a few months' sojourn in Mornington Crescent, she decided it was time once more to move. Her landlady had no idea where she was going.

Days later, Matilda Hacker disembarked from a horse-drawn cab and presented herself at the doorstep of number 4, Euston Square. Now, she was 'Miss Uish'.

9

The Book of Dreams

In the summer of 1877, 'Miss Uish' was a welcome addition to the household at 4, Euston Square; several lodgers had just left. At the time, the only other resident was the salesman Francis Riggenbach. Another travelling salesman, an American called Mr Findlay, had departed with surprising haste; and even though there was every expectation that he might be back – it was thought there had been urgent business in America that he had to transact – the arrival of 'Miss Uish' brought both stability and also a welcome tone.

Thus it was that 'Miss Uish', together with her strong box, her wicker trunk and *The Book of Dreams*, was installed in the front room of the second floor. We can imagine her first walking into the house, noting its clean smell; glancing at the handmade furniture in the ground-floor drawing room; then following the maid-of-all-work up the carpeted stairs, along the quiet and dark landing of the first floor – Mr Riggenbach's door shut until his return that evening – and thence to her own rooms.

Although not quite as grand as the tall ceilinged apartment of Mr Riggenbach immediately below, this would have been a slightly cosier prospect. In the dusty high summer of London, there was little need for the fire in the grate; the warmth from the kitchen below would have risen through the house. And the room was tastefully furnished; other than the bed, there was an easy-chair, a desk, and pictures and ornaments, including an attractive cut-glass lamp.

The young Bastendorff family occupied the top rooms. For 'Miss Uish', this would have been a charming and pleasingly middle-class prospect: rooms which looked out over the leafy garden in the centre of Euston Square; the endlessly fascinating bustle of horse-drawn traffic riding to and from the mighty railway terminus; and then the household itself which occasionally pleasingly echoed to the noise of laughing children.

Without the children, the house might have occasionally felt a little disconcerting. The habits of the departed Mr Findlay, for instance, had caused his fellow tenants a few moments of discomposure. He seemed excitable; prone to exaggeration. He imagined himself to have violent enemies. He kept irregular hours. As a valued resident, he had a latchkey to the house. He was not alone in this. Others had keys too.

Deep into the night, Matilda Hacker, lying in her bed, would have occasionally heard an unfamiliar footfall on the landing outside her room; there would have been that moment of curious suspense when listening to the steps of one outside the door who is hesitating in the dark. These were steps of a furtive nature, when the rest of the house was still: careful footfall on carpet and creaking board.

There were other houses nearby where such movement in the middle of the night was commonplace and tolerated. There were some squares in Bloomsbury in the late 1870s that had acquired a reputation for licentiousness and promiscuity; rooms occupied by women who invited men back. This was not the case with number 4, Euston Square. So far as the outside world knew, the Bastendorffs kept a decent house. Those footsteps in the dark were a secret never to be spoken of.

Of the other resident, Francis Riggenbach, there would have been little congress between himself and 'Miss Uish'. Mr Riggenbach was a very busy German travelling salesman, specialising in the sugar trade. He had a great many clients across Bloomsbury and neighbouring St Pancras, and down in the south London suburbs of Brixton and Camberwell. When Germans had first started coming to the city in great numbers in the earlier years of the century, many had set up bakeries; and in the late 1870s, a great many maintained this line.

As a commercial salesman, Riggenbach had at that time an unusual amount of influence for one who might have simply been seen as a middle man between importers and customers. His business also took him frequently to the continent; and his buyers were reliant on him to obtain the most favourable prices for large purchases of sugar.

His clothes, in which he took great pride, were expensive and colourful: brightly patterned waistcoats, eye-catchingly rich neckties. He would have been very little trouble as a tenant, were it not for the fact of his dog. He had only been allowed to keep the animal on sufferance, and there were suggestions that others in the household found it a short-tempered animal. When he went out – which was frequently – the unhappy dog was confined to Riggenbach's room.

And 'Miss Uish' would have been very swiftly aware too of the thriving industry that lay across the back yard of the house: the specialised furniture-making workshop. Severin Bastendorff was not often to be seen around the house. But whenever she met him, 'Miss Uish' would have been struck by his distinctly accented English.

Nor was Mary Bastendorff a particularly pronounced presence around the house; all the work was delegated to the housemaid Hannah Dobbs.

But if any of the residents found 'Miss Uish' a little unusual, the children of Severin and Mary Bastendorff apparently took to her immediately. There was something a little child-like about this lady of a certain age who promenaded up and down the street in sashes. It was later to emerge that during that autumn of 1877, 'Miss Uish' would take the younger Bastendorff children to play in the gardens immediately outside.

It would not be long before 'Miss Uish' was charming all the Bastendorffs with her seemingly gentle eccentricity; beguiling them with *The Book of Dreams*.

The full title of this work was *Napoleon's Oraculum: or the Book of Fate*. It was also sometimes referred to as *The Book of Dreams* and a competitor later published a version entitled *The Imperial and Royal Book of Dreams*. The publishing hook was this: during the campaign in Egypt, Napoleon's forces had in 1799, happened across an ancient mystic text that could offer a guide to the future. Napoleon himself had this work translated from the ancient Egyptian into French and German and was said to have become addicted to its prognostications.

It worked by first requiring the sitter to draw out five sets of rows of stars on a piece of paper, at random and paying no heed to the number of stars in each row. Then the sitter was required to count up the number of stars in each line, noting which rows had odd numbers and even numbers. These stars would then produce their own code-like pattern.

At the start of *The Book of Dreams* was a table of questions that might be submitted. Among these were: 'Shall I have to travel far by sea or land or to reside in foreign climes?' 'Inform me of all particulars relating to my future husband.' 'Will my beloved prove true in my absence?' 'Shall I ever be able to retire from business with a fortune?' 'Will it be my lot to experience great vissicitudes in this life?'[1]

Then by use of a table of numbers and letters, the sitter would delve through *The Book of Dreams* to find the page with the corresponding pattern of stars. And on each page of this book, ancient nameless powers, it was said, had formulated oracular answers. Among these were: 'Be not buoyed up by hopes of inheriting property which thou has not earned.' 'Be prudent, and success will attend thee.' 'As the glorious sun eclipseth the light of the stars, so will the partner of thy bed be accounted the fairest among women.'[2]

This book, 'translated from the German' had been a terrific sales success for some time in London. It was published by George Purkess, who also produced the hugely popular (and torrid) weekly journal the *Illustrated Police News*. (Ironically, Purkess's shadow was soon to loom greatly over 4, Euston Square.) The advertisements for *The Book of Dreams* ran in the *Police News* alongside other quasi-mystical services: 'Important!' ran one regular advertisement. 'Any unmarried person sending their description, including date of birth and 18 stamps will receive in return a beautiful and artistic likeness of their future husband or wife and date of marriage – also my wonderful secret on fascination, carefully sealed. Address J. Henry, 42 Cooper's Road, Old Kent Road, London.'

But there was something rather guileless about Matilda Hacker's fascination with *The Book of Dreams*; later, various acquaintances would recall how she would happily spend hours poring over the artful prophecies.

And it would certainly seem to be the case that this was part of the way that she charmed the Bastendorff children. When the children were invited up to Matilda Hacker's room for a tea party of ginger biscuits on one occasion, the event would certainly have featured an atmospheric reading from *The Book of Dreams*, the children clamouring to know of the awful powers gathered beneath Egypt's desert sands.

In amid the old lady's pathological skittishness – her deceit, her adoption of various new names – it is possible to imagine that she found 4, Euston Square a more agreeable lodging than the others; that after an initial disinclination to have anything to do with the life of the house, she found herself becoming a part of it none the less.

All of which only made it more inexplicable that her ill-used corpse came to be found beneath that coal.

In May 1879, the inquest at St Pancras was about to conclude. And before it did so, a key figure in the final days of Matilda Hacker's life was taken to survey her decomposed remains.

10

'No, Not Me'

He was an expert on the intoxication of greed. Inspector Hagen's career had been built upon cases where money as a motivation blotted everything else out. But here instead he was confronted with something chillingly nihilistic; the emotional vacuum in which a woman could be murdered, dumped like rubbish and wholly forgotten. The detective was fixing his focus upon the tangible valuables, rather than the absence of love.

The CID had been following the trail of the gold watch. It led to a pawnbroker called Mr Parkinson, who operated from a shop around the corner from Euston Square in Drummond Street. Could Mr Parkinson identify the person who had brought the watch to his shop and exchanged it for money? Inspector Hagen had an instinct that this person would be found at the Tothill Fields prison. And he arranged for a line-up to be staged.

Hagen was thinking of the former maid-of-all-work Hannah Dobbs, serving her sentence for petty robbery; she 'and over a dozen other criminals were placed in one of the passages of the gaol for this purpose', reported a local newspaper, 'and as soon as Mr Parkinson entered and scanned the features of those present he, without a moment's hesitation, singled out Hannah Dobbs'.

The press was immediately fascinated by Hannah; and most particularly by the question of her physical appearance and allure (although one newspaper noted ungallantly that prison had made her 'stout'). Her coolness was also a source of fascination. 'She did not deny having a knowledge of Mr Parkinson,' one report stated, 'and indeed it is stated that she was so often in the habit of pawning articles at . . . Drummond Street, it was merely a matter of formality to visit her at all, as he remembered her perfectly well and indeed knew that the watch and chain had been pawned with him by her.'[1]

Inspector Hagen had been alert with interest to this, not least to the detail that Hannah had pawned this item not in her own name, but under the pseudonym 'Rosina Bastendorff'. This was the name of one of Bastendorff's daughters.

Added to this, one newspaper report ran, 'Hannah Dobbs has been questioned as to . . . £50 she is alleged to have stated she received as a bequest from a dead uncle, but she can offer no explanation. It is well known to the police that she had no relative who was able to make so substantial a bequest.'[2]

Hagen was freely briefing the press concerning his instincts about Hannah and her acquisitive nature. And the gravitational push of the reporting was linking Dobbs closer and closer with Matilda Hacker's death. So much so that even before the inquest had had its final session to pronounce on the cause of that death, the police were letting the press know their theories.

'It is supposed,' ran one report, 'that Miss Hacker must have been first struck . . . by a heavy instrument, which doubtless drew a quantity of blood. Then it is thought either that the half-lifeless body was carried to the cellar, where it soon showed some signs of returning life, and was instantly strangled by the rope which was found on the neck of the victim; or that the rope was attached immediately after the first blow was struck and that she was dragged by the cord down the stairs and thrown into the cellar.'

In addition to this, the report continued, it seemed certain that 'some kind of acid' was thrown over the corpse 'by some person'.[3]

It was now that the neighbour of the Bastendorffs, one Mrs Talbert, who lived with her husband at number 5, Euston Square, came forward with a curious and unsettling memory of one dark afternoon in the autumn of 1877. She told the police that she had been in her first-floor sitting room, facing the square. It was a Sunday, and the streets were quieter than their weekday bustle; and there was little sign of life in the streets and the gardens below. Mrs Talbert, enjoying the silence, suddenly received a jump-inducing shock.

It was, she said, 'a scream'; and one that was of a most unnatural kind. It was drawn out, it seemed to be the scream of a lady, and hurrying to the window, she could not ascertain the source of it. Presently, the square returned to the muffled quiet of the dark autumn afternoon. And very soon after, Mrs Talbert had forgotten all about it. Only by reading of the sensation in the newspapers, and observing with some distaste the sightseers who had been gathering and jostling outside 4, Euston Square, had her memory been jolted.

Hagen meanwhile had a further instinct about Hannah; that it would be constructive to have her view the remains of the corpse at St Pancras mortuary. 'Hannah Dobbs arrived in a carriage with Inspector Hagen and one of the matrons of Tothill Fields prison,' reported one newspaper. 'She was attired in deep mourning, which had been supplied by the authorities.' Again, there was some fascination with her appearance. 'She was noticed to be in splendid physical condition,' noted the journalist. 'She was perfectly calm and collected.'

Once escorted inside the mortuary, white-tiled walls flickering with the reflected gaslight: 'She walked over to the coffin where the skeleton lies and looked very calmly upon the hideous and foul smelling sight.

'She shook her head,' the report went on. 'She did not remember anyone whom she would expect to see in that state. She was shown a piece of floor cloth marked with a diamond pattern. She recognised it as having been on one of the landings in Mr Bastendorff's house. This had been thrown over the body in the cellar.'

Another item, this time clothing that had belonged to Matilda Hacker; Inspector Hagen was watching Hannah Dobbs with raptor eyes as these presentations were quietly made. 'She thought the shawl was much lighter than Miss Hacker's,' ran the report, 'but she remembered the lace shawl, or fichu, which Miss Hacker had worn. During all this time, Hannah Dobbs never lost her self-possession.'[4]

It might have been precisely this apparent insouciance that was causing Inspector Hagen's instincts about her to grow ever more concrete.

Yet Hannah had her own instincts too; and when she wrote to her parents in Bideford, immediately after this visit to the mortuary, someone in her family ensured that the eager journalists in north Devon and in London knew about it.

'She has written a letter to her parents from Tothill Fields prison,' stated one local newspaper report, 'expressing her deep regret at the disgrace that she has brought upon them.' But this disgrace, it was to be understood, was for the petty theft that had consigned her to that jail. 'She makes no allusion in her letter,' stated the report, 'to the Euston Square murder.'

Yet Hagen was now ever more certain that he had the killer before him. 'In consequence of the information which has lately come into the hands of the police-officers who have been engaged in the elucidation of what is known as The Euston Square mystery,' ran a report in the *Daily News*, 'it was decided by the authorities of the Treasury Solicitor's Department to prefer a charge of murder against Hannah Dobbs.'

There was to be a form of pre-trial hearing, the purpose of which would be to determine if there was enough of a case to bring to full trial. This 'examination', was to be heard before a magistrate, Mr Vaughan, at Bow Street court. 'She was brought to the court in a cab,' ran the *Daily News* report, 'accompanied by the chief warder of Tothill Fields prison, where she is serving her time, but owing to the extreme secrecy which has been preserved in the matter, there was scarcely anyone present to witness her arrival, and in fact she had been in the precincts of the court some considerable time . . . before it was generally known who she was.'[5]

This meant that the court reporters, as well as public onlookers, were unaware at first; they soon realised. 'On being placed in the dock,' wrote one reporter, 'the prisoner, who is a tall, good-looking woman, showed little sign of nervousness and during the whole time the examination lasted, she had a wonderful self-possession.'

Also present in that small, square, white-walled court at Bow Street, looking on at the proceedings, were Severin and Mary Bastendorff.

After a few minutes of preliminary business in the court, the formal charge was at last read out to the young woman at the stand: that of wilful murder.

Hannah Dobbs' crisp response to this was: 'No, not me.'

The prosecutor appointed by the Treasury was Mr Poland. Hannah, for this initial hearing, did not seem to have a defender in court. Looking after the legal interests of Severin Bastendorff was one Mr Jones. And also present were the police inspectors Lansdowne and Hagen.

Mr Poland opened the proceedings, describing Matilda Hacker, her 'eccentric habits' and her adopted identity of 'Miss Uish'. He outlined her tenancy at 4, Euston Square; and then he told the court of the day when it was supposed 'Miss Uish' had moved out, information supplied by Hagen.

'[Hannah Dobbs] had been a servant in that house somewhere about August 1877, when she had left for a month's holiday,' said Mr Poland, 'but she came back, and in October of that year, she was again in the service of Mr and Mrs Bastendorff . . . [Hannah Dobbs] about that time told Mrs Bastendorff that the lady, Miss Uish, was going to leave, and she brought downstairs to Mrs Bastendorff a 5*l* note, the bill having previously been made out, and Mrs Bastendorff gave the change for the note.

'The bill was receipted and there was also a charge made of two shillings for a lamp glass, which it was said this lady had broken.'

Mr Poland told the magistrate that the rent for the room was 12 shillings a week, and that change for the note was procured. 'Mrs Bastendorff did not see Miss Uish leave the house,' said Mr Poland, 'and it was only from the statement of the prisoner that she became aware that the lady intended to give up these lodgings. Shortly after Miss Uish was supposed to have left the house, Mrs Bastendorff went up into the room on the second floor. She found that a lamp glass was broken and there was a stain on the floor, on the carpet, a patch which she describes, I think, as appearing to have been washed out, and she made the remark to the prisoner at the time that if she had noticed it before Miss Uish left, she would have made her pay for the damage done to the carpet.'[6]

He seemed to be emphasising that the lady of the house had placed herself beyond any suspicion. He then moved to make the same point about her husband, Severin. It was Mr Poland's contention that 'Mr Bastendorff was not aware at all of what had become of the lady Miss Uish. He never suspected that anything was wrong, and the prisoner remained in his service up to September of last year.'

Without intending to, Mr Poland had evoked a slightly puzzling image: that of a servant having murdered an old lady in cold blood, concealing the crime brilliantly – then brazenly continuing to work in the same house in which the deed had been committed; and doing so without giving either Mr or Mrs Bastendorff any sense that something might be wrong.

But what of the sad fragments of Matilda Hacker's life? Mr Poland told the court that after the rent money was received, and after 'Miss Uish' was supposed to have left, Hannah Dobbs 'told Mr Bastendorff that the lady had left behind her dream book'. This book of predictions was 'afterwards given to the children'. Added to this was 'a cash box', also given to the children; Hannah Dobbs had claimed that it was hers, but that she had lost the key. 'Miss Hacker,' said Mr Poland, 'had a cash box and also a dream book, and there was no doubt that these were her property.'

As the months passed, said Mr Poland, 'Mrs Bastendorff had no suspicion that anything was wrong.' The prosecutor seemed eager to press this point. It was only on that morning several weeks back, when it was decided to have the coal cellar cleared in readiness for the Brook, that the horrific truth was uncovered. Mr Poland described how the remains had 'a rope round the neck'; he described the lace shawl, the brooch. He discussed possible witnesses, such as Matilda Hacker's lawyer Mr Ward, who would help to identify her. He described how, on 10 October 1877, Matilda Hacker wrote to her informal Canterbury property manager Mr Cozens, instructing him in her usual cryptic fashion that his reply was to be addressed to: 'MB, Post Office, 227 Oxford Street.' And how Mr Cozens did, indeed, reply, enclosing a cheque for £9 and 14 shillings – the letter remained at the post office, 'never having been called for' and ultimately it was returned 'through the Dead Letter Office' to Mr Cozens in Canterbury.

'So you have the fact,' said the prosecutor, 'that she was last seen alive on the 5th of October 1877.'

Mr Poland, via the offices of Inspector Hagen, had been furnished with some intelligence concerning the movements of Hannah Dobbs in the weeks and months after the murder was supposed to have been committed. When she left the employment of the Bastendorffs in September 1878 – almost a year after the disappearance of 'Miss Uish' – Hannah Dobbs went to live in lodgings around the corner from Euston Square in George Street. 'She left those lodgings in debt, and here she left behind some boxes,' said Mr Poland, 'and ultimately these boxes . . . were found to contain clothing belonging to the missing lady who lived at Euston Square, and also the eyeglass which will be identified as the property of Miss Hacker.'

The trail of purloined possessions did not end there. 'In November 1877,' said Mr Poland, 'a gold watch was pawned in the name of Rosina Bastendorff, at a pawn-broker's shop in Drummond Street. Rosina is the name of a daughter of Mr Bastendorff. There was attached to the watch a chain and locket. These were pawned in the month of March of the following year in the same name of Bastendorff. The locket will be identified as that of Miss Hacker, and was pawned in March 1878.' Again, this was some months after her disappearance.

There was one more item which did not go to the pawn shop, but which instead ended up being passed around within the Bastendorff household. It was a basket trunk, also 'the property of Miss Hacker'. 'This,' said Mr Poland, 'was left behind and was afterwards given by Mr Bastendorff to his brother, and is now in the possession of the police. There is also a tray belonging to the basket, which was found some time afterward in the loft of 4, Euston Square.' The trap door of the loft had apparently been 'fastened down' before Hannah Dobbs left her employment at the house. It was Mr Poland's intention, he said, to demonstrate that so many of the old lady's belongings had ended up nefariously in the possession of the servant girl.

He also meant to ensure that the Bastendorff family themselves were considered completely respectable. 'During the day,' said Mr Poland, 'Mr Bastendorff, who is a bamboo cabinet maker, usually works in the back shop. Mr and Mrs Bastendorff occupied the parlour and the kitchen. It would be difficult to believe,' the prosecutor told the magistrate, 'that this lady was murdered in the room during the week and the body removed down the stairs to the cellar. But on the Sunday, Mr Bastendorff is always away from home. He goes out to shoot small birds in the country.' Equally on Sundays, he stated, 'Mrs Bastendorff also goes out with the children.' In other words, he said, 'on such an occasion, the prisoner would be alone with the lodgers in the house.' Mr Poland added that even though he could not quite fix the date, it certainly seemed that on one Sunday in the October of 1877, both Mr and Mrs Bastendorff were away from the house.

He would also address the puzzling question of motive: why would anyone murder an eccentric old lady? He would, he said, 'prove that Matilda Hacker was in the possession of certain means, and a person might have been murdered for them. The body was found with a rope around the neck. Whether this was the cause of death I cannot say, or whether there were some other acts of violence.'

There seemed at any rate to be one other sign of lethal struggle. There was, he said, a stain on the carpet of Miss Uish's room. 'A piece of the carpet was examined . . . there are patches of blood upon it,' declared Mr Poland. 'Whether death was the result of violence, or by strangulation, it is impossible for me to say. If this woman was murdered, then the rope may have been put round her neck and by these means she may have been dragged down the stairs through the kitchen, into the cellar, where the body would remain concealed to all persons except the person who would be in the daily habit of going into the cellars.'

That person, he emphasised again, was not the lady of the house. 'Mrs Bastendorff did not go into the cellars herself,' he said. But Hannah Dobbs did. 'The prisoner was in the daily habit of going to the cellar, and nobody else,' said Mr Poland. Moreover, he added, it was 'impossible for the prisoner, if she was in the habit of going there, not to have seen it'.

This seemed a curious logical jump; for if Hannah Dobbs had concealed the body, then she would not have subsequently 'seen' it; and if she didn't, she wouldn't necessarily have seen it either. It all depended upon the disposition of the coals. Nor had Mr Poland completely established that Hannah Dobbs was the sole occupant of 4, Euston Square who somehow had access to the cellar.

'They made inquiries of the prisoner in the House of Correction at Westminster,' he continued, '. . . as to whether she could give them information relating to this matter.' And it would appear that during this questioning, Hannah Dobbs was caught out in one key admission about the eccentric old lodger. 'She stated at first that she could not recollect the lady's name.' But then, a little later when being interviewed by Inspector Hagen, she changed her account. 'She said she had been thinking the matter over and she remembered the lady's name which was Miss Hacker.'

But the old lady had resided there under the pseudonym 'Miss Uish'; how did Hannah Dobbs know her real name? 'It may be that the name of Hacker was in the Dream Book because looking into that book we find that there are two or three front pages torn out, where the true name of Matilda Hacker might possibly have been,' Mr Poland told the magistrate. 'Whether she got it from that book or in any other way, there is at least the fact that she did state to the inspector that the name of this lady was Miss Hacker; and she also further said that (Miss Hacker) had gone to the country to collect her rents and left behind her a Dream Book which (Hannah Dobbs) took to her mistress after this lady had left.'

Mr Poland was fixating on one particular Sunday in October 1877 being the day of the murder.

Why? 'I believe I shall be able to give evidence,' he told the magistrate, 'that on a Sunday about this date, a scream was heard by a lady living next door who has seen a photograph of the old lady, which she is able to identify as that of the lodger she had seen at the house . . . This scream, I am told, is not of an unimportant character because it alarmed the lady so much that it caused her to faint, and she was found in a fainting condition by her servant.'

All that said, concluded Mr Poland, 'I do not pretend, Sir, to have put before you all the facts I intend to prove. A great many important facts have been ascertained – but I give you a mere outline of them to show that the police are justified in bringing the prisoner before you and charging her with this very serious crime.'[7]

Even though this was the pre-hearing to determine the need for a larger trial, Mr Poland was allowed to call one key witness: a curious proceeding when it is remembered that at this stage, Hannah Dobbs had no-one to represent her defence.

And the witness seemed there not merely for the value of her testimony, but also to present a wholesome image of ordered domesticity, cruelly shattered by the horror brought upon her house. Mary Bastendorff took to the stand.

Possibly it was because of the nervous way that she responded to pressure; but quite quickly, the proceedings – in laying bare the daily life of her household – would make it seem as if Mary Bastendorff was on a form of trial herself, for gross domestic negligence. She swore her oath and declared: 'We went to live at Euston Square in March 1876. The prisoner Hannah Dobbs was in our service as general servant.

'She first came to live with us in the summer of 1876,' said Mrs Bastendorff. 'She stayed with us until September of last year (1878). She had been away once, but had re-entered our service between those dates. She had the management of the place, and entirely attended to the lodgers.'

Mr Poland's first question was: 'Do you remember a lodger named Uish?'

'She occupied a front room on the second floor,' replied Mrs Bastendorff. 'I saw her on two occasions as she was going to church. Those were the only times I saw her.' The rent she paid was 12 shillings a week.

And how long did she live there? 'I see by the rent book (which was produced in court) she stayed with us three weeks.'

And when was this? 'There is no date in the book,' said Mrs Bastendorff, 'and I cannot call to mind on what date Miss Uish came to us. A Mr Findlay lodged with me . . . before the deceased and before him there was a Mr Lefler . . . The last entry after Miss Uish is Mr Willoughby, 21st November to January following.'

This established 4, Euston Square as a busy and well-used house; landlords and tenants alike apparently unaware of the hideous crime that had taken place. 'Though I cannot fix the dates exactly,' continued Mrs Bastendorff, 'Miss Uish must have been with me between the 25th of July and the 21st of November.'

And what then of these other lodgers? Did Mrs Bastendorff have many dealings with them? 'Mr Lefler was an American,' she said, 'and went back to New York. I don't know what Mr Findlay was.'

The court heard of Mary Bastendorff's detachment from day-to-day housekeeping; the fact that the tenants' needs were met by others. 'I have never seen Miss Uish's luggage,' said Mrs Bastendorff. 'From what I saw of her, I should say she was about five feet 4 inches in height, and she wore her hair in curls. It was very light . . . the prisoner spoke of her as either Miss Uish or the old lady. At the time she was stopping with me, I had another lodger called Riggenbach. He was the only other lodger there when she was there.'

Mr Poland wanted to know a little of her husband's craft, and of the layout of the house. 'My husband works in a back (work) shop on the dining room floor,' said Mrs Bastendorff. 'There are two cellars, and there is a passage from the kitchen into the cellars. One of the cellars was used for coke and some of my husband's bamboo.'

Was that the front cellar, she was asked? 'Yes,' she said. 'The other was always used by us for coals.'

And was Hannah Dobbs in the habit of going there? 'Always.'

And could she recall 'the prisoner' speaking about the departure of Miss Uish? 'Yes.'

Was that at the end of the three weeks after she came? 'Yes,' said Mrs Bastendorff. 'The prisoner asked for Miss Uish's bill for £1 16 shillings, which was due, and gave it to the prisoner . . . As near as I can tell, (this was) between 11 and 12.' But she could not remember which day of the week this was. Did Mrs Bastendorff have any prior indications that Miss Uish was going to leave? 'Only by Hannah telling me,' she said. 'She came down and said Miss Uish was going away and then I made out the bill and gave it to the prisoner.'

Shortly afterwards, 'she brought me a £5 note and I took the £1 16 shillings out of it. I don't remember how the change for the note was obtained. She brought the bill with the note and I receipted it.' And that, she was asked, was about 12 in the day? 'Yes, as well as I can make out.'

'Now,' said Mr Poland, 'that day had you seen anything of Miss Uish?' 'No, I saw nothing of her.'

'Did you see her leave?' 'No, I did not see her leave the house, nor did I see anything leave in the way of boxes.'

It was established that it might have been several days before Mrs Bastendorff went into Miss Uish's former room on the second floor. She could not recall exactly. But she did remember 'perfectly' going into the room one morning, accompanied by Hannah Dobbs. 'She either followed me in or was there before me, I don't remember.'

There was the matter of a 'broken lamp glass'; that is, an ornamental gaslight fitting that had been somehow smashed at some point in Miss Uish's tenancy, for which the old lady had apparently given a small financial consideration to Hannah Dobbs in order to be passed on to the lady of the house.

And when Mary Bastendorff entered the room, what did she notice? 'A large stain on the carpet.' Whereabouts? 'Down by the side of the bed.' And what sort of stain was it? 'It appeared as though it had been scrubbed with water.'

Was it, asked Mr Poland, 'a felt carpet with a good deal of green in it, and had the colour been affected?' 'Yes,' said Mrs Bastendorff, 'for the colour had come out by the washing. When I saw the state of the carpet, I said, 'you are a dreadful girl to trust things to. I would much rather have no lodgers at all than have my things destroyed so.'

She added of Miss Uish that 'if I had seen her before she left, I should have made her pay for the carpet.'

Mr Poland asked her: 'Do you remember the prisoner showing you a book?' 'Yes, she brought me a book. I cannot say how long it was afterwards.'

With this, *The Book of Dreams* was flourished before the court. 'The first two or three pages are missing,' said Mr Poland, 'but is this the book?'

'Yes, that is the book she brought to me,' said Mrs Bastendorff. 'She said that Miss Uish had left her Dream Book behind. I said, 'I should think that she will come back for it.'

The book had been in the kitchen of 4, Euston Square until it was acquired as evidence by Inspector Hagen on 19 May. 'It was in better order when I first saw it,' said Mrs Bastendorff, 'for my little girl has since had it to play with, and leaves would very likely come out.'

What of the movements of the accused, Hannah Dobbs? Did Mrs Bastendorff remember her leaving her house at around the time of the disappearance? 'No, I do not,' she said. 'She went away for a few days, around the Christmas of the same year – from a Saturday morning to a Monday night, I think.' And where was it that Hannah Dobbs went? 'She said she went to her home at Bideford in Devonshire.'

And when she returned, had she in her possession any item that particularly attracted Mrs Bastendorff's attention? 'No, sir.' Had Hannah Dobbs mentioned anything about her relations – about 'their position and circumstances'? 'I always thought they were well-to-do people,' said Mrs Bastendorff, 'for she said her uncle had left her some money, and I thought that she had gone home to fetch it.'

And had she said anything else on the matter? 'Only about the gold watch and the chain, which she said were her uncle's.'

When, asked Mr Poland, did Hannah Dobbs say that? 'I could not say when it was,' said Mrs Bastendorff. 'I only know I had seen her wear it.' Was it before she went home at Christmas? 'I could not say.' Was it before or after that last rental bill had been paid? 'I could not say.'

Mr Poland was trying to convey to Mrs Bastendorff the urgent importance of these timings. He said: 'Have you tried to think this matter over?' As if in frustration, Mrs Bastendorff replied: 'I am very irregular over dates and can't remember.'

Now the magistrate, Mr Vaughan, interceded. 'When did (Hannah Dobbs) tell you her uncle had left her some money?' he asked her. 'I can't say,' said Mrs Bastendorff.

Yet, the magistrate said, she had stated 'just now' that she thought that Hannah Dobbs had gone down to the country to 'fetch the money'. Had Hannah Dobbs told her that? 'I don't know.' Then why should she have thought that? 'I had heard some time before that she expected him to leave her money.'

And afterwards she learned that he had? 'Yes, sir.'

It was at this stage in the proceedings that this chief witness was starting to seem at best vague about many of the facts that she was being asked to recall. One generous explanation might simply have been that Mary Bastendorff would have understood very clearly that Hannah Dobbs, when put on full trial, would be facing the possibility of the death penalty. An extraordinary weight of responsibility rested on flitting memories of seemingly trifling events that had happened eighteen months beforehand.

But the court had curiously limited patience. Accordingly, the questioning from both Mr Poland and Mr Vaughan became increasingly terse; nothing is recorded concerning the reactions of Hannah Dobbs, who was looking on. Mr Poland, with what sounded like a note of exasperation, tried another angle on Mrs Bastendorff. 'Just look,' he said. 'I think you saw a basket trunk?'

'Yes, in the cellar,' said Mrs Bastendorff. 'I can't say when, but I have seen it in there.'

'Just try and think when you first saw it,' said Mr Poland. 'Have you seen it since the discovery?' By this, he meant the disclosure of the corpse.

'No, I have not.'

'When did you first see it?' he asked.

'I can form no idea,' said Mrs Bastendorff. 'At Christmas last, we had it moved into the scullery.'

At this, the basket itself was wheeled into the Bow Street courtroom. It was described in the reports as a 'large basket trunk of a very ordinary kind, used for travelling, covered with American cloth.'

'Was that,' Mr Poland asked Mrs Bastendorff, 'the basket you saw?'

'It may be the same,' Mrs Bastendorff said, 'but it looked different, and I don't think it had a cover on when I saw it.'

'That basket does not belong to you?'

'No.'

'Was the one you saw about that size?'

'It was a different shaped one.'

'Are you able to say,' said Mr Poland, once again trying to pin down some certainty, 'that this was the one or not?'

'No,' said Mrs Bastendorff. 'I have seen one similar to that, but the one I saw looked higher.'

Once again, the magistrate pressed for greater clarity. 'Is the cellar where you saw it dark?' he asked her. 'No,' she said.

Mr Poland tried again, with what now sounded like angry impatience. 'Was (the basket) similar to that?' he said. 'Yes, it was.' 'And it did not belong to you?' 'Not that I know of. I did not examine it. I thought it was a wine case.'

'Now, pray consider,' said Mr Poland. 'Have you ever had a basket like that?'

'We have many cases sent to us.'

'Like that?'

At this, the magistrate lent in and said to her: 'Just consider.' Mr Poland added: 'Like a clothes basket, you know.' Mrs Bastendorff then said: 'No, I have not.'

'When did you first see that?' said the magistrate. 'I could not possibly form any idea,' said Mrs Bastendorff. 'Last year?' pressed Mr Poland. 'Yes, last year,' she replied.

'What time?'

'I could not tell at all,' she said. 'It is twelve months since I went into the cellar. I go there very seldom.'

'Was the prisoner in your service,' said Mr Poland, 'at the time you first saw it?'

'I believe so.'

'Did you speak to her on the subject?'

'I did not.'

And where was this basket-trunk then moved to within the house? 'It was moved into the scullery,' said Mrs Bastendorff, 'and filled with empty bottles.' Who moved it? 'I don't know.' Was Hannah Dobbs still working at the house when it was moved? 'I think not.' So this was after September of the previous year, 1878? 'It was brought in at Christmas last year,' said Mrs Bastendorff.

What became of this trunk afterwards? 'I never knew until the detectives asked for it,' said Mrs Bastendorff, 'and then it was found that it had been taken away from the house and that my husband's brother had it.'

Could she 'fix the day' that Hannah Dobbs had left her employment? 'No, I can't, but it was some time in September.'

The resident Mr Riggenbach had lodged some complaint? 'Yes.' He had 'lost some things'? 'Yes.'

When Hannah Dobbs left her employ, said Mr Poland, he understood that Mary Bastendorff was 'some time without a servant.' 'Yes, sir.' 'And then Louise Barker came?

'Yes sir.' And could Mrs Bastendorff remember 'one evening her bringing you some towels and drawers – three or four towels and a pair of gentleman's drawers?' 'Yes,' said Mrs Bastendorff, 'she said she had found them in the cellar. I looked at them, and saw the drawers belonged to Mr Riggenbach.'

The implication was that these were among the items that had been stolen by Hannah Dobbs from this most respectable of tenants. And the fact of male underwear in this context once more threw a light on the novel intimacy of this sort of living: items that would be normally bundled off to the St Pancras laundress were among those effects that could be purloined from supposedly private rooms. When were these drawers found, asked Mr Poland. 'Barker was only with us seven weeks,' said Mrs Bastendorff, 'so they were found during that time.'

And what servant was engaged for 4, Euston Square after that? 'A girl named Sarah Carpenter,' said Mrs Bastendorff.

And did 'that woman' afterwards show her 'a bone'? 'She brought me a bone,' said Mrs Bastendorff. 'I looked at it and I said

I believed it belonged to a wild boar my husband had, which he had shot in Germany.'

And thence to the day of the discovery in May 1879: she herself did not go into the cellar? 'No,' she said, 'but I heard afterwards that a human body was found. I went up to tell my husband and during that time, a policeman had been called in.'

There was one last matter that Mr Poland wanted to find out about: the matter of Miss Uish's eyeglass, which had now been retrieved by Inspector Hagen from a local pawnbroker and which seemed to correspond to an eyeglass sported for a time by Hannah Dobbs.

'I remember Hannah used to have an eyeglass by a peculiar incident,' said Mrs Bastendorff. 'My mother wears glasses . . . and she compared the sight of hers and Hannah's on one occasion when she came to visit me.'

And was the eyeglass 'one of that description'? 'It was a single glass and it had a gilt frame,' said Mrs Bastendorff firmly.

Did Mrs Bastendorff ever hear from Hannah Dobbs where 'Miss Uish came from, or where she had gone to?' 'No,' she said. 'Very little reference was made to her at all.'[8]

There is no record of how the accused Hannah Dobbs was responding to any of this in the dock. But as this pre-trial examination was adjourned, the magistrate, Mr Vaughan, caught her eye. He said to her: 'Have you any questions to ask?'

Hannah Dobbs' answer was shocking – and as a result, greatly relished by all the court reporters.

'I have no questions to ask of *Mrs* Bastendorff,' Hannah Dobbs said, drawing out the 'Mrs' with startling contempt, adding: 'When Mr Bastendorff is present, I shall have some questions to put.'

This elicited no comment from either prosecutor or magistrate; nor is there any record of how Mary Bastendorff responded. A date was set a week hence for one more pre-trial examination. Since Hannah Dobbs was already serving a sentence in Tothill Fields, there was no difficulty about remanding her.

'Shortly after leaving the dock,' ran one report, 'the prisoner, who still preserved her nonchalant demeanour, was placed in a cab, and, accompanied by the warder, driven back to the prison.' There was also a wry afternote concerning the attractions of such cases to the general public: there were few crowds outside to witness her departure from the Bow Street court that afternoon – the reason being that 'all those who took an interest in the case . . . apparently found means to enter the court which was very full indeed while the examination lasted.'

The pre-trial resumed a few weeks later – it appeared that Mary Bastendorff had fallen ill and was in no state to attend until she had recovered. Now back to health, she was present as a new gobbet of evidence was given by Hannah Dobbs' guards at Tothill Fields; she had been telling them of a previous resident of 4, Euston Square called Mr Findlay. The chief warder of the prison, Robert Vermeulen, said that Hannah Dobbs told him of how Findlay had 'a seven-chamber loaded revolver'. Dobbs also told him that Findlay 'had committed a murder and that he wanted to confide his secret to her . . . he wanted her to go away with him to America and offered her £50 to do so but she refused the offer.' Mr Vermeulen had not taken a note of this conversation but it was lodged in his memory.

Having heard this – with some interest – the court moved to examination of the movements of Severin Bastendorff; of his visit, that weekend in October 1877 to see a friend in Erith, on the Kent marshes. He and another friend, a 'Mr Whiffling', were there for some shooting.

Severin Bastendorff had got his shooting license some two months beforehand; despite that, he had had a minor dispute with a local policeman who accused him of 'shooting in the roadway' rather than clearly into the country. Despite this minor vexation, he and his friends continued their marsh shoot that weekend; he arrived back in Euston Square late on the evening of Sunday, 14 October 1877; he remembered seeing his wife Mary in the kitchen in her 'walking hat' and dress; she and the children has just returned from a trip to Hampstead. Then, he recalled, all retired to bed.

Following this evidence, there were further witness statements concerning boar bones, rent receipts, the gold chain that Hannah Dobbs had been seen with. The prosecutor Mr Poland now asked for the official 'committal' of the prisoner for full trial: and at this point the magistrate Mr Vaughan repeated the charge to her.

'I am not guilty of it,' Hannah Dobbs said.[9]

There was, according to reports, the first sign of some agitation from her; but she very quickly recovered; when she was presented with a declaration to sign, she did it with a firm hand.

Though Hannah Dobbs was the one standing accused of the murder of a perfectly harmless and eccentric lady, there seemed much unspoken about the arrangements within number 4, Euston Square. There had been the first suggestion of lodgers like Mr Findlay who could seem rather disconcerting.

Those had not been the only nocturnal footsteps on the stairs in number 4, Euston Square. Journalists picking up gossip were starting to hear of some intriguing and unexpected sexual relationships in that house. There were rumours involving another of the Bastendorff brothers.

And as a result – as Inspector Hagen and his colleagues were still piecing together as much as they could of the earlier life and career of Hannah Dobbs – there were other legal figures who were now anxious to swiftly learn more about the lives and experiences of a family who had emigrated from continental Europe to London and who had, with some dazzling success, reinvented themselves as English middle-class gentlemen.

11
The Brothers Bastendorff

The Bastendorff children – all sixteen of them – had grown up on a farm amid the rich forests and rocky hills and castles of the Ardennes; in the mid-nineteenth century, the Grand Duchy of Luxembourg, under the wing of Belgium, was still largely untouched by the Industrial Revolution. It was only in later years that new forms of steel production suddenly made the country a viable prospect for manufactories. Indeed, Luxembourg only got its first railway line in 1859, some distance behind its neighbours in Belgium and France.

The Bastendorff family lived in a village called Berdorf, near the bustling town of Echternach, which stands very close to today's German border. The area had its own, close dialect, and held tenaciously to its Catholicism; and the children who were later to emigrate to London – Joseph, Severin, Elizabeth, Anton and Peter – would have been brought up on local folktales[1] that blended religion and the lush wooded landscape with the faerie realm; there were the little people that dwelled under the hills, who aided virtuous farmers; a satanic fiddler who could possess people with his music; the chilling nocturnal chants of long-dead monks in the ruin of an abbey despoiled by invaders. There was nothing in this childhood that could have prepared them for life dwelling among millions in the fog of a vast city.

Perhaps it was the belated coming of the railway to the city of Luxembourg which opened up the possibilities of that new world. sixteen-year-old Elizabeth Bastendorff, was the first to leave her home; she was married to a young German called Wilhelm Hoerr. Their horizons were ambitious; rather than heading in the direction of Belgium, they were set on Paris. And they arrived there in the late 1860s. They were joined shortly afterwards by Elizabeth's brother, Severin, released from his rural labour.

'At the age of fifteen, I was hired to a farmer for one year,' Severin later wrote, '. . . I remained with him the whole year, looking after the horses, and he maintained me. After that I went to Paris and learned the cabinet-making trade.'[2]

Of all the times to hope to make a new life in Paris, this was hardly ideal. Napoleon III was confident that France's military skill and strength would act as deterrent to a newly unified Germany and its leader Bismarck. It did not. By 1870, there was war.

Elizabeth and Wilhelm Hoerr and Severin Bastendorff left just before the disaster overwhelmed Paris; the thunder of war made them think not of returning to Luxembourg, but venturing further. There had been a few instances of their young Berdorf neighbours sailing out to America. But they decided upon London.

And it was Severin, then 22-years old, who moved first. He set sail on a steam packet across the grey Channel and came into port at Southampton. 'I knew no-one, and could not speak a word of English, only French and German,' he later wrote.[3]

When Bastendorff arrived, there was no oppressive police presence at the docks to follow him; no officials to tell him that his time in the country was limited; no overbearing government departments insistent on monitoring his employment or housing. There was just a quick note on a register. (Indeed, it was only in the 1880s that official passenger disembarkation lists started to be kept; and the first serious efforts at controlling immigration came later yet at the turn of the century.)

On the other side of that, Bastendorff was left to make his own way in this alien realm. It must have been a tremendous adventure for the young man with no English; but the docks were very cosmopolitan. 'A man at Southampton gave me the address of a hotel in Nassau Street,' he wrote. 'I went there and had some refreshment and he (the proprietor) sent a waiter with me to take a room at the tobacconist's shop in Ryder's Court, which I took for two shillings and six pence. The shopkeeper was a Pole.' It seemed also that he was connected to a wider network of émigrés. 'Next day, this Pole gave me addresses to look for work.'

One of those addresses was in the East End of London; using what remained of his money, Bastendorff caught the train from Southampton; here, in this swaying carriage amid fellow passengers, he will have had that exhilarating butterfly sensation of being a new arrival in a foreign land. He would have glanced around and wondered if the others could tell he was a foreigner.

His approach into London from the south took him past plump green hills dense with suburban villas, and thence more close-built yellow-brick terraces, and on from there towards the dense smoky clusters of tall chimneys and low roofs denoting riverside industry. The air of this new world – coal, chemicals, gusts from breweries, the close, fusty reek of others' clothes – must have tasted extraordinary to him. His train arrived at Victoria station. And from here, there was what must have been the stomach-swooping prospect of the underground Metropolitan District Railway: the recently constructed ingenuity of which was described by some as 'a descent into Hades': again, we must imagine a young man from a rural land standing looking into the black mouth of the tunnel, cacophonous with the approach of the deep green steam engine; then, the yellow gaslight in the swaying brown-painted wooden carriages, the rich darkness out of the windows, punctuated with gas-lit stations, until reaching the terminus at Mansion House.

However he did it, Bastendorff eventually made his way east to Union Street in Whitechapel.

There he met 'a German, Mr Keller', and immediately started working for him. Bastendorff's skill sharpened; over the weeks, he began to acquire a little of the language, and then more. Though there were many other German speakers in Whitechapel, the area was in sloping decline; bitterly overcrowded housing, pervasive street violence, a labyrinth of close-built courts that reeked of dung and animal blood. For a young man who had come from wide-open country, it must have been bitterly unpleasant.

But as Bastendorff's craftsmanship improved, so his ambitions rose. He took on another cabinet-making job, near Clerkenwell. This business was not so successful; he considered at one point returning to Paris. (This was commonly the case with numbers of French immigrants at this time, who for some reason, possibly to do with language, often found it harder than others to maintain their grip on the city.)

Instead, he found another position, this time closer to the centre of town, with 'Mr Vortier, of St Martin's Lane'; and his speciality was bamboo work. Bastendorff stayed with him for a year, ever more profitably; then decided to take his own workshop in Denmark Street, and go into business for himself. (Though the timings are unclear, his sister and brother-in-law must have arrived around this time and established themselves elsewhere; similarly, his other brothers, Anton and Joseph, came to London too; Peter followed later.)

Commercial success now came quickly for Severin: he started simply, making one table, a blend of timber and bamboo. He sold it to a large retailer on the nearby Tottenham Court Road. He recalled that by the time he had delivered this table, and returned to his workshop, there was already a messenger boy there to place an order from the retailers for more of his work.

Bastendorff had found a place, and a skill that was serendipitously in demand. For some decades out of fashion, 'chinoiserie' – furniture inspired by Chinese designs – was desirable once more. It was now blended with influences from Japan, and the art of working with bamboo as a material resulted in furniture – chairs, desks, firescreens, occasional tables – that could be relatively cheap, as well as light and durable. In the early 1870s, only a handful of manufacturers were specialising in it. Although not a part of the nascent Arts and Crafts movement, which focused on the aesthetics of handmade designs, this sort of furniture making – highly elaborate patterns, careful lacquers and varnishing – was in the same spirit. And as Bastendorff grew his new business, he entered into partnerships with English furniture makers. His assimilation was fast. It was natural for him to think soon of taking a wife.

By the 1860s and early 1870s, there was in a wider sense quite a degree of cultural fusion between the British and German people. The most obvious link – emotional, rather than constitutional – was the Royal Family, with its antecedents and branches reaching deep into Germany. Not only was German the first language of Queen Victoria, but many of the aristocrats who patronised the flourishing arts and sciences in London and throughout the land were very closely bonded with German landed power. Far from being either a suspicious or hostile environment, London was a very open city at this point. Continental Europe was more than neighbouring nations; it was a closely integrated part of the capital's life.

Bastendorff had to continually move his work premises; for his growing success meant he had to hire more hands and rent yet more space. In the middle of the nineteenth century, the streets that ran north from Oxford Street towards Somers Town were filled with workshops specialising in everything from easy chairs to pianos. By the time Bastendorff's brothers had arrived in London in the early 1870s, there were an estimated 6,000 people working in the furniture trade in the small area of London around Fitzroy Square alone. Filmer and Sons, for instance, produced 'couches and chairs' that were 'celebrated . . . for their grace and comfort'. Oetzmann in the meantime took immense pride in the finish of its mahogany furnishings. C. Nosotti offered 'a choice selection of dining room, bedroom and boudoir furniture'.[4] For soft furnishings such as 'Brussels Carpets', Druce and Co. were advertising heavily.

And the busy thoroughfare of Tottenham Court Road was opening up yet more possibilities: furniture shops that had once been small and cramped were expanding, and blossoming in colour and style. John Maples had looked at his eponymous outlet and saw the wisdom in constructing a much larger store that could be divided into departments. In the 1860s, Maples was offering a shop which could offer everything from Jacobean-themed sideboards, blackened and elaborately carved, to more voguish Chinese lacquered cabinets.

Soon this approach was attracting a more upmarket sort of customer: there were ladies in Belgravia who would summon the brougham to take them to Tottenham Court Road. Heal and Son – which still stands on the Tottenham Court Road today – was reconstructed 'in the Italian style' with galleries and 'a considerable amount of colour introduced in the pilasters and panels'.[5]

And the workshops that clustered around these smart emporia had for some decades seen a dazzling mix of European nationalities: French, Swedish and Dutch craftsmen had all, in time, come to own their own concerns. The working conditions were, for the time, very reasonable. This was not the case all over London. Cheaper, more basic furniture, manufactured on the fringes of the City and the Hackney Road, was a sweated enterprise; for less-skilled workers, the pay was very poor and the hours were debilitating. Here just off the Tottenham Court Road, however, the craftsmen were treated with respect.

The journalist and social observer Henry Mayhew visited The Woodcarver's Society just off Charlotte Mews in 1861 and found 'a fairly paid class of mechanics' surrounded with proud examples of their work, 'discussing the affairs of their trade'.[6]

Here was intelligence, and diligence, and also the prospect of social mobility. Severin Bastendorff – and brothers Joseph, Anton, and a little later, the young Peter – acquired skills and business acumen very quickly. The entire family went into the business of bamboo.

Working with bamboo was quite a different discipline to the more conventional forms of carpentry; it required an understanding of the unique nature of the reeds and patience when it came to moulding with flame the different elements of each furniture item, the varnishing required for lacquered cabinets and the production of a tortoise-shell finish on items such as chairs and sofas.

But, in the early 1870s, the time was perfect for hard-working young men from the continent; not least because, through contacts and assiduous research, they would have found very quickly a German-speaking market for their goods.

By this stage, the German-speakers in London congregated most around three areas: Bloomsbury (which seemed largely to attract the younger incomers who would live in the boarding houses); Camberwell, an increasingly prosperous suburb four miles south of the Thames; and Sydenham, some three or four miles further south yet, and sitting on the high wooded hill that was dominated with the vast glittering structure of Joseph Paxton's Crystal Palace.

The composer Richard Wagner had spent a few months in the 1850s being 'entertained by some of the wealthy Camberwell Germans' as well becoming infuriated with 'inattentive' English audiences and having his Tannhauser overture performed before Queen Victoria and Prince Albert.[7] But, by the 1870s, it was the native Germans in Sydenham who were the most well-to-do; these were families of merchants living in large, pretty villas, with pleasing views ranging from the City to the green fields of Kent; these were the sorts of customers that the Bastendorffs would seek out.

Many of the small furniture businesses clustered around Fitzroy Square and Charlotte Street were run as partnerships; skilled tradesmen joining forces and sharing their enterprises. Then, as the Bastendorffs grew in confidence, there was a move to start building a family-based business.

And as they did so, they also started to form romantic attachments that would come to give them even more permanent roots in this bright, exciting city. The eldest, Joseph, found himself a sweetheart who was a parlourmaid. And, in time, handsome young Severin, aged 25, began stepping out with a striking young lady whom he had met locally. It must have seemed for a time, to him and Mary Pearce, that the possibilities of this extraordinary time and city were endless.

Yet it might also be asked whether even at this early point Severin was finding it difficult to maintain his mental stability.

12
The New Age of Light

It took a French artist, recently arrived in London in 1870, having fled the Franco-Prussian War, to see the exquisitely romantic spirit: Claude Monet's 1871 painting *The Thames Below Westminster* bathed the new Victoria Embankment and the rebuilt Houses of Commons in the rosy smoke of sunset. Where others might have seen pomp wreathed in the vapours of industry, Monet's vision softened the heart of this imperial realm. He gave it a glowing twilight evanescence, the river and the buildings and the jetty sitting on it suggestive of silence. But lovers had seen the possibilities too; the river had only been recently embanked, a vast engineering project undertaken by Joseph Bazalgette, and what he had conjured for the first time in London was a riverside esplanade.

The trees had been planted but were as yet young and slender; the road for horses and carriages was wide but not always busy. Thanks to Bazalgette's other terrific innovations in terms of London's sewerage, the river itself, although still filthy with a variety of waste, was no longer noxious; the strong tides bore the effluvia fast down into the darkness of the east.

Severin Bastendorff would surely have come here with his sweetheart, Mary Pearce, in the early days of their courtship; how could a recent arrival in London not be desperate to see both the heart of government but also the sophisticated marvel of a curving riverside path, lit prettily with gas flames, and gazing across south at the misty darkness of the Lambeth shore? How could he and Mary not spend a hazy summer's evening talking and walking, taking in the splendour of the new Somerset House, or the quiet gardens leading to the Temple Inns of Court? Couples walked from Westminster to Blackfriars arm in arm; stopping to look up as mighty locomotives on the bridge above heaved from their platforms at Charing Cross across the water towards the countryside of the south. To a young man from Luxembourg, all of this must have dazzled and beguiled with possibilities.

This was a time in which German-speakers were met with a growing measure of friendly curiosity (except in the East End, where young Irish men fought furiously with young Germans); one syndicated newspaper article detailed what kind of evening one might have in a German restaurant (of which more, such as Kuhn's, were being established in the area just north of Oxford Street). The article described a cosy room, lit with gas jets and wreathed in rich cigar smoke, where one would sit at long wooden tables with random companions to partake of soup and meat and then drink Bavarian beers and lagers while engaging in lively political debate.

The sense was given that the atmosphere of these establishments was a shade more thoughtful than the typical English pub.

A native Luxembourgian like Bastendorff might also have been heartened to see a large number of rather fashionable little French restaurants around Leicester Square and Soho, advertising their *tables d'hote*, and serving such items as veal cutlets in white sauce with onion puree. There was also the sumptuous continental sophistication of the recently opened Café Royal, just off Piccadilly, noted not only for its Gallic cuisine but also its magnificent cellar. But if this was rather beyond the means of a young furniture maker, then there was still good wine to be found in small French bars a few yards up the road off the Shaftesbury Avenue.

For Mary Pearce, who as far as can be gathered was a native Londoner, the prospect of romance with a German-speaking man (fast becoming fluent in English but still heavily accented) might have carried a sense of removing herself from the more straightforward class expectations. She lived with her mother amid the close-built terraces of Kentish Town, a mile or so north of King's Cross. It is not recorded how she and Bastendorff met; but it is known that he was a restless soul, given to long evening walks. And there is every possibility that she was in service. Throughout the middle years of Victoria's reign, the number of young women employed as domestic servants increased enormously. Severin's older brother, Joseph, had met his wife-to-be when she was in service.

However they first encountered one another, Severin and Mary must have made a handsome couple; she, dark and grave, and he, red-haired and whiskered and healthy.

This was a city on the edge of electricity; while the thick industrial fogs of night were being softened with the pale flicker of gas light, there were men of science demonstrating their remarkable new developments in electrical illumination, in the streets and in the music halls. And some of these important innovators were German. (Indeed, in May 1879, the Royal Albert Hall, already bathed in the cream-tinged glow of early electric light, devoted a widely attended evening to the possibilities of this science, including incandescent lamps designed by the firm of Dr Siemens. He had already demonstrated how electric light might be used at sea; now he was telling his audience that this new luminous age would soon be changing homes and streets.)

Meanwhile, the city had other more immediate wonders for young courting couples to enjoy. The vogue for Germanic entertainment extended mostly to orchestral music, but there were other attractions too: 'Professor Herrmann, the world-famed conjuror, unique in his style, and the celebrated Praeger Family, performing every evening at eight' announced the advertising for the Egyptian Hall theatre in Piccadilly. Elsewhere, 'Herr Carl Fittig, Professor of the Zither, who had the honour of performing before their Royal Highnesses the Prince and Princess of Wales' was pleased to announce his return to the London stage.

And there were charitable events to be attended too. 'The Chevalier de Kontski, pianist to the Emperor of Germany, and Herr Wilhelm Ganz, Grand Organist of the Grand Lodge of England, will play a grand duo on two pianos to raise money for the City of London lifeboat fund,' announced *The Times*. And to the east of the City, where there had stood for some years a dedicated 'German Hospital' for German speakers in the suburb of Dalston, there was another fund-raising event which was to be attended, among others, by Count Bernstoff, Count Buest and Gustavus Kottengell.

The Bastendorffs were sharp and fast adapters to nuances of class. And the romance between Severin and Mary deepened to the point in 1872 when he asked for her hand in marriage, and she accepted. The wedding was in St Pancras parish church.

The furniture trade was expanding fast for the brothers. The Bastendorffs were honing their Chinese-styled bamboo work. As well as cane chairs with latticed geometrical motifs suggestive of Chinese architecture, they also produced occasional tables, fireplace screens, and ornamental stands for flower vases. The growing popularity of such pieces reflected a young and upcoming middle class, moving to the new suburbs in Kentish Town, Holloway and Plaistow, and favouring lighter furnishings than the previous generation.

The Bastendorff brothers soon broke away from partnerships with others just off the Tottenham Court Road and made their enterprises more family-oriented. It would not be too long before they were hiring more staff.

When Severin and Mary had the first of their children, whatever lodgings they had the lease on were not going to be sufficient for very long. The ideal was to combine more comfortable surroundings for the babies while also possibly finding room for a much larger furniture workshop.

In the streets all around, putative landlords were taking leases on the four and five storey houses that clustered around the University of London and the British Museum. The economics were straightforward: if one could keep the house filled with tenants, one would have no difficulty paying for both the lease and the maintenance. And so it was that Severin alighted on 4, Euston Square.

And while the Bastendorffs were not rich, they had certainly hit a plateau of financial ease; enough for them to acquire their own horse and trap (though the horse might also have been used for deliveries for the furniture business throughout the week). And what this city also offered – as well as a kaleidoscope of different entertainments – was the weekend prospect of escaping into the airy heights of Hampstead Heath. These would have been marvellous adventures for the Bastendorff toddlers; the horse drawing them up past Euston and Camden New Town, and then the foothills of the Heath at Gospel Oak. In the summer, the heath was wild with hares; and as well as the middle-class picnickers, there were also numbers of boys and girls who had trailed up from humbler homes in Clerkenwell and Islington, and who were enjoying foraging for horseradish, sorrel and wild garlic.

It was in the mid-1870s that Severin Bastendorff expanded his interests in sporting pursuits; he was keen on fishing, for instance, and acquired a circle of friends with whom he would ride out to the Welsh Harp reservoir to the north-west of London. Added to this, the fast and regular railway services from London out into the countryside of Kent facilitated his other burgeoning enthusiasm. The silent marsh country close to where Charles Dickens had set the opening chapters of *Great Expectations* was a lure to a number of men with shotguns aiming to pick off as many birds as they could.

The appearance of respectability seemed very important to Bastendorff. He cultivated a thick beard. Unlike many craftsmen (and according to later illustrations taken from photographs) he sported a collar and tie and frock coat.

Nor did Severin or his brothers confine themselves to England in the mid-1870s; they made journeys back to Luxembourg, and across that border to Germany.

And at some point in the mid-1870s, Severin's younger brother, Peter made the voyage to England to join his brothers. Peter was said to resemble Severin quite strongly, except that his hair was more blond than red and when he first arrived in the capital, he scarcely had any facial hair at all. Peter was also very shy in those first few weeks; he had no English. Among his brothers, he could quite happily speak either in German or the local Luxembourgian dialect, but it was said that when faced with female company, he became blushingly tongue-tied.

This was not to remain the case for long; indeed, as the courts would soon hear, there was one young woman that Peter would call, in a joke cockney accent, 'his missus'. And there were none who could have foreseen just how toxic young Peter Bastendorff's first serious sexual relationship would be.

As with the tenants at number 4, Euston Square, who came and went with some regularity, so too was there a changing roster of servants. In 1876, Mary Bastendorff placed an advertisement in a local St Pancras newspaper for a maid-of-all-work. There was a reply from a 22-year-old, who had been in a situation in a Bloomsbury house just a few streets away in Torrington Square. She seemed efficient and intelligent; it was clear that Mary wanted to delegate as much of the running of 4, Euston Square as possible.

And three years later, it was this maid, Hannah Dobbs who was sitting in Tothill Fields House of Correction awaiting her arraignment on a charge of wilful murder. No-one – not even Hannah herself – could have anticipated the shocks that were to come.

13

He Kept Company with Her

The press and police were freely referring to it as murder; but even as the trial of Hannah Dobbs was being prepared, the members of the inquest jury in St Pancras were still deliberating the horrifying discovery. They convened for the final time at the beginning of June, 1879, with the coroner Dr Hardwicke. By now, the jurists had heard a number of local rumours concerning relationships within 4, Euston Square. For this hearing, Hannah Dobbs was recalled from Tothill Fields; strikingly, her mother Susan was also present. She had travelled from Bideford with Hannah's sister and her son-in-law. Mrs Dobbs clearly understood that there was now a danger to her daughter.

Also in that coroner's court were solicitors representing Hannah Dobbs and, indeed, the Bastendorff family. There was a general awareness that all now had to proceed carefully.

This was at a point when a greater regularity was being brought to a previously chaotic system of inquests and trials; in earlier years, jurors at such inquiries had inadvertently galloped ahead of police, speculating wildly on motives and means in murder cases, as well as the identities of the yet-to-be accused, before the police had even finished questioning all concerned. Not too long afterwards, specific legislation was brought before Parliament concerning this very question.

In the event, the first witness called to Dr Hardwicke's stand was Edward Hacker, the brother of Matilda. Mr Hacker explained how his sister supported herself. 'She had some independent property,' he said, 'a freehold in Canterbury. She received rents on this property and lived on the money so derived.'[1]

And how much was she receiving? 'Her property realised about £1 30 a year,' he said. (This would be about £9,000 a year now, though such a sum would have gone very much further in the 1870s than it would now.)

When was he aware that she was missing? Mr Hacker's answer was somehow both cold and piercingly sad. 'I first came to know of her disappearance,' he told the court, 'when Inspector Hagen came to see me.'

Now Mary Bastendorff was called; and a chair was requested. The strain she was under seemed to be the cause of her fatigue. Might she also have been anxious about the course that the questioning was shortly to take? The coroner began by asking her how Matilda Hacker came to take her room? '[S]he gave the name of Miss Uish,' said Mrs Bastendorff, 'and came in the end of 1877.' Did she pay a deposit? 'I can't remember,' she said. 'But I see in a book the entry, 'three weeks rent, 36 shillings – 12 shillings a week.'

Dr Hardwicke asked if she knew why Hannah Dobbs was currently being held in Tothill Fields prison.

'I was told for having robbed furnished apartments,' said Mrs Bastendorff.

When did Hannah Dobbs leave her employment at 4, Euston Square? 'About last September,' she said. That is, September, 1878.

Did Mrs Bastendorff know 'of any person' that Hannah Dobbs robbed 'who lodged with' the Bastendorffs? 'Yes,' said Mrs Bastendorff. 'I was told that she had taken things which belonged to Mr Riggenbach.'

And had Mr Riggenbach now recovered the items which had been purloined? At this juncture, Inspector Hagen – always sharp on matters of finance and property – arose to declare: 'The things stolen from Mr Riggenbach have been found pledged.' In other words, they had been taken to a pawnbroker. The coroner turned back to Mary Bastendorff. Was she aware that Hannah Dobbs had had a gold watch and chain? 'Yes,' she said. 'She wore one.' And did Mary Bastendorff remember when she first had it? 'No,' she said.

Was she aware that it had been pawned in her name? 'Yes,' she said, 'one of my family.'

This was the gold watch and chain that had belonged to Matilda Hacker. Now the court focused on Mrs Bastendorff's relationship with her servant girl. Did Hannah Dobbs go home to Devon during her time at 4, Euston Square? 'Yes,' said Mrs Bastendorff, 'several times.'

Now came the moment when it became clear how far Inspector Hagen's inquiries had reached.

Was Mrs Bastendorff aware, the coroner asked, that Hannah Dobbs was 'keeping company' with Peter, the young brother of her husband, Severin?

'Yes,' replied Mrs Bastendorff.

And did Mrs Bastendorff know that Hannah Dobbs had had a child by this brother, Peter?

'No,' she said, 'I did not.'

The revelations would have been shocking and extraordinary enough – but, in fact, as later emerged, the inquest had been a little misled on this point: the child had apparently not survived pregnancy.

None the less, the fact was established of a sexual relationship between servant and brother of the master of the house, outside of marriage: precisely the sort of seamy connection that respectable boarding houses tried furiously to avoid.

And more: why was the coroner seeking to establish some kind of link between this affair and the corpse in the coal cellar? He pressed on with the questioning of Mrs Bastendorff. Did she suppose that Peter Bastendorff had perhaps become engaged to Hannah Dobbs? 'Yes,' said Mrs Bastendorff.

And did Peter Bastendorff pay visits to 4, Euston Square to see Hannah Dobbs? 'Yes,' she said, 'he came to see her.' But he did not live with them? 'No.' What business was Peter Bastendorff in? 'A carpenter.' And, the coroner repeated, did she believe that Peter Bastendorff and Hannah Dobbs were engaged? 'Yes.' And when she returned to her home in the country, in Devon, did Peter Bastendorff go and see her? 'Yes,' she said, 'I believe he went, but I do not know.'

And how long was Hannah Dobbs away for? 'Once for a month,' said Mrs Bastendorff, 'and then two or three days.' And so when she was away from 4, Euston Square, who carried out all the work? 'I did it myself,' said Mrs Bastendorff. 'I had no charwoman until after she left.'

And was she in the habit of going into the coal cellar? 'Not while Hannah was there,' she said. But when Hannah was not there, pressed the coroner – did she then go into that cellar? 'Yes,' she replied.

And did she see anything? 'No,' she said, 'nothing but what I thought was rubbish. She used to throw a great deal of dust there instead of putting it into the dust hole.' The 'dust-hole' was the area into which the household's spent ashes and cinders from the fires were dumped; the 'dust' would be collected frequently, and could be recycled into the manufacture of bricks.

Mr Poland stepped in to ask some questions. He wanted to be quite clear on the dates. 'Hannah Dobbs was in your service from the summer of 1876 up till the September of last year?' 'Yes,' confirmed Mrs Bastendorff. 'Do you not find from the entries in your rent-book,' said Mr Poland, 'that Miss Uish must have been lodging in your house from the 24th of September to the 15th of October – that these were the three weeks she was a lodger of yours?' 'Yes,' said Mrs Bastendorff, 'that was about the time.'

'I believe,' continued Mr Poland, 'that it was a Monday that Miss Uish left your house?' 'I think so,' said Mrs Bastendorff.

'She left £5 after her,' Mr Poland said. 'Did Hannah Dobbs give you this £5 to take the three weeks rent out of it? 'Yes,' said Mrs Bastendorff. 'I saw the £5 with Hannah Dobbs but what she did with it I do not know. All I know is that she gave me out of it the £1 16s that Miss Uish owed me.' And about what time of day was this? 'Some time about 12 o'clock,' she said. 'About the dinner hour.'

'You say you never saw Miss Uish's face?' asked Mr Poland. 'I never did,' she said. 'Did you ever see her at all?' he persisted. 'Yes, on two occasions, when she was going out to church.' And how was she dressed on those occasions? 'All that I noticed,' said Mrs Bastendorff, 'was that she wore a blue silk dress.'

Mr Poland ran through several items that had once belonged to Matilda Hacker – an eyeglass and a bunch of keys among them. Could Mrs Bastendorff confirm that the eyeglass had been seen 'in the possession of Hannah Dobbs'? 'Yes,' she said. Did Mrs Bastendorff ever see 'Miss Uish's' luggage? 'I never did,' she said. And after Hannah Dobbs had left her employment, did she thereafter 'come to see' Mrs Bastendorff? 'Yes, she called at my house afterwards.'

And while 'Miss Uish' was resident, asked Mr Poland, was Mr Riggenbach the only other lodger at that particular time? 'Yes,' she said.

One juror asked Mrs Bastendorff if she had seen 'Miss Uish' after Hannah Dobbs had presented her with the £5? 'I did not see her after that time,' replied the lady. How could the elderly resident leave 4, Euston Square without the mistress of the house knowing? 'I was otherwise engaged,' was her response.

The coroner was bemused at how unperturbed the witness seemed by the old lady's dramatically abrupt departure. 'You felt no surprise at her going?' he asked. 'No,' said Mrs Bastendorff. 'I did not expect her to stay long.'

Another juror interjected, and this time clearly armed with local gossip that had clearly been circulated for some time, long before the discovery of the body. 'Do you know of anyone at your house,' the juror asked Mrs Bastendorff, 'being given to intemperance and making a disturbance?'

'No – never,' said Mrs Bastendorff, with some feeling. 'There was never any disturbance and the police were never called in.'

Once more, the good reputation of her house and business was being challenged. That insinuating juror was not finished. 'I can produce a constable in the Metropolitan Police,' he said, 'who can speak to having been called in at number 4. I can also produce an ex-constable, who has retired after 23 years' service on a pension, who will state that he was repeatedly called in to a foreigner at 3 or 4 (Euston Square), he cannot say which, but he could identify the foreigner if he could see him.'

Another juror interjected, probing further what seemed ill-defined domestic borders. Did Mrs Bastendorff make 'a confidant' of her servant Hannah Dobbs? 'Not at all'. And when new prospective lodgers came, did she personally take them to view the rooms on offer? 'I never did.' How many children did Mr and Mrs Bastendorff have? ''Four,' she said. 'The youngest is a year-and-a-half old.'

The juror questions were becoming more quickfire. Did Hannah Dobbs ever wear a gold watch when she was in service to the Bastendorffs? 'Not all the time,' said Mrs Bastendorff. 'When she began to wear it, she said she bought it with some money left her.' Did she believe this story? 'Yes,' she said, 'I was always told her relations were well off.'

The foreman of the jury stepped in. When was Hannah Dobbs 'most flush of money?' 'After she came back from the country,' said Mrs Bastendorff. 'After that, she wore better clothing.' And did Hannah Dobbs 'sit at the same table' as the family sometimes? 'No.' Did she wear a watch and chain before she went to the country? 'No.' And she was 'not so finely dressed before that?' 'No.' And how long was Hannah Dobbs kept on after her mistress had discovered 'her pilfering'? 'I gave her a month's notice.'[2]

At last, Mary Bastendorff was allowed to retire from the dock.

With the next witness came a resumption of the focus upon the victim. John Sandilands Ward of Lincoln's Inn was a lawyer who had been engaged by Matilda Hacker in 1877 during the course of her singular legal disputes. Did he observe her 'particularly'? 'Yes, she was dressed in an eccentric way,' said Mr Ward. 'Her dress was usually of a light colour. She wore a light sash and a fashionable hat and feather. And she generally had a light lace shawl thrown over her shoulders.

'When consulting me,' he added, 'she generally held up her eyeglass.'

And when was the final time that he met with her? 'She last called at my office on the 5th of October 1877,' he said. 'On the occasion of our last interview, I told her that I would have considerable difficulty in effecting the transfer of the mortgage which she required. And I recommended her to go to another solicitor, whom she might know.'

Mr Poland wanted some clarification about that final meeting. 'The 5th of October 1877 was a Friday,' said Mr Ward. 'Miss Hacker wanted an advance of £250.'

Then there was the matter of her supposed 'curvature of the spine'. Mr Poland asked Mr Ward if Matilda Hacker had been 'at all lame'? 'I think she had a slight limp,' he said, 'which I attributed to her fashionable shoes.' This remark drew a burst of laughter from jurors and onlookers.

The next witness had the effect of subduing the court once more.

Peter Bastendorff was called to the stand. The jurors and spectators would have taken in the blond hair, the flushed cheeks and the respectable clothes: this still young man would certainly have worn a collar, with a tie for this occasion.

The jurors may also have been aware that he had only recently acquired his fluency in English.

Yet the jurors would also have been intrigued beyond measure at the apparent smiling confidence of this young man, and at the glance that he threw to Hannah Dobbs at the start of the proceedings. 'As he entered the witness box,' reported the *Illustrated Police News*, 'he looked at the prisoner, who quickly turned her eyes away and a broad grin stole over his face.'

Peter Bastendorff swore the oath and confirmed to the inquest who he was: 'I am 22-years old. I live at 32, Francis Street. I am a bamboo worker, and used to work at my brother's, no 4, Euston Square. I have been about four years in this country.'

The coroner asked how he first heard of 'the discovery' at Euston Square? 'I heard of it through the newspapers,' said Mr Bastendorff.

Was he 'acquainted' with Hannah Dobbs? 'Yes.' Did he 'keep company with her'? 'Yes'. For 'how long'? 'About two years.'

How did he first meet Miss Dobbs? 'I became acquainted with her when she was in the service of my brother,' he said. Was he 'engaged to her?' 'No'.

'You had not gone so far as that?' asked Dr Hardwicke, at which there was another loud outbreak of laughter from among the onlookers. He went on: 'You only kept company with her?' Peter Bastendorff replied: 'That is all.'

The next question was lethal. 'You do not know then,' the coroner asked him, 'that a child had been born?'

Nothing is recorded of Peter Bastendorff's facial reaction to this; but his answer was: 'I know nothing of that.'

'You do not know then,' persisted Dr Hardwicke, 'that you are the parent of one?'

'I do not,' said Peter Bastendorff. 'I did not know that she ever had a child.'

Did he ever go to see Hannah Dobbs 'in the country'? 'Yes,' he told the court. 'On one occasion I went to Bideford to see her and her father and mother. I remained there a day and a night. I went there in consequence of a telegram I received.'

This was left hanging in the air. A juror wanted to know if 'mention had been made of a lamp that was broken'; this was a reference to a lamp in the room in Euston Square that had been occupied by Matilda Hacker. 'On one occasion,' Peter Bastendorff said, Hannah Dobbs 'said that she had broken a lamp and that it had cut her hand and caused it to bleed.'

A juror asked if he had heard why she had left Euston Square. 'I was given to understand that she was accused of taking something belonging to one of the lodgers,' he said. So what then 'became of her' afterwards? 'She went to live in lodgings.' And did Peter Bastendorff continue to visit her after she left her situation at Euston Square? 'I went to see her at her lodgings once afterwards,' he said, 'and another time when I was sent for in consequence of her illness.'

So when did he 'come to know' that Hannah Dobbs was in prison? 'I did not know what had become of her,' said Peter Bastendorff, 'and I did not hear of her being in prison till I saw it in the newspapers.' And when he did so, did he go to visit her in Tothill Fields? 'No,' he said.

'Have letters passed' between them both? 'Some,' he said, 'but not many.'

He must have seen her wearing a watch and a chain, said Dr Hardwicke; did he ask 'what became of them?' 'I never asked what became of them,' he replied.

Did he go by his 'own name while on a visit to Hannah Dobbs in the country? 'I did.' And did she? This was a cleverly lateral question: the juror must have heard one account that the maid was describing herself in Bideford as 'Hannah Bastendorff'. And Peter Bastendorff's answer was equally lateral: 'I do not know that she did not.'

During this sojourn in Bideford, asked the same juror, clearly pursuing local gossip, 'was an attempt made to pass' Peter Bastendorff off 'as a father of two children?' The question again related in a sideways fashion to the fact that Hannah Dobbs had arrived in Bideford with two of Severin and Mary's children. Peter Bastendorff replied: 'No'. And at this, Dr Hardwicke asked more straightforwardly: 'Did you pass as man and wife on that occasion?' 'No.'

Peter Bastendorff was asked where he came from. 'From Luxembourg.' 'Have you been in the habit,' asked the coroner, 'of going back to Luxembourg?' 'I have been over there on one occasion with my brother,' he said.

Did Peter Bastendorff 'know Miss Uish' who lodged with his brother? 'I do not remember,' he said. And did Hannah Dobbs ever mention her at all? 'Never.' A juror interjected to ask if he ever went 'into the cellar where the remains were found'? 'Never'.

Perhaps this was a nervous reflex, or a reaction to tension, but it was reported that the young man started laughing at the questions.

Mr Poland asked him if Hannah Dobbs had said where she had got the watch from? 'No.' Did she say anything about her uncle dying and leaving her some property? 'No.' And with this, there was more grinning from Peter Bastendorff; so much so that the lawyer was moved to tell him 'in a stern, ringing voice': 'Don't laugh, sir, don't smile. Just attend to the questions.'

The coroner lent in. 'Did you know anything,' he asked, 'about her uncle coming into property and did you notice at any time that she was in possession of more than a usual amount of property? 'I did not,' said Peter Bastendorff, 'and I never noticed her having much money.'[3] He was released from the stand.

And so the proceedings finally moved to what might have been perceived as the cause of death. The jury heard from Dr A.J. Pepper, of nearby 122 Gower Street. He declared: 'I have heard the medical evidence of Dr Davis and I have seen the remains and made certain examinations. The body . . . was far advanced in decomposition – that decomposition which takes place when remains are subjected for a long time to moisture.

'I saw no evidence of chloride of lime having been placed over them. Probably the body had been dead between one and two years – assuming it had been in the same position all the time, and covered with clothes. The greater part of the scalp had gone. The hair was curly and of light colour, turning grey. The colour was apparently normal.'

Had there perhaps been a serious blow to the head? Dr Pepper did not seem to hold this view. 'In the skull, I detected no fracture,' he said. 'There were some fluid remains of the brain and the lower jaw was that of a person beyond middle life. From the conformation of the jaw, I should say the person probably had a prominent mouth. And from the general conformation of the skull, I should also say that the person had an elongated face.

'The whole of the front of the neck was absent,' he continued, 'but the back and sides of the neck were present, and there was a deep groove both at the back and at the sides.' This 'groove' would be returned to. But he also wanted to point out that the 'heart was distinctly recognisable, the lungs had entirely disappeared, and the back of the chest was simply a black layer'.

Did he think, asked the coroner, that these body parts had perhaps 'been eaten away by vermin?' 'No,' said Dr Pepper. 'The liver was very much shrunken but kept its natural form. The kidneys were better preserved than any other portions of the body. The person must have been quite stout. Of the stomach I could find no trace.

'I found portions of the uterus,' he continued. 'The bladder was well preserved. The foot was almost entire. The hip-joints were perfect.'

Dr Pepper was asked if he had made an examination of the carpet that was in her room at 4, Euston Square. 'Yes,' he said. 'The stain was undoubtedly produced by blood. But whether it was the blood of an animal or a human being, it is impossible to say.' (Such tests would not be formulated until the final years of the nineteenth century.) And so the jury returned to the mystery of the cause of death. 'No mineral poison had been found in the intestines,' said Dr Pepper. 'No organic poison was expected, and none was looked for.' There was, he said, still the outside possibility of 'self-destruction'. 'The person found may have hung herself,' he said, adding 'or she may have been strangled. On that point I have nothing to say. There was nothing to prove that such a thing had occurred during life.'

Dr Hardwicke was eager for more certainty. He asked the doctor: 'Do you think that the rope found in the cellar would have caused death?' 'Certainly,' said Dr Pepper. 'The woman may have hung herself, or she may have been strangled. But it was utterly impossible to say.'

There was nothing left but for Dr Hardwicke to sum up to the jury. 'Foreman and gentlemen,' he said, 'it is for you to consider whether you are not in a position to give your verdict. The evidence as to identification I think is complete. But as to the cause of death, I do not think any other evidence will assist you one iota.'

The gentlemen of the jury withdrew at 6p.m. to consider their verdict; and after twenty-minutes' discussion, they returned to the inquest chamber. The foreman of the jury declared: 'We find and believe that the remains found in the house, 4, Euston Square, were those of Miss Hacker, and that there was a strong belief that she has been murdered by some person or persons unknown.'

'By strangulation?' the coroner asked.

'No, we do not say that,' said the foreman.

'That is all the verdict you have to give?' the coroner then said.

'Yes,' said the foreman.

So the verdict was then 'formulated' thus:

> That the deceased, Matilda Hacker, was found lying dead in a coal cellar at number 4, Euston Square. And we further say that some person or persons unknown did feloniously, and with malice aforethought, kill and murder the said Matilda Hacker, against the peace of our sovereign Lady the Queen, her Crown, and dignity.

As Hannah Dobbs was taken from the court and escorted back to the coach which would return her to Tothill Fields, the press observed 'she tripped lightly' while 'smiling at the small crowd hoping to catch a glimpse of her'; in this tableau, she seemed less a possible murderess and more an actress leaving a theatre through the stage door.

Given the fact that she could have been facing the prospect of capital punishment, Hannah Dobbs had behaved with remarkable insouciance. But despite her apparent confidence, was there a sub-conscious prejudice against her in the minds of the police and public alike sparked by quite a different murder case that was just concluding elsewhere in London?

14

The Boiling Bones

One of the effects of the 1870 Education Act was a dazzlingly fast rise in rates of literacy; but this improvement had, in turn, been fuelled by the increasingly salty and sensational nature of popular newspapers, periodicals and literature. Reading as a mass pursuit had become a terrific source of escapist entertainment: as young boys became addicted to the bloodthirsty adventure stories to be found in weekly 'penny dreadfuls', so it was noted that those young women in service were gripped by romances and in particular, scandal. And there was no question that for readers around the country, lurid real-life stories of murder were particularly satisfying.

As well as the thrilling element of Grand Guignol,[1] and the attractive notion that these were baffling mysteries that could be penetrated by the exceptional minds of Scotland Yard – with readers following each fresh development on a daily or episodic basis – there was also a sense of these stories speaking to deeper, more general, fears and prejudices.

By some dark coincidence, as the Euston Square mystery was deepening, the public was immersed in another sensational domestic murder. And for many middle-class readers, the story of the 1879 atrocity that occurred in the pretty Surrey town of Richmond upon Thames would perhaps have had them glancing in the dark at their bedroom doors at any suggestion of a creak outside. Indeed, there was a ghastly necromantic luridness about this particular story that seemed to have some echoes with the Euston Square coal cellar.

In the early frozen weeks of 1879, with the riverbanks crusted white with frost, a woman called Kate Webster made her way through the leafy lanes of Richmond to a pleasing cottage; this was the home of an elderly lady called Julia Thomas who was had been seeking domestic help. She required no references from her new maid. If she had sought them, she might have found that Webster, born Kate Lawler, had lived an unusually turbulent life and had been in prison frequently for prostitution and theft.

But Julia Thomas was hardly the ideal employer either; she was excessively contrary and demanding. She would follow her new maid from room to room, offering venomous criticism of her work and demanding that tasks be repeated endlessly. Kate Webster, who was an avid drinker, started finding the local public house an increasingly congenial sanctuary.

The relationship deteriorated fast; the old woman becoming more vituperative, Kate Webster becoming more drunk. Finally, one Sunday, as they argued in an upstairs room, there was an explosion of violence. First, Webster pushed the old lady hard, sending her crashing down the stairs. Then – in an apparent panic about Mrs Thomas screaming and alerting the neighbours – she ran down the stairs after her, grabbed the prone woman by the throat, and strangled her.

Out of this apparently spontaneous homicide came subsequent actions that were, to say the least, remarkable. Webster decided that she was going to dispose of Mrs Thomas's remains in such a way that no-one would ever find her. Using a hacksaw, she set about dismembering the corpse. Then, the next day, she filled the laundry copper – in essence, a large metal cauldron that clothes were washed in – with water, heated it over the fire, and then started boiling the removed body parts. Flesh softened in the molten water, tissue melted, fat ran into the mixture. Webster spent the day reducing the corpse of the old lady to a form of obscene soup.

Her next steps in the subsequent days had the suggestion of a fugue state about them; visits by omnibus to upriver Hammersmith, with boxes filled with boiled bones, that she dropped in the water; and then her extraordinary decision to remain living in her murdered employer's house and wear Julia Thomas's clothes quite openly in the street.

One of the boxes was washed ashore at Barnes; the unlucky man who poked at it curiously on the riverbank found it filled with unidentifiable melted flesh.

The fact that the head was missing (and was to remain missing for many decades) made the crime seem insoluble; until Kate Webster's strutting behaviour in Richmond – combined with the absence of the old lady – at last alerted neighbours and solidified the lines of suspicion.

She faced trial in London in the late spring of 1879 – concurrent with the Euston Square drama.

Journalists made careful note of the fact that Webster wore gold earrings for the hearing; perhaps to suggest that her desire to rise above her servile station was intertwined with the horrific crime.

And with the guilty verdict came sentence of death. In July 1879, Kate Webster was executed at Wandsworth Prison. Her wax effigy was placed on show in Madame Tussauds almost instantly. All of this was happening as public and potential jurors alike were reading of Hannah Dobbs, another maid-of-all-work.

(As a curious and macabre footnote, a few years ago Sir David Attenborough, long a resident of Richmond, acquired a little extra land upon which had once stood a pub near some cottages; when work began, builders unearthed a skull. Tests were carried out; and confirmation was given. This was the long concealed skull of Julia Thomas.)

The real fascination of the story among the reading public – and this meant not only middle-class householders, but also those whom they employed as servants – was the nature of the relationship and the balance of power between the mistress of the house and her maid.

For countless young women who worked long and physically demanding hours in the grander houses of Kensington and Belgravia, subject to the whims of masters and mistresses whose behaviour might be oppressive and overbearing, how many derived a vicarious thrill from the story of a servant who turned upon her malicious mistress? Equally, for wealthy householders, was there an echoing chime of recognition in terms of the difficulty of dealing with wayward and ungovernable staff?

The weekly journal *The Spectator* picked up on this seam of fascination and the apparent parallels with the Euston Square mystery and a still unsolved murder from a few months beforehand in another Bloomsbury street, Burton Crescent. 'The conviction will, we trust, relieve that portion of the public which appears to have felt so very strongly the danger of old ladies living alone in houses with only one servant,' declared its editorial in June 1879. 'An alarm of this kind always arises after every great murder, and sometimes rises to singular proportions…

'As a matter of fact, however,' the journal continued, with a note of near-joviality, 'servants very rarely commit murder, their comfortable lives not developing either the desire or the nerve for such crimes; and thousands of old ladies are attended for years by single servants whose peccadilloes are, at the worst, limited to petty thefts, minute impositions, and very numerous small tyrannies and exhibitions of jealousy.'[2]

The other murder mentioned by *The Spectator* had occurred six-months previously in the December of 1878. The Burton Crescent killing had also centred on a landlady, Mrs Burton, and a maid called Mary Ann Donovan. In this particular story, one of Mrs Burton's lodgers returned home on a dark afternoon and found, to his horror, her body with her throat cut wide.

The only suspect in the case appeared to be Miss Donovan, who was noted by the newspapers as being of an unusually 'heavy build'.

There was a pre-trial hearing in which the accusation was put that the killing had been spurred by acquisitiveness and rage. Yet the pre-trial hearing was as far as the case got; the judge decided there and then that there was simply not enough – or indeed, any – evidence with which to mount an effective prosecution.

Donovan was released. *The Spectator*, using this and the case of 4, Euston Square as examples of why their readers were not likely to be murdered in their beds, had this to say of the Euston Square enigma: 'As to Miss Hacker, she lived in a house which a policeman would have declared as little likely to be the scene of a murder as any in London, in one of the noisiest and most frequented of squares, and a house where one would have supposed solitude impossible.

'No sensational novelist would dream of fixing on Euston Square as the scene of a violent murder, with a body hidden away for months; nor could anyone, however timid, have dreamt that in her own bedroom, in a frequented lodging-house in the heart of London life, and within sight of policemen, she was in greater danger than in any lonely farm-house in a remote county.'[3]

That might well have been so; but within all these stories was a thread of modern middle-class unease with the question of servants, and how to retain one's authority within one's own household. Just several decades beforehand, the subject would not have arisen with such frequency. There were aristocratic families who had always employed servants; men and women who had been attended to from birth who knew (or thought they knew) how best to deal with those who did this work. For the rising Victorian middle classes – especially those in London taking on just one or perhaps two servant women – there were lessons to be learned. Equally, those going to work with them – even those with no apparent traction or agency to improve their circumstances – still had to find a way of negotiating awkward questions of power and hierarchy.

An example: a lady of the house who entertains many guests decides that they should all dine late. What thought is there for the servant girl who has to rise before six in the morning, yet cannot hope to complete her duties of washing the china and the glass and cleaning the kitchen until the early hours of the morning? Many Victorians were not wholly insensitive to such questions. In a popular mid-century journal called *The Englishwoman's Domestic Magazine*, there was an essay entitled 'The Cry of the Maidservant'. It stated that 'in the homes and kitchens of the middle classes in England, "white slavery" is rampant. How many of these (servants) labour and slave in their vocations sixteen, eighteen and even more hours a day . . . continuing on foot "upstairs and downstairs" with only "slight inter-regnums" and "comfortless meals . . . past midnight?"'[3]

There were no employment rights as they are understood now; simply the understanding between the employer and the servant. And certainly for many young women in service at that time, there must have been a great many secret tyrants who, because they gave them the roof over their head, felt able to make the most outrageous demands.

Yet at a time of rising prosperity – and in London in the 1870s at least, the fast-expanding middle classes meant a whole new range of employment prospects – it was also quite a simple matter to leave an unsatisfactory master or mistress. This was a ballooning labour market with increasing demand; and as is clear from the classified advertisements in the newspapers of the time, households were continually seeking new staff. The ease of finding such work meant that the responsibility lay with these middle-class householders to try and make the position seem as agreeable as possible.

In houses such as 4, Euston Square, run by ladies such as Mary Bastendorff who might once have been servants themselves, such equilibrium could not be taken for granted; no-one had taught these new employers either how to keep full control or indeed how to do so without behaving monstrously. And it was these delicate questions of household management that the women's magazines of the day addressed continually. According to *The Lady's Own Paper* in 1870, even the most well-meaning lady of the house might find difficulty getting the best out of her domestic staff; for these young maids themselves would be quite new to the very idea of being in service.

'Unfortunately, most of that class upon whom many of us have to depend have had no opportunity for systematic training,' the magazine declared. 'So they pick up a few ideas here and there and use them very inefficiently. For example: notice the manner in which many girls remove the dishes at the dinner table. It makes one uneasy and nervous to sit by and observe the slovenly manner in which this work is often accomplished.'[5]

Could one learn authority? Equally, from the point of view of the put-upon overworked maid, could one acquire a habit of sincere subservience and obedience? By the 1870s, there were countless magazines devoting much feature space to these and associated problems. There were some books too, among them *The Lady's Maid* published in 1877, which featured advice both to employers and servants on tricky matters such as privacy and discretion.

It is especially interesting to think that while Karl Marx was studying and writing in the British Museum reading room in Bloomsbury, there were daily outbreaks in the houses all around him of a perfectly invisible and yet important class struggle. It might perhaps have been one thing to be in the service of a bejewelled Duchess; but in so many households in London and the larger cities, the ladies of the house had only just attained their middle-class eminence; to what extent did a certain social insecurity drive their dealings with their staff?

Even as early as 1853, a journal called the *North British Review* was dispensing tips when it came to the troubling question of servants witnessing domestic disharmony. 'Everything that you do, and very much that you say, at home is related in your servants' families,' ran the article, 'and by them retailed to other gossips in the neighbourhood, with appropriate exaggerations, until you almost feel that you might well live in a glass house or a whispering gallery.'[6]

Meanwhile, in *The Lady's Maid*, the servant in question was advised on how to deal with capricious employers and domestic tension. 'If your master should be unfortunate in his temper or in any of his habits,' it read, 'if you should hear harsh words, or see your mistress in distress, you are bound in honour to be as silent upon the whole matter, whether you are so desired or not, as if it were a secret committed to your keeping.'[7]

The secrets were on both sides, though, and other journals counselled the lady of the house to keenly monitor those who came to visit their servants; to 'double-check the kitchen accounts'; and also to set strict curfews. Intriguingly, this particular aspect of life for servants was soon to be focused upon as the Euston Square trial got underway.

In the case of Kate Webster, it seemed understood that here was a woman with no sense either of moral boundaries or class boundaries: that she killed and then dismembered her mistress in an apparent frenzy after being scolded for her domestic shortcomings was one thing. But there was also outrage, as expressed in the press coverage after her execution, that she should then have had the impertinence to assume the identity of her dead employer. She appropriated the clothes and jewellery of Mrs Thomas and began to pass herself off as a lady.

And the trial of Hannah Dobbs for the murder of Matilda Hacker at 4, Euston Square was also set to create interest in how a maid and her employers negotiated the working relationship; and it was also set to illustrate just how easily the balance of power in certain households could be swayed this way and that. Inspector Hagen and the newspaper correspondents had been working on the assumption that, like the Webster case, this was a straightforward affair that would be easily settled by the court. They were all perfectly wrong.

15
'Everything Was Sweet'

In her white-washed cell – and out of it – Hannah Dobbs was unusually garrulous; and whether talking to fellow prisoners, or the guards watching over her, she was discussing the Matilda Hacker case as if she herself was distanced from it and might be able to reach some valuable deductions. All this would emerge in later testimony. It is difficult to know whether this was some reflex caused by a growing dread of the trial; or an extraordinarily strong self-assurance that her own innocence would be taken for granted.

Her talkativeness was not light-hearted though; Hannah spoke very seriously to those around her. Indeed, she was often conspiratorial. She seemed to have a taste for suggesting that all was not as it seemed with certain Euston Square tenants . . . and then she would stop herself, as though somehow forbidden to say more.

The streets outside the prison were glistening with rain that never seemed to stop over those first weeks of summer; and the bruised sky brought with it dampening cold. But outside pubs around Westminster and Hyde Park, there were brilliant splashes of scarlet: the uniform of soldiers from barracks celebrating the news of British victory in the Anglo-Zulu War after the Battle of Ulundi.

Here was a city effervescent with confidence, a dazzling spectacle to visitors; a city that was now fully conscious of its own splendour. The view to Ludgate Hill, and thence to the dome of St Paul's, was bisected by a railway line; a perspective that placed Christopher Wren's seventeenth-century ideal of a reborn London next to the exuberant vigour of nineteenth-century industry. Under this railway bridge was driven the police cab taking Hannah Dobbs to the nearby Old Bailey. The case was heard in the New Court in June 1879. Even in that drab summer, the light would have flooded through the three large windows of the court; and there would have been ample opportunity for all present to study the most minute of Hannah Dobbs' reactions as the proceedings unfolded.

The prosecution was to be led by the Attorney General, on behalf of the Treasury; he opened by outlining the nature of the case against Hannah Dobbs; this was weighted with additional information concerning the stained carpet in Matilda Hacker's room; a 'piece had been cut out' and tests confirmed not only that the stain was blood but that also 'there must have been a considerable quantity of it'. The case was that Matilda had been most probably killed by a blow to the back of the neck (differing from the inquest's supposition that strangulation had been the chief method of dispatch). There was also mention of the old woman's watch and other items of jewellery, which ended up being pawned by Hannah.

It was the intention of the prosecution to prove that on an autumn Sunday in October 1877, 'Hannah Dobbs and Miss Hacker were the only grown-ups in the house'; Severin Bastendorff was out shooting on the Erith marshes, Mary Bastendorff was visiting her sisters and her mother, respectively in Holloway and in St Pancras. The other lodger, sugar merchant Francis Riggenbach had been out in the morning, 'returned for a short time in the afternoon to get something, and went away with a friend, and he would be able to fix the date by the character of the conversation he and his friend had'.

The prosecutor was quite firm about what might seem to some circumstantial evidence. He told the jury that many 'cases of this description – cases of murder – depended on circumstantial evidence but such evidence might happen to be stronger and even more trustworthy than direct evidence'.

He did not explain exactly how this might be so; he added that what the jury 'had to do was satisfy themselves as to the facts which it was alleged could be proved and from which they were asked to draw their inferences'.[1]

Yet this was certainly not going to prove either straightforward or easy for the jurors; the very first witness on the stand instead seemed to weave further layers of ambiguity into the case. This was Dr H. Davis of number 1, Euston Square, who had been called almost immediately after the hideous discovery in the cellar was made. Now, some weeks later, he had his notes: and he was pleased to take the gentlemen of the jury through the charnel house details.

The 'separation of limbs from the body was no doubt due to decomposition', he said. 'The whole of the flesh had gone from the face and front of the leg, and also from the scalp except the back part.' There was the indentation caused by the cord around the neck and the 'flesh was in a very decomposed state'.

All that said, there 'was no indication by which he could judge of the death'. He 'should have expected that there would have been a flow of blood – probably not a copious flow – from a body which had been strangled. This would have been from the eyes, mouth and nose.' He added that if the jugular vein had been severed, 'the body would have been emptied of blood directly'.

Mr Mead, the defence counsel, was intrigued by this. 'So as far as you saw,' he said to Dr Davis, 'there was nothing inconsistent with a natural death?'

'No,' said the doctor.

'There would have been a flow of blood,' continued Mr Mead, 'had a blood vessel been broken?' The doctor agreed, and withdrew from the stand. In his place came 'Mr A.J. Pepper, pathologist' at St Mary's Hospital. Again, confusingly, he threw doubt upon the very idea of murder. He told the court he had made 'two examinations of the body at St Pancras mortuary'. And that he 'agreed generally with the evidence of Dr Davis'.

In his view, 'strangulation would make a considerable indentation'. In the case of this corpse, the mark 'was higher than if the person had been strangled'.

The Attorney General cut in to ask Mr Pepper if he could clarify that. 'The marks were consistent with hanging,' said Pepper, 'or of the body's being dragged by the cord.'

There was a sliver of further medical evidence from Mr W. Luck, analytical chemist, who told the court that he had made 'an analysis of the internal organs of the stomach and found no trace of poison'.[2]

The question was left hanging in the air: was there the chance that this was a murder trial for a murder that had not actually been committed? But there was also an impatient velocity to the proceedings; such cases rarely ran beyond one-and-a-half or two days. There were many more witnesses to be heard.

Matilda Hacker's brother, Edward, took the stand. He confirmed that he 'never saw her alive after October 1877' and that before then, their communications had been sparse. 'She usually called every four months,' he said, 'and generally at Christmas.' He said that 'last Christmas, she did not call.' He thought this 'very strange and made inquiries, and found that she had not applied for her rents as usual'. The prosecutor was apparently too sensitive to make the awkward point that this would in fact have been the second Christmas he had not seen his sister, the first being that of 1877; this meant that over a year-and-a-half had passed before he began to find his sister's absence strikingly odd.

And what of the residents of 4, Euston Square? The German sugar merchant Francis Riggenbach – who now lived in Brixton Road, south of the river – told the court that in August 1877, he took an apartment in the Bastendorff home, 'occupying the whole first floor'. He lived there, he said, until September 1878. Hannah Dobbs, he said, was the servant there and she 'waited upon him the whole of the time he was there, excepting when she went for a holiday'.

Mr Riggenbach said that he 'did not recollect the lady who occupied the room over him' (this was Matilda Hacker) 'but on one occasion – a Sunday – in October 1877', he met 'a lady in the passage'. Mr Riggenbach explained that he 'usually left about nine o'clock in the morning and returned about the same time in the evening' and that on Sundays, he would go out at about lunchtime and return at about nine or ten o'clock in the evening. The implication was that even if he had wanted to, he would never have spent enough time in the house to get to know his fellow lodgers to any great degree.

So what then did he recall of that autumn Sunday when it was being assumed that Matilda Hacker had been murdered? Mr Riggenbach said he remembered 14 October 1877 because 'it was the day of the French elections'. He went out that day 'to see a friend who resided at Torrington Square (just two or three streets away), leaving at about 12 o'clock (noon)'. He told the court that he returned to Euston Square with his father and a friend 'for a few minutes about 4 o'clock' and then went out again, remaining out until about eleven o'clock that night.

This evidence if anything made the puzzle more unsettling. If the contention of the prosecution was that this was a vicious killing carried out when the murderer knew that the house was empty, then when did the murderer strike? Before or after Mr Riggenbach had returned at 4 o'clock for that few minutes? When he went back to his first-floor apartment, was there already a corpse lying on the floor above his head? Or had the body already been taken down to the coal cellar? There was clearly no sense of disturbance, or of violence, or none at least that Mr Riggenbach noted. Had it happened after he left, as the house swiftly darkened in the autumn night? Such questions must also have caused the jurors to look at Hannah Dobbs in the dock and wonder about motivation and, indeed, opportunity. In a house where people generally were coming and going without warning, how had she timed this shocking slaughter?

Mary Bastendorff was now called to the stand; if the inquest had been an ordeal, this must have been doubly so. She told the court that it was in the summer of 1876 when Hannah Dobbs came to work for them. The servant's salary was £14 a year. Mrs Bastendorff remembered that in August 1877, Hannah 'went away for about a month'. She did not elaborate on why the maid-of-all-work had been granted such an unusually long leave, but again, the question must surely have struck many of the jurors.

Mrs Bastendorff remembered 'Miss Uish' coming 'to lodge with them'. Her rent was 12 shillings a week and it had particularly stuck in the landlady's memory because they day the old lady arrived, she had gone out specially to buy a new glass lamp, which would go in 'Miss Uish's' room.

She maintained that she 'only saw Miss Uish twice while she was at 4, Euston Square'. It was, she said, 'on Sunday morning on each occasion'. Indeed, Hannah Dobbs had borrowed 'a church service' for her. Three weeks after 'Miss Uish had been in the apartments – viz, on Monday, October 15, 1877', her husband, Severin, asked Hannah Dobbs for Miss Uish's rent. Mary Bastendorff told the court of Hannah Dobbs taking the bill upstairs and returning with the £5 note. Mrs Bastendorff was certain that she never saw 'Miss Uish' again.

It was 'a day or two' afterwards that Mary Bastendorff went into the old woman's former room on the second floor and immediately noticed 'a large stain on the carpet'.

There were now questions directly about Hannah Dobbs and her movements. Mrs Bastendorff testified how, at the latter end of October 1877, just after 'Miss Uish' was thought to have left, that Hannah Dobbs went 'away for three days'. She had told her employers that she was 'going to her home in Bideford' and that 'her uncle had died leaving her a watch and a chain and some money'. And, indeed, Mrs Bastendorff noted that her servant was wearing a watch and chain, although she could not swear to them being the same as those produced in court.

And what then of the coal cellar, where this body had lain hidden for over 18 months? Mary Bastendorff told the court that while Hannah Dobbs was in her employ, she herself never went into that cellar.

Hannah Dobbs, she said in response to another question, left her situation in 4, Euston Square eleven months later in September 1878. She had told her employer that 'she was going into apartments' in nearby Gower Street. After she left, Mary Bastendorff spent a few weeks 'without a servant'. And on the very rare occasions she did go into the cellar, all she saw was 'rubbish'. She recounted the story of the bone, and of the wild boar, and then of the discovery of the body. Mrs Bastendorff told the court that up until that time, she 'had not the slightest idea that there was any body in the cellar'.

She was asked to think back to the presumed date of the murder, that dark October Sunday, and to think hard about the whereabouts of all who lived in 4, Euston Square. Severin Bastendorff went off to the Kent marshes on the Saturday and did not return until late upon the Sunday evening. Mrs Bastendorff went to visit her sister in north London. And she was aware that Hannah Dobbs took the children 'to be photographed at Hampstead' but she 'could not say' that this was in October.[3]

None the less, this left open another intriguing element; if the Bastendorffs' children were in the care of Hannah Dobbs that day then where exactly were they in the Euston Square house when the murder was supposed to have been carried out? And how could Hannah Dobbs have wrought such an act of violence without the children having detected any disturbance? This was a loose thread: but for some reason, the defence counsel Mr Mead 'reserved his cross-examination' by the 'permission of the court'.

The proceedings moved at speed and next to be called to the witness box was Severin Bastendorff. The first thing that he recalled about the lodger 'Miss Uish' was *The Book of Dreams*, which, he said, she 'was very fond of reading'. It is difficult to know how he formed this impression because, as he subsequently said, he 'never saw her'. It was not his habit, he said, 'to see the lodgers'.

Bastendorff was happy to recount his shooting outing that key weekend; how he was accompanied by his friend Mr Whiffling, and the minor disagreement with the local Erith constable about his 'shooting near the high road'. He was required to pay a hefty fine of £2. That aside, the weekend had clearly been enjoyable; the sportsmen entrained back from Erith to London Bridge on the Sunday evening; and Bastendorff's friend accompanied him 'to the corner of Euston Square'. This was about 11p.m. When Bastendorff let himself in, and went down to the kitchen, he found his wife there – she herself had only just returned from her sister at Holloway.

It could only be assumed that their children had been tucked up in bed for some time; and given that neither husband or wife mentioned seeing Hannah Dobbs, that the maid must have retired too. This again must have struck some of the jurors as curious; surely it would take blood of the coldest sort to murder, to hide the body, and then to remain in the house and go to bed as though nothing had happened?

Bastendorff related how the following day, the Monday, he had particularly directed Hannah Dobbs to go upstairs and collect the old lady's rent – and that if she did not do so, he would do it himself. The reason, he said, 'for speaking thus sharply was that (she) had shown a disinclination to collect rents from the lodgers'. But when spoken to, Hannah Dobbs said: 'Then I will go.' And as his wife had stated, Dobbs came back down the stairs with a £5 note.

Added to all this, Bastendorff told the court that he 'afterwards found a cash-box lying about the house'; he asked where it had come from. Dobbs had told him that it belonged to her, but 'having been compelled to break it open, as she had lost the key, it was no use'.

Like his wife, Bastendorff said that he had no inkling of what might be lying beneath those coals in the cellar; he did remember 'one occasion' when he 'smelt something rather strong' and spoke to Hannah Dobbs about it. He thought that 'it was some bad eggs on the shelf' and he admonished Dobbs 'to keep the place more sweet'. Indeed, she seemed to have attended to the problem, for he remembered that a little later, around Christmas 1877, that he ventured into the cellar when there were coals there and 'everything was sweet'. His holiday to Germany – and the wild boar he shot there – was a little later. The salted boar was stored not in the coal cellar, but in the adjacent cellar.

There was just one last thing the prosecution wanted to know: did Mr Bastendorff have any memories of the lodger called Findlay? Yes, he said; that he 'left in August 1877' and 'had a small American revolver'.[4]

Once again, the defence counsel Mr Mead decided to 'reserve' his cross-examination. And with this, the court was adjourned until the following day. Hannah Dobbs had apparently lost none of her composure. This in itself was quite remarkable.

16

'It Was Not My Place'

Whatever the source of her outward strength, Hannah Dobbs would surely also have been helped by the dizzying pace of the proceedings. The following day in the New Court of the Old Bailey, the defence was ready to begin cross-examinations. And Mary Bastendorff was the first to be recalled to the witness box. She was first asked once again about the gold watch and chain that Hannah Dobbs had started to affect around the house.

Mrs Bastendorff recalled that just before Dobbs left her service, she found two pledge tickets in Dobbs' box; these were for a pawnshop run by a Mr Thompson. And while Dobbs worked at 4, Euston Square, how much latitude did the servant have in terms of taking time off? She was, said Mrs Bastendorff, 'in the habit of frequently going out. Sometimes she went out on Sunday – whenever she chose to ask, she went out'. And if the lodgers needed anything in these absences, a 'little girl' would step help. This 'girl' was a 'nurse' or nanny but she was not there in October 1877 – or indeed, at any point when Matilda Hacker was in the house. And Mrs Bastendorff added that she could not recall Hannah Dobbs 'going out at all' during the time 'that Miss Hacker was lodging'.

The defence counsel was interested in this. Could Mrs Bastendorff be quite sure on this point? It seemed not; she could not 'swear to it'. What were the more precise terms of Hannah Dobbs' duties when it came to the lodgers? 'She provided for all the requirements of the lodgers before she went out,' said Mrs Bastendorff. Occasionally, she herself would send Dobbs on errands. But yes, she conceded that lodgers might occasionally come into her own room if there were any requests.

Mr Mead continued, could Mrs Bastendorff swear that Matilda Hacker never spent an afternoon with the landlady? 'I do not recollect it,' said Mrs Bastendorff. 'It is very improbable that she did.' However, she conceded, 'on one occasion, she might have taken my children into the square'.

Could Mrs Bastendorff also be quite certain about the stained carpet in Matilda Hacker's room? 'The stain was not on the carpet when Miss Hacker came,' she said, adding that she only saw it 'after she left'. She did not, she told the court, go into the room when Matilda Hacker was staying there.

And yet, the defence asked, 'managing this lodging house, will you swear that you never went into their rooms?' Mrs Bastendorff became quite vehement, telling him: 'No. I never went into Miss Hacker's room. I was too much engaged with other things. It was not my place to look after lodgers.'

This received a startlingly aggressive response from Mr Mead: 'I should rather think that it was your place to look after the comfort of your lodgers.' The cross-examination went on.

Did Mrs Bastendorff see Matilda Hacker's luggage being taken away in a cab? No, she did not. Was it normal for Hannah Dobbs to look after the children? She 'was in the habit of taking (the) children'. And so could it have been the case that Hannah Dobbs had the children on that fateful Sunday when 'Miss Hacker went away?' Mrs Bastendorff 'could not say that she did not do this'.

So what were Matilda Hacker's daily habits? As a rule, said Mrs Bastendorff, she 'dressed in the morning and went out'. Mr Mead returned to the children; and Mary Bastendorff was forced to concede that it was a possibility that on that Sunday, Hannah Dobbs had taken them up to Hampstead.

And so when precisely did Hannah Dobbs relay the news that 'Miss Uish' had gone? It was on the Monday, at around lunchtime. But how could Mrs Bastendorff not have noticed the inevitable disturbance – the noise of belongings being taken downstairs, the footsteps above moving back and forth, checking that all had been packed, the summoning of the cab outside – that comes with departure? 'Anyone,' she said, 'could come downstairs and leave without (her) hearing.'

Indeed, when pushed on this, she added that she 'should not have seen the cab unless she had watched for it'.

From the business point of view, was it not the case that her lodgers would have to give her notice of at least a few days if they were planning to leave? No, said Mrs Bastendorff. It was 'not at all usual for the lodgers to give notice'. The judge leaned in, interested, and asked: 'Not usual?'

'Not in furnished apartments,' said Mary Bastendorff. 'At least,' she added, she 'did not make it a rule.' The judge asked if all her tenants had departed similarly. Mrs Bastendorff 'could not remember whether the next lodger who came gave notice or not'. But on that occasion, she had seen the lady – Miss Willoughby – depart.

Something by this stage had started to visibly irk the judge, Justice Hawkins. Perhaps he thought Mary Bastendorff was being wilfully evasive, or hostile – perhaps he simply thought that she was a neglectful landlady – but his own questions stepped up. He wanted to hear more from her about the nature of the coal cellar. 'The cellar would hold a large quantity of coals,' she said. 'They had had four tons in it.' And 'it was a light cellar' (meaning that with the door open, it got the light).

And what of the day that Matilda Hacker arrived and moved into number 4, Euston Square? Mary Bastendorff was once more blank. She 'did not see her arrive, but understood that she brought luggage'. No, she did not 'hear the luggage being taken upstairs'. Someone might more fairly have pointed out that as the mother of four young children, she might have been elsewhere attending to other matters as the old lady was let into the house by Hannah Dobbs. But Justice Hawkins now volubly lost his temper, as though he felt that Mary Bastendorff was being deliberately obstructive.

He turned to the jury. And he asked them: 'Is there any other question I can try to get answered? I never saw such a witness. We cannot get answers to questions which ought to be answered.'[1]

Mrs Bastendorff was asked then whether she noticed the comings and goings of the tenants in the unfurnished rooms, for which they supplied all their own needs. And yes, this was the distinction that she had wanted to make: she remembered the departure of Mr Riggenbach, for instance, 'as he had his own furniture'.

This had clearly been an ordeal for Mrs Bastendorff; but perhaps where the judge thought he saw sullen silence, there could have been a range of other emotions, one of which might have been an inward terror. Each of these encounters was scraping layers of respectability and security off the life of her home and family. She might also have known that there was worse to come.

Now Severin Bastendorff was re-called, and he swore his oaths. Without any kind of preamble, Mr Mead – who had now clearly been briefed very much more comprehensively by his client – began his questioning aggressively.

The inquest had heard about Hannah Dobbs' relationship with Peter Bastendorff. Mr Mead was now about to allege that there was quite another relationship going on at the same time.

Was it the case, Mead asked Severin Bastendorff, that he had been 'keeping company' with Hannah Dobbs?

The denial was instant and hot. Bastendorff declared that all the time Hannah Dobbs was in the family's service, he 'was never out with her'.

Was Mr Bastendorff perhaps familiar, Mr Mead now asked, with the Princes Hotel in Argyle Street?

Bastendorff replied that he 'knew Argyle Street, not the Prince's Hotel'.

Was he ever there with Hannah Dobbs?

No, he said. He 'was never in Argyle Street with her'.

Now Mr Mead mentioned an inn in the Surrey town of Redhill, some 30 miles south of London. Had he ever been there with Hannah Dobbs? Or after she left his service, did he perhaps go and see her at her lodgings just off the Edgware Road? Again, the denial was most insistent. He 'did not go to Redhill to see her, nor to her lodgings in the Edgware Road'.

But, it was put to him, she had also been observed in the vicinity of Euston Square after she had left service there. Yes, Bastendorff said, he had on occasion seen her outside his house but he 'never walked one inch with her'.

Mr Mead suggested that there was a local publican who thought otherwise. Bastendorff 'knew a publican named Johnson and his brother', but he 'did not tell the latter' that he 'had been out' with Hannah Dobbs.

The defence counsel would not leave the subject. Was Severin Bastendorff 'not attached' to Hannah Dobbs? 'No,' said Bastendorff simply. 'I liked her very well because my brother was keeping company with her.'

Wasn't younger brother Peter uneasy about Severin's affection for Hannah?

'My brother never complained that I was too fond of her,' said Bastendorff. 'If he says so, it is untrue.'

All of this must have been profoundly shifting the views of the jury. At the start, and through newspaper speculation, Hannah Dobbs had been presented as a defiant, shameless young woman; her sexual relationship with Peter Bastendorff shockingly free and casual. But into this portrait of modern amorality was thrown a further element of seaminess; sexual betrayal.

Mr Mead wanted to know still yet more. Did Severin Bastendorff ever give Hannah Dobbs any presents? His answer had an unintentional element of Pooterish humour about it. 'Never of more value than two shillings and sixpence,' he said. 'That was the value of a cabinet I gave her.'

And, continued Mr Mead silkily, did Hannah Dobbs ever lend Severin any money? 'Yes,' he said. 'Three pounds in the year 1877.'

That was a startlingly large sum – almost a quarter of her annual salary. And now Mr Mead was ploughing into murkier territory; what else, Mead asked, did Hannah Dobbs give him? Bastendorff told him that she lent him 'her watch for half a day'. She also 'gave him a pencil case'.

And did he ever give her a gold watch? He said no.

Did he not give her the gold watch and chain, persisted the defence counsel, 'and tell her to say that her uncle had given them to her, and that because you did not wish your wife to know the circumstance?'

'No,' said Bastendorff, 'I did not.'

'Nor the gold eyeglass?'

'No.'

The sequence of questions had the appearance of trying to move the shadow of guilt away from Hannah Dobbs and on to Severin Bastendorff.

When, Mr Mead wanted to know, did Bastendorff first see Matilda Hacker's basket trunk? 'Last autumn,' he said (which would have been the autumn of 1878). 'It was then in the scullery. It might have been in the house a long time,' and, he said, he would not have seen it.

And what of the cash-box? Bastendorff said he 'used it for Christmas 1877'. It was Hannah Dobbs who had given him the box. Why, asked Mead. Bastendorff had 'asked her for it,' he said. 'It was standing on the dresser.' And Dobbs gave it to him.

Mead abruptly turned to rumours concerning the moral nature of 4, Euston Square. Was he right to state that on the sabbath, there was frequently drinking and gambling taking place there? 'On Sunday, card-playing sometimes went on,' in his house, Bastendorff said, 'and drinking.' But then he had got into a routine of going away for the weekend, and so such activities stopped. Indeed, he told the court, he absented himself precisely because he wanted to 'turn-up' the card-playing, meaning give it up. He 'did not like it on Sundays'.

This had the effect once more of shifting impressions; not merely an apparently respectable man using his house for gambling, but also a man for whom the card-playing was becoming a problem. Mead had astutely established the unusual fact of the servant lending money to her employer; and he had also fixed in those minds the image of the cashbox, also being handed by the servant to the employer. And the thread of this narrative was becoming more and more pronounced; if perhaps the old lady had been murdered opportunistically for money, might there not have been a likelier suspect?

And these weekend sojourns in the country, continued Mr Mead. Did Mrs Bastendorff ever join him in these jaunts? 'On one occasion,' he said. And yet could he not recall having said at the police court that Hannah Dobbs had joined him on a Sunday, bringing one or two of the children? He said he had not 'had time to think over the matter'.

There were yet more curious mysteries to be considered. Why, asked Mr Mead, had pages been torn from the general rent book of 4, Euston Square? Bastendorff declared that he could not say. Then there were the guns in the house: the lodger Mr Findlay apparently had a revolver – but he was not the only one, was he, said Mr Mead. Bastendorff replied that in 1876, he had had a revolver 'which he sold in that year'. He conceded though that he 'borrowed a revolver from his brother'.

The prosecution returned to the subject of Hannah Dobbs; he was interested in the amount of latitude that she had within the house. Mr Bastendorff testified that she was 'in the habit of going out'; and that if the lodgers ever required anything while she was out, sometimes the childrens' young nursemaid would help. Though Bastendorff also recalled one occasion when Hannah went out and a lodger started ringing for her attention. The lodger was ignored by everyone else and indeed carried on ringing for hours until the maid returned.

This gift of a cabinet to the maid; the prosecution was interested in hearing more about it. Bastendorff told him that it was a 'Japanese cabinet'; he had 'allowed her to choose'. And for what reason had Hannah Dobbs lent her employer the sum of £3? 'It was to pay the carriage of a cask of claret,' said Bastendorff. He had the wine imported specially from France; the reason for the loan was that he 'happened to be very busy at the time' (thus not being able to get to the bank) and he 'paid the money back the same week'.[2] But where had Hannah Dobbs obtained the money from?

He was also asked about the layout of 4, Euston Square in terms of sleeping arrangements; this presumably was to help narrow down the hours in which Matilda Hacker was fatally attacked. Bastendorff told the court that 'the children slept on the floor above that which Miss Hacker had her room'. He added that they 'were usually put to bed at 7 o'clock'.

This seemed to suggest that the murder had certainly taken place earlier; surely the young children would have been awoken by any disturbance from downstairs? Equally though, it might have pointed in the other direction: the tired little children soundly asleep, and the house otherwise empty save for Matilda Hacker and whomever her assailant might have been.

Bastendorff was now relieved from the stand. He would have known that the suggestion of a sexual relationship with the woman accused of murder would be featuring in all of the newspapers the next day; that it would be there in the eyes of all his neighbours in Euston Square. It cannot be known how much, after the hearing, he protested innocence to Mary.

His friends were next to be called as witnesses, to prove that on the day of the murder, he had indeed been out in the country. Taking the stand was John Richards of Brook Street, Erith, to tell how Bastendorff had been visiting at the weekend for the last two years, and how he would accompany him 'on Saturday and Sunday morning shooting small birds'. Mr Richards remembered the 'one occasion' when Mary

Bastendorff came down for the weekend to join them. And he also testified that on that crucial October weekend, Bastendorff was there as usual, leaving late on the Sunday evening; Mr Richards remembered that particularly as 'he had to go after him with a string of birds' that Bastendorff had presumably forgotten.

Mr Whiffling, Severin's friend from nearby Gower Street, gave corroborating evidence, adding in his recollection of Bastendorff being fined by the officious Erith policeman.

Then came the turn of Mary Bastendorff's mother, 'Mrs Pearce, Charrington Street'. She was there to testify about the gold watch; how Hannah Dobbs had handed her the watch to get it cleaned in October 1877. It was the watch that had been produced in court; the property of Matilda Hacker. The reason Dobbs had sent it her way was that Mrs Pearce had a lodger in Charrington Street called David Rhodes who knew a specialist in jewellery cleaning. He in turn passed the watch to Mr Julius Jeuchner, 'watchmaker, Soho'; and the watch was duly returned to Hannah Dobbs.

But Mrs Pearce recalled rebuking Hannah Dobbs, telling her that 'it was very out of place to wear jewellery in the presence of lodgers'. She remembered also that Dobbs appeared to have acquired an eyeglass.

One of Severin Bastendorff's employees in the furniture workshop at the back of the house was called. William Hanwell, who had been working for Bastendorff since the start of the decade, remembered Hannah Dobbs leaving Euston Square to take a trip to Bideford; and he also recalled how she took little Peter, one of the Bastendorff children. He had repaired a gold chain for her (a chain that was identified in the court as also belonging to Matilda Hacker) and had also noticed the watch. Hannah Dobbs had told him these items had been left to her by her uncle. There were other pieces of jewellery in her possession too, including 'one or two rings' which again she said had been a bequest.

And now the pawnbroker was summoned. 'Mr William Partington, assistant to Mr Thompson, Drummond Street, Euston Square, identified one of the watches produced as having been pledged in the name of Rosina Bastendorff,' ran the court report. Mr Partington told the court that 'it was never redeemed' so in the spring of 1879, the watch was put up for sale. 'But not being sold, it was taken back into stock' and held until being given up to the police. Added to this, the gold chain and another watch were brought into the shop, and again pledged under the name 'Rosina Bastendorff' of '4, Euston Square'.[3] For these items, Hannah Dobbs received £2 and 10 shillings.

Next to testify was a St Pancras laundress: Hannah Earls of 68 Stonehurst Street. She regularly cleaned the clothes, linen and bed-linen of all the lodgers in 4, Euston Square. She recalled that in the autumn of 1877, she noticed that Hannah Dobbs had started wearing a gold chain. She told the maid that 'it did not look very well of a servant wearing this chain in her work and that she might lose it'.

To this, Hannah Dobbs had apparently made no reply, but then told the laundress about her late uncle's bequest. She then gave Mrs Earls 'eight to ten handkerchiefs to wash'. But they 'were not dirty'. There was a handkerchief belonging to Matilda Hacker produced in court; and the laundress confirmed that it corresponded to the 'character' of the other items.

Rather more haunting evidence was given by another former servant to the Bastendorffs, Louisa Barker, who worked there for a couple of months, following Hannah Dobbs. During that time, she said, she was 'in and out of the cellar'. There was, she said, 'straw, rubbish and coal . . . and in one of the corners, there was a larger heap of something'.

It was clear she did not care for the cellar (although it might now be wondered how much of this was hindsight). She said that whenever she had to go in there for coal, she always fetched the lumps that were 'nearest the door'. She also recalled seeing 'two or three white towels in the cellar' and that 'they were rotten'. But no, she told the court: she had 'no idea there was a body in the cellar'.[4]

The court reports did not relate whether the next witness – Peter Bastendorff – had composed himself into a more sombre attitude than his previous public appearance.

In the autumn of 1877, he told the court, he 'lived in the Hampstead-Rd' (which ran a little north of Euston Square) and 'worked for a cabinet maker'. He was, he said, 'in the habit of visiting his brother' at 4, Euston Square; and he saw Hannah Dobbs there. 'For some time,' he said, he 'kept company with her.' Did he recall Dobbs taking time off to go to Bideford with one of Mary and Severin's children? He did. Did he recall the lodger Matilda Hacker or 'Miss Uish'? He did not.

But now once again the electric crackle of scandal was in the air. Was it the case that Peter complained to his older brother about Severin's relationship with Hannah Dobbs? He did not, he said, 'complain of his brother's too great familiarity . . . but he heard something in a public house and spoke to her (Hannah) about it several times'.

So Peter did have suspicions concerning his then lady-friend? The young man now contradicted himself. He said that he 'thought himself that there was something between (Hannah) and his brother and he complained of it to both'.

At this pregnant moment, he was allowed to step down.

The court now addressed the question of Hannah Dobbs' late uncle, from whom she claimed to have inherited her jewellery. Called to testify was 'Mr James Hamelin, of Newton Tracey, near Bideford'; he declared that he was the uncle of the prisoner. But, he pointed out, there was another uncle, called Clarke, who had died almost two years beforehand in 1877. He too 'lived at Newton Tracey', he said. 'It was after harvest time when he died. He left a widow and five children.' What Hamelin did not say was whether he had left much money or indeed a bequest for his niece.

There was a break as Justice Hawkins adjourned for lunch. Hannah Dobbs was removed to her cell; then she was brought back up as the court rose for the afternoon session. There seemed little prospect of fresh clarity: new witnesses were set to make the mystery even murkier.

Dr Pepper, one of the experts who had initially examined the remains of Matilda Hacker, was recalled for more questioning. This time the defence counsel Mr Mead asked him if he could really be quite certain as to the cause of death; given the old lady's age, might there not have been the possibility of natural causes? Dr Pepper stated that if 'a person had a large varicose vein which burst suddenly, death might ensue'. He 'had known of such cases. The bursting would produce a great flow of blood and would account, had it occurred with the deceased, for the blood upon the carpet'.

Such cases are indeed very rare; had the vein burst in this fashion, the bleeding might have been akin to a pierced artery. But, it would have produced much more blood than the carpet stain suggested.

The prosecutor might well have been justified in demanding that Dr Pepper furnish the court with more exact details. But the Attorney General objected: and on closer questioning, Dr Pepper reluctantly conceded that actually 'there was nothing to show that the deceased suffered from varicose veins'. So did he perhaps have any other possible theories that might have involved violence? Dr Pepper, now clearly irked, was reluctant to be pulled down this path. He suggested that 'pressure applied to the throat might rupture a small vein, though it would not effect a great flow of blood.' And, he added, 'the stain on the carpet was probably caused by about four ounces of blood'.

The jury and the judge were now left with the confusing sense that neither natural causes nor murderous assault could explain the matter. If there was no sign of a blow to the head, then what caused the bleeding? Similarly, if Matilda Hacker had been strangled, then why was there blood? But even more pressingly, if she had died of natural causes, then quite why had her body been dragged all the way down four flights of stairs and hidden at the back of the coal cellar? The more witnesses were called, the cloudier the case became.

This confusion – plus the seeds of more danger for Severin Bastendorff – were carried by the next witness Robert Barnley, 'warder at Westminster prison', who had accompanied Hannah Dobbs in a cab on her way to the hearing at Bow Street. In the course of that journey, he said, Dobbs 'had told him there had been a lodger called Findlay living in the house and that he was in the habit of carrying a seven-chambered revolver. She believed,' Barnley continued, 'it was he who had committed the murder and stated that (Findlay) wanted to commit a secret to her keeping, and offered her £50 to go to America with him.'

Dobbs, according to Barnley, also had an explanation for the goods belonging to Matilda Hacker that she had pawned: it was 'to clear off what she called Mr Bastendorff's bastard debt'. There was another prison warder present in that cab; Francis Hawkins confirmed that this is what Hannah Dobbs had said.

It is easy to imagine the frustration of Inspector Hagen throughout all this; to see his case being torn this way and that in cross-currents of hearsay and scandalous speculation. Now he had the chance to stand up before a court to press his case.

After swearing the oath, Inspector Hagen took the court through the sequence of his movements. 'On May 12th, 1879, I went to see the prisoner, against whom there was then no suspicion,' he said. This was just after news of the discovery of the corpse had been featured prominently in newspapers all over the country; though there was no indication of whether the prisoner Hannah Dobbs had any access to newspapers. 'I went in company with Inspector Gatlin,' Inspector Hagen told the court. 'I made a memorandum of what she said.'

And now he proceeded to take the court through that first interview in the prison cell: questions about Hannah Dobbs' memories of lodgers, about any recollections she might have had of an elderly lady. Hannah Dobbs did remember what she termed a 'shabbily' dressed and rather mean old lady. She did not see her depart the house, she told the inspector, because 'I had to go out sometimes with the children. I went once with them to Hampstead Heath, and I rather think it was then that the old lady went away.'

In that cell, Inspector Hagen had asked Hannah Dobbs about the old lady's habits; what she ate and drank; and how her rents were collected. Then Hagen asked Hannah if she ever went to the coal cellar. She answered him: 'Every day.' Had she noticed anything 'wrong' about the cellar? 'No.' The inspector had then asked her: 'There has been a dead body found there; do you know anything about it? Hannah had replied: 'A body? A body in the coal cellar!' She said she knew nothing about it.'

Intriguingly, Inspector Hagen now told the court that after a few more questions about the lodger, Hannah said that 'the lady's name was Hacker – Miss Hacker'.

This was the first time that Inspector Hagen had heard the name. He told the court: 'I asked her if (the name) was not Uish. She said, "no, it was Hacker". She told me the lady had come up to collect her rents.' [This, it may be presumed, was a reference to Matilda Hacker's rental incomes.] I asked, "had she plenty of money?" She said she did not know; she had a gold watch and chain and that she only wore it on Sunday.

'She said, "I am sure now I was with the children at Hampstead when she went away and when I returned I was told she had gone and left a shilling for me." I asked her, "who told you that?" and she said, "Mrs Bastendorff". She said, "after she had gone, I found a dream book in her drawer, and I gave it to Mrs Bastendorff. She used to be always reading this dream book."'

The defence counsel Mr Mead asked Hagen how he had drawn the conclusions that he had. 'It was in great part through the prisoner that I was enabled to trace the case to Miss Hacker.'[5]

The Attorney General informed Mr Justice Hawkins that concluded the case for the prosecution. And it was at this point that Mr Mead, with some force and flair, submitted that there was no case to go to the jury.

'There was no evidence,' Mead added, 'that the deceased person, whoever she was, had been murdered, except for the mere fact of a rope having been found around her neck, and which might have been put there after her death. Besides, all the other appearances of the body were inconsistent with the theory of strangulation.' He returned to the possibility of a burst varicose vein, 'from which complaint Miss Hacker, whose body it was supposed to be, was suffering. There was,' Mead added, 'no evidence of any murder having been committed' and therefore he wished it to be submitted that 'the prisoner had nothing to answer.'

It was an intriguing gambit; but the judge was not convinced. He said he 'could not withdraw the case from the jury'.

Mr Mead now turned, in his legal passion, to the jury. He told them that he thought they would 'hesitate some time' before they came to their conclusion, 'especially when the life of a fellow creature [is] in danger, that a murder had been committed'. The defence counsel mused a little on the rope found around the neck of the remains. This was the only evidence of 'a violent death'. He averred that some may think the cord 'might have been drawn with considerable force' but after such a long time, 'there would have been considerable decomposition'. He did not elaborate on quite what he meant by that; was this the opinion of any of the doctors called as witnesses? Mead told the jury that there were 'two theories that might be put forward as the cause of death – that it was by strangulation or hanging'. He suggested that a 'portion of the evidence' about the 'position of the rope' was that it was consistent with a person being 'suspended' rather than strangled. Mead did not go so far as to use the word 'suicide' at this point; he simply left the suggestion in the air. Whatever happened, he said, there was no evidence of strangulation.

But now Mead pressed home what he saw as a more persuasive theory: that it might have been 'that someone had discovered that Miss Hacker had died. There was, perhaps, nobody in the house at the time'. He added that 'an avaricious person would at once conclude that the best thing to do would be to hide the body and take possession of any property she left after her. That,' he said, was 'a more likely theory than that a murder was committed by strangulation.'

Was it? One or two of the jury might have asked themselves if it was actually more likely that an avaricious person happening across a dead body might first swiftly appropriate and hide any valuables, rather than hiding the corpse itself: and then with the valuables safely stashed, then alert the household to the death. It would be some time – in a household of strangers – before anyone would establish beyond doubt that valuables were missing. Surely all that would be rather less effort than finding the body, fetching a cord to wind around its neck, dragging the corpse down the stairs and stuffing it into an alcove that was used daily, and where it was certain to be discovered in time.

Mead also addressed the blood stain on the carpet, and the difficulty of getting this part of the evidence to fit with strangulation. In all, he said, in a case like this, where there was 'mystery', he was satisfied that the jury would not overlook these alternative theories as to the cause of death. 'Before long,' he said, they would give their verdict, which would 'affect the life of a fellow being'; and so he redoubled his plea for them to consider all possibilities.

The defence counsel summed up with bravura the genuinely puzzling elements of this story: he told the jury that in order to find Hannah Dobbs guilty, it would have to be proven that Hannah Dobbs was alone in 4, Euston Square with the old lady on 14 October 1877.

'Mr and Mrs Bastendorff were away,' he said, and yet 'it was shown' that Mrs Bastendorff was not away. (Mead did not say who had 'shown' this – the vital fact appeared not to have been mentioned in court.) Mead added that indeed, Hannah Dobbs had the Bastendorff children with her in the house that day; were the jury really to believe that 'such a murder could be committed without making a noise and that the children would not have heard that noise?'

He was quite right to focus on the curious timings of the prosecution case: at what point of the day was this murder committed, given that 'Mr Bastendorff and some of the lodgers' had latchkeys and when Hannah Dobbs knew 'that at any time any of these persons might return and come in?' And had Hannah Dobbs herself not gone out that day? And 'supposing' she had been 'alone in the house'; 'was it to be believed that without concert or assistance she would have committed the deed? What weapon had she? And how was the body to be carried downstairs into the cellar?' More, 'was it conceivable' that 'the girl had the nerve' to 'go through all that proceeding unaided?' There was also the matter of 'washing up the blood and various other things' that she would have had to do. Where was the time?

Mead conceded that the gold watch subsequently seen in the possession of Hannah Dobbs was Matilda Hacker's; but he said that he was less certain about the chain which might simply have 'resembled' one of hers. The handkerchief: no proof that it was the property of Matilda Hacker. *The Book of Dreams*: it 'might be conceded that that had belonged to the deceased lady'. But not, he said, the eyeglass. So all in all, the only item that could really be traced to Hannah Dobbs was the gold watch.

At this, Mr Mead once more deftly swerved the focus of the case away from Hannah Dobbs and more firmly on to the master of the house, Severin Bastendorff. Hannah Dobbs, he said, had declared that 'Mr Severin Bastendorff had given the watch to her and,' added Mead, 'looking at the relations which had existed between the two, was there anything unreasonable in that account of it?' In other words, he was saying that there was no doubt whatsoever that there had been a sexual relationship between Bastendorff and his maid. 'Mr Severin Bastendorff's brother,' continued Mead, 'had shown that intimate relations existed between the master and his servant.

'As to Mr S. Bastendorff's account of the matter,' Mead added, 'he had denied what his brother had sworn, that there were those relations; and if he could deny the one thing, might he not also deny the other?'

Mead was relentless in his theme. 'There was the cabinet,' he said, which Hannah Dobbs' master had admitted 'he had given her as a present. Was there anything unreasonable in supposing that other things had been given as presents in a similar way?'

Mead also tackled the issue of class rather neatly, suggesting that part of the reason that there seemed to be such suspicion attached to Hannah Dobbs sporting fine watches was the idea of her 'being possessed of property unsuited to her condition'. In conclusion, he told the jury that even if the possessions told against her, the jury would have to suppose that Hannah Dobbs 'acted like a mad woman' if they thought her guilty. Given that anyone might have come calling for Matilda Hacker after her death, was it likely or rational that Hannah Dobbs would have been answering the door flaunting the jewellery of a dead woman?

He also pleaded with the jury to consider whether – if she had committed murder – she would have 'stopped in the same house . . . displaying no fear of being found out, and not exciting the suspicion of those about her'.

Now, in his efforts to turn the charge away from his client, Mr Mead once more fixed his attentions upon the house's other occupants. How was it, he asked, that nobody in the house, after all those months, ever noticed the body of the dead woman? Hannah Dobbs, he said, had behaved with the utmost candour ever since Inspector Hagen went to see her at the House of Correction. And nothing happened to arouse any suspicions when Dobbs was taken to the mortuary to see the remains. Now, it was the case that she had told her wardens of the lodger Findlay, and his revolver; but Mr Mead wanted the jury to be sure that that was just 'gossip'.

The principle, though, was this: he 'had a right to suggest that the murder was committed by some other person'. He 'did not care whether the jury thought Mr Bastendorff or Mrs Bastendorff were guilty or not guilty'. Their main aim was to rid themselves of any prejudice that might have attached itself to the defendant who 'had but small opportunity of saying anything for herself to remove that prejudice'. He also asked the jury to consider 'the lady of the house', and the oddness of Mrs Bastendorff's 'want of knowledge' concerning the business of the people who lodged under her roof.

Indeed, he said, 'what evidence there was, was stronger . . . against the Bastendorffs than it was against Hannah Dobbs'. He concluded with a peroration about the 'poor defenceless woman' who instead had been forced to stand trial, and that this 'poor defenceless woman' should be given the benefit of any doubt.[6]

Rising to counter this extraordinary defence, the Attorney General speaking for the prosecution was crisp: he declared that 'the circumstantial evidence on which that charge was founded pointed conclusively' to guilt. Even as late as 1879, circumstantial evidence was still regarded as having perfect legitimacy; that such evidence provided a kind of moral signpost in a case.

And so now it was time for Mr Justice Hawkins to sum up; he admitted that the case had a remarkably 'narrow compass' despite the 'considerable time' that they had spent on it (a two-day trial in 1879 was unusually lengthy). He then went on to talk of Matilda Hacker, and of the landlady who seemed 'never to have seen her, nor cared to see her'.

He talked of the corpse, and certain striking features, including the curvature of the spine and some condition of the leg. 'It was not suggested that the body had been mutilated,' the judge said, '. . . but it was imputed that the death was due to violence, this being shown by the coils of rope tied tightly round the neck and by the dragging of the body into the coal cellar.'

The judge seemed as bewildered as even the defence counsel had sounded. 'There was . . . no suggestion she had committed suicide,' he said. But 'if the woman had died a natural death, what earthly object was there in hiding the body except, perhaps, for the sake of possessing the few little articles which she had worn?' The judge also pondered the point that if it was indeed murder, then the jury had to consider if the defendant had committed the crime alone.

Matilda Hacker had been last seen on 10 October; she was supposed to have met her death four days later. It could be shown beyond doubt that

Severin Bastendorff was in Erith; Mrs Bastendorff was out most of that afternoon; and no other lodgers were present. It was just her, Hannah Dobbs, and the Bastendorff children. The judge said that it had to be asked why the next day, Hannah Dobbs, when sent to fetch Miss Hacker's rent, 'immediately returned' with a £5 note. If she was innocent, why had she simply not said that Matilda Hacker was not in her room, and had gone?

Hannah later stated that the old lady was intending to go; and then announced that she had gone, although no-one saw her leave. Matilda Hacker's basket trunk and *The Book of Dreams* remained. The jury had also to consider that blood stain on the carpet, which had not been there when the old lady took the room.

What the jury had before them was the evidence, and it was on that that they should 'firmly discharge their duty'.[7]

It was five minutes to eight on the summer's evening of 6 July 1879 when the jury retired; they did not take long. Twenty-five minutes later, they returned to the courtroom.

'The prisoner,' ran one court report, 'who was very pale, and in a half-fainting condition, was brought back to the dock.'

The 'clerk of arraigns' asked the foreman of the jury whether they had all agreed upon their verdict. He 'replied in the affirmative'. The clerk then asked if they found Hannah Dobbs 'guilty or not guilty of the charge of wilful murder'.

The foreman replied: 'We find her not guilty.'

'You say she is not guilty,' said the clerk, 'and that is the verdict of you all?'

'It is,' said the foreman.

With this, according to one report, 'a sigh of intense relief escaped from the prisoner, who during the whole trial had behaved with the greatest possible decorum and evidently with a full appreciation of the serious position in which she stood. She was then removed from the dock.'[8]

Hannah Dobbs was not free, not yet; she still had a few weeks of her previous sentence for theft to serve. And despite the verdict, this was only the end of one act of this tragedy.

For both Hannah Dobbs and the Bastendorff family, there were to be ricocheting, shocking consequences extending far beyond the legal system. The darkness that had gathered in and around 4, Euston Square was set to intensify.

17
'Working Women Like Herself'

The mother of Hannah Dobbs was reported to have said, prior to her main trial, that she always knew her daughter would be the one to bring disgrace on the family. Yet on the morning of 8 August 1879, as she completed her jail sentence for fraud, it was clear that Hannah had moved beyond disgrace to a subtly different form of notoriety; she was now in a curious way a celebrated figure. That morning, outside the Tothill Fields House of Correction, not far from Westminster Abbey, a crowd had gathered, having heard advance intelligence of the young woman's release. It was possible they were there to jeer; it is equally possible that many of them were simply agog with curiosity having followed the twists of this intriguing case in the *Illustrated Police News*.

Also standing close to the gates of the prison was Peter Bastendorff. He, like all the others, was not allowed too close to the entrance.

No risks were being taken. When Hannah emerged from the main door of the jail, a pre-arranged hansom cab immediately drew up. There was no time for Peter Bastendorff to step forward in greeting; his lover was hustled fast into the vehicle. And before any of the 'mob' as the crowd was described in the press could so much as glimpse her,

Hannah was being driven off in the direction of Paddington Station from where, it was assumed, she would be catching a train to Bideford.

And yet how curious it must have been for Hannah, and her family and, indeed, the people of that small harbour town, to have her return. There would have been many in the area who would have recalled the young woman's childhood years; now, declared innocent of murder, yet daubed in the gaudy colours of sexual scandal, many must have wondered how Hannah had progressed from a bucolic childhood to the sophisticated amorality of London.

Hannah was born in January 1855, in Barnstaple, on the rushing River Taw, a town with a thriving harbour and quays, and a handsome square. Although some distance from any large city, Barnstaple was in some ways a mercantile hub; imports such as tobacco and wine sailed in from the ocean up the river into the calm harbour; and the fertility of the plump countryside around brought the wool trade, and many dairy farms. A few miles west lay a dramatic coastline that even by 1855 was drawing wealthy and fashionable visitors from London and other cities; there were headlands such as Hartland Point, where the roaring Atlantic winds would disperse any lingering sense of pervasive city smog. But inland, the countryside was soft; vivid deep green under the clouds after rainfall, dips and hollows plunging to secret river valleys and rich woods.

The visitors were being inspired by the recently published novel *Westward Ho!* written by Charles Kingsley. This was an historical romance set in the Elizabethan era concerning the high sea adventures of a young man from Bideford. The fame of the novel – combined with the completion of a railway line running to Barnstaple in 1855 – brought a new class of tourist.

This was an age where, under the dark skies of intense industry, urban romanticism concerning untouched landscapes was reaching a new intensity. Well-to-do travellers from London might have gazed from the railway window as they passed through the tiny villages, thatched houses in the midst of lavishly wooded hills, and imagined that they were looking at a perfect vision of what rural life could be. Such visitors would not see just how hard that life actually was.

Soon after Hannah Dobbs was born – one of three sisters – her parents moved the family to live and work on a farm just outside Barnstaple. At that stage, her father, William, was a shepherd, her mother Susan worked as a dairy hand, as well as attending to other tasks 'about the farm-house'.[1] Neither of these roles were easy: relentless hours, brutal winter weather, the oppressive fly-humming torpor of the summer; for Hannah's mother, it must have been extraordinarily difficult, combining all the physical labour of the dairy with bringing up young children. There were no complex items of farming machinery to ease the work; the business of caring for cattle continued much as it had done for centuries – though by the mid-nineteenth century, and with the advent of rail travel, the scale was slightly larger. Even without any wholly effective form of refrigeration, the arrival of trains meant that it was now possible to transport milk and butter to large towns such as Exeter.

In 1856, the railway line that wound through the valleys from Exeter to Barnstaple was now extended further to Bideford and a few miles south to the market town of Great Torrington. For a generation of children growing up amid these green valleys, this would have re-shaped their entire view of the world in a way that their parents could not have imagined: bringing cities such as Bristol and even London within easy reach. For children such as Hannah Dobbs, who were educated in Bideford at what was termed the 'British School', the piercing cry of the locomotive whistle, the distant thunder of the departing train, will have sparked many new dimensions of daydreaming.

William and Susan Dobbs, with their children on that farm at Gameston Moor, had clearly been thinking that there must be less physically arduous means of getting a living. This was a difficult life for those of advancing years to maintain. As tenants, the Dobbs' would have had few entitlements or rights.

Yet equally for their children – when they were not labouring at chores – this was a life filled with strong colour, long hilly paths upon which the wind would bring scent of the sea. Hannah herself would certainly describe it later as a 'happy' childhood; if there were privations, then there were seemingly none that had lingered in her memory or indeed had sparked any aversion to this rural life.

But this landscape could be paradoxically claustrophobic. As they grew older, Hannah and her sisters, who would have attended the summer dances at the agricultural fairs, would have seen that the trajectory of their lives was either marriage and homemaking, combined with further varieties of farm work; or entering into service with the local gentry. As she grew up, it is possible to envisage how Hannah might have become dissatisfied with the limits of north Devon life. She and her family had little money but the fashionable tourists from the cities had brought more than glimpses of material wealth; they had brought ideas. Added to this, in the 1860s and 1870s, there was an ever greater number of colourfully written journals and magazines. And literate girls like Hannah read voraciously.

This was a booming period for such literature; a serendipitous conjoining of a widely spreading railway network, opening up new markets, and a new generation avid to absorb news and amusement and scandal of all varieties.

In 1870, *The Ladies' Own Paper* carried an amusing A–Z feature concerning that perennial preoccupation now widely termed 'The Servant Problem'; how were middle-class people, inexperienced in such matters, to deal with truculent staff? In this case, 'E' stood for the 'elegant person' who has been hired as the new maid-of-all-work to the Browns in London; she wears 'a lady-like bonnet' and 'a trimly fitting dress'. And that evening, she prepares an excellent dinner. No-one can find fault 'with the fish or the roast'. However, after a few days, the mask of perfection slowly slides away; and the girl becomes sulky, disobedient, angry. It comes to the point when the family try to sack her.

And then the feature moves to 'F' for 'fracas' as the maid steadfastly refuses to budge upon being fired, while also unleashing 'the torrent of her eloquence' upon the lady of the house and the lady's daughters. As the magazine reports the servant saying, 'They might send for as many constables as they liked. 500 men couldn't stir her till she chose to go, and that would be soon enough when she got her wages. Call them ladies! They was working women like herself – common working women. She had been deceived.'[2]

A hugely popular magazine of the 1870s called *London Society* turned the servant problem the other way around; it told the wry story of a maid in London's Mayfair called Jane Bell, and how she was lured away from her household to work for 'Lady Mary Fauxanfier' of Belgravia. Jane Bell's previous mistress was highly sceptical of this arrangement; why, Jane had no experience in arranging hair or supervising the extensive wardrobe of an important society lady. She would surely be hopelessly out of her depth in a grand Belgravia house.

And some days later, Jane Bell indeed returns to Mayfair, and asks her former mistress if she still has a situation for her. But the tale she has to tell is not quite what the lady is expecting: the fact was that Lady May Fauxanfier's extensive retinue of servants were non-existent. Jane Bell was required to fill every role herself, from answering the door to supervising her ladyship's hansom cab. This was Belgravia household economics: every appearance of aristocratic grandeur but acute shortage of cash. Jane Bell wanted to return to a nice middle-class house where the family might not have had any sort of aristocratic lineage but it did at least know how to live comfortably and how to treat its servants.

By her own admission, Hannah Dobbs became entranced by fashion early in her life; and magazines such as 'London Society' were filled with beautifully textured illustrations showing ladies on 'fashionable promenades' or in resorts such as Brighton. The slang term 'fashion plate' derives from these illustrative plates in the journals; the images accompanied by extensively detailed descriptions of cashmere with velvet, 'all in shades of blue'; of 'striped, plaited skirts' matched with 'striped waistcoats', 'fastened with cordelieries' and 'velvet buttons'.[3] The illustrations conveyed a life of elegant leisure; ladies in the Regent's Park, at flower shows, taking tea. Hannah Dobbs had a voracious interest in the fine clothes of the models; and surely also for the elegant world that they represented.

When Hannah Dobbs left school, she immediately joined her mother in dairy work on the family farm. Such work – from the cajoling of reluctant cattle with 'teats as hard as carrots',[4] the milker's face resting against the beast's hot flank, to the carrying of great pails to the repetitive churning of the butter pail – would have left most so physically tired that at the end of the day, sleep would have been yearned for.

Hannah Dobbs had a fecund imagination (as she would abundantly prove later when the Euston Square mystery darkened further); it is possible to imagine how in the soft glimmering darkness of summer's nights, as she lay in bed, she might have heard the last train puffing through from Great Torrington, through Bideford, towards Exeter. It is possible to imagine how she might have yearned to be on that train.

She did not stay long on that farm; as a sixteen-year old in 1871, Hannah Dobbs decided to find work of her own. Her first domestic situation was at the rectory in Parkham, a few miles south of Bideford; but her next move took her closer to the realm depicted in magazines. She went into service – albeit initially at the level of dairymaid – for the Stucley family at Moreton House just outside Bideford.

The Stucleys – or Bucks – were the most prominent local aristocrats, and Morton House was beautiful (they also had possession of the picturesque Affeton Castle and the more imposing Hartland Abbey). Moreton House, built in the eighteenth century, was a white-washed mansion, looking out over carefully tended gardens and parkland. The lives of those within must have seemed, to a creative and intelligent young woman such as Hannah, extraordinarily desirable: the mistress of the house would have been attired in the finest new modes, and the house itself played host to a range of society figures drawn not only from the immediate county but invited from London.

The Stucley family enjoyed a particularly fast social ascension in the previous century; their wealth had been produced by the harbour at Bideford, and the extensive importation of ever-more popular tobacco from America. Wealth brought a seat in Parliament; and in the mid-nineteenth century, Sir George Stucley was made a baronet.

Hannah's time came to be divided between the farm house and the big house; she had many dealings with all the other staff. She was on a salary of £10 10 shillings a year; enough for the necessaries, but not enough to plan, and nowhere near enough to be able to edge closer to the finery that she craved: 'I could never resist the desire to dress well,' she later stated.[5]

As might be expected in such an establishment, there were flares of passion between the younger staff; and by her later admission, Hannah became 'intimate' with one of the footmen.[6] The affair did not last; for not long after this, Hannah became involved with a young butcher from the nearby village of Holsworthy. It was also around this point, working in various capacities in and around the big house, that her apparently troubled relationship with money – specifically, money belonging to others – began. Hannah's own account of the trouble was ambiguous and patchy; the lady of the house had intended to give another servant girl a cheque for £3 for some unspecified reason. But then, in a twist of complexity, Hannah somehow had this cheque pressed upon her so that she might get it cashed in town, or indeed use it as security to lend against. What was clear in the admission was that at the time, Hannah was fixated by a particularly desirable bonnet that she had seen in the window of a Bideford milliner.

The cheque was somehow used as security for Hannah to have the bonnet; it was left with the milliner. And it was then, as she put it, that the 'trouble' began.[7] Hannah said that she failed 'to return' for the cheque in time and it was then that it was discovered that it had not gone to the intended recipient. In her own account, Hannah declared that this happened at exactly the point that she was leaving the service of the Stucley family, in order to marry that young butcher from Holsworthy. But as a result of this garbled affair – what would appear to be a fairly straightforward case of theft – she left without any favourable references. And her engagement to the young butcher was terminated. At the age of 18, in 1873, Hannah found herself forced to return to her parents.

As she had fallen, so their circumstances had seemingly improved; for by this time, William and Susan Dobbs had left the dairy farm. William had taken a lease on a public house in Bideford called The Blacksmith's Arms.

This was (and is) a handsome Georgian building, with a fanlight over the door, a whitewashed front elevation, and a view over the river of sailing masts and the rich sunsets beyond. The upper storey had rooms for family and guests alike. The arrival of the railway in the 1850s had been a boost to the business.

Crucially, this was also to become something of a haven for Hannah Dobbs; but it was impossible for her to find a new domestic situation in Bideford or Barnstaple. Word carried.

So Hannah now had an obligation to think beyond the local hills. The impatient sighs of the locomotives on the railway behind the tavern might just have been the spur. It might have been expected for her to look towards Exeter, or Bristol. But her imagination had already taken her a great deal further than that.

And as her luggage was loaded on to the railway carriage that day, and as she bade farewell to her parents, it must also have taken quite a great deal of courage. Hannah Dobbs was fixed on London. She clearly felt that this was where she would find the life that she yearned for. But even in the mid-1870s, even armed with all the knowledge gleaned from magazines and journals, it must still have seemed as if she was travelling to a new and unknown world.

18

Avowed Admirers

There would have been days without number when the sky above was broiling brown; and the air was thick and suffocating with chemicals, with the piercingly caustic smell of burning rubber and ammonia, and the weightier stench of animal dung and urine. Under the shadow of the vast railway viaduct that stretched out from London Bridge station for four miles down to Greenwich was an infernal world of leather tanneries and rubber works; there were distilleries too, although their own distinct aromas were wholly smothered. Hannah Dobbs' first view of her new city neighbourhood must have been – in the most literal sense – breath-catching and daunting.

Before she left Devon, she had secured herself lodgings in the district of Rotherhithe, on the south side of the river, near the vast timber warehouses of the Surrey Docks. Hannah did not know any better; but did the cheapness of the room on offer cause her any kind of premonitory flutter of disquiet or unease? Hannah's train, after a change at Exeter, would have arrived at Waterloo; and after a tiring seven-hour journey, she would have stepped off the train into a shattering clamour of noise and smoke. A young woman, quite alone in this vast metropolis; how was she to establish herself? And once she had engaged a horse-drawn cab to Rotherhithe, how was she to adjust to that new realm of narrow, glistening alleys and damp walls and rotting weather-boarding, where the nearest green space was a mile away and where the close-built streets at night were alive with the pervasive menace of male drinkers?

A satisfactory domestic situation seemed elusive. There were employment agencies for servants; but her references were by necessity limited. And Hannah Dobbs was also in precisely the wrong location to walk around looking for work in grander houses; though there were some middle-class households to be found a little further south in Peckham and Camberwell, it would have been an increasingly trying business for the former dairy-maid to trudge from door to door asking if there were any jobs to be had. The real focus of work lay north of the river.

In addition to all this, a young woman living quite alone in a mean rented room close to the noisy pubs that served the hard-drinking dockers, in moist passages that by night were a malign maze, would surely have found this first taste of London deeply unsettling. After a month, when Hannah's meagre funds had dwindled, she was forced to leave.

But she was not ready to give up altogether; somehow, she got to hear of a position at 'Mrs Nicholson's, Woodlands Road, Redhill'[1] – a town in Surrey swaddled in the lee of the North Downs.

The work must have been relatively agreeable; Hannah stayed there for fifteen months and indeed might well have stayed longer. The reason for the termination of this job was once again her compulsion to steal. This time, she purloined 'a piece of silk, and £1 3 shillings from a box'. Mrs Nicholson not only dismissed Hannah, but also wrote to her parents in Bideford about her 'conduct'.[2] Hannah had no choice but to return to Devonshire in disgrace.

Despite the failure of her last attempt, she yearned to return to London. Again, there may have been subliminal encouragement offered by newspapers and magazines; daily gossip items increasingly focused on female stage performers from unprivileged backgrounds, and where they were next appearing. The capital, it seemed, was welcoming women of talent; and newspapers were fascinated by these new celebrities, moving in such a world of glamour and colour. Hannah (who was later to have the term 'celebrity' sardonically attached to her own name) and countless others would have been gripped by stories about those who began as humble dancers or chorus members. The rooms of Bloomsbury played host to many women who sought such work.

Journals such as *The Era* were printing articles about music hall artistes such as Bessie Bellwood (famous for her ditty 'What Cheer, Ria'), Lizzie Coote ('Froggy Would A Wooing Go') and Jenny Hill – 'The Vital Spark' ('Maggie Murphy's Here' was a favourite). Bessie Bellwood had risen from great poverty in Bermondsey; but with her newfound stardom, her devoted fans were thrilled to read that out of her tremendous earnings, she regularly paid for Masses for the poor. Jenny Hill, meanwhile, was using her fantastic earning power to invest: in 1879, she bought The Star music hall in south London.

The public fascination for these female performers lay in the fact that they were seen to have agency and traction; an unusual level of control over their lives.

Added to this, the rise of the popularity of photography saw singers and stage actresses now having their images sold in special photograph shops. These shots were known as 'shilling beauties'. There was an inevitable element of salaciousness involved in a lot of the photographs; as actresses, music hall singers, even dancers in ballet companies, the women portrayed might justifiably pose in scanty clothing. By the 1870s, this trend for slyly shocking photography receded a little when the newspapers and magazines noticed, and signalled disapproval.

'The photographic shops are now purged of the prurient portraits of half-dressed actresses,' observed one London gossip column entitled 'West End Notes', 'which used to make it impossible for modest women to study the celebrities of the day.' But 'celebrity' photographic cards of a more decorous nature were still pervasive and popular with women. And despite censoriousness, they still pointed towards a sense that their subjects understood the power of sexuality.

In the mid-1870s, there was a national flurry of fascination over the famous young cockney actress and singer Nelly Power, who had become involved in a most intriguing off-stage scandal. Under her real name, Eileen Maria, she was married to a man called Richard Israel Barnett. As Nelly Power sang on stage: 'He is something in an office, lah-di-dah/ And he quite the City toff is, lah-di-dah.' But the marriage had soured. And now there was the prospect of a very public divorce which sensationally would reveal Nelly Power's affair with another man. For a woman in any other social situation, this would mean blazing humiliation, if not ruin. The case of Nelly Power, who was only twenty-years old, appeared to re-write the conventions.

As the marriage disintegrated, Power moved out of the nuptial home and went back to stay with her mother, Mrs Lingham who lived in Islington, not far from the canal. But Nelly Power's estranged husband was roiling with fury, jealousy and suspicion; and spent many evenings simply standing positioned across the road from the mother's dwellings, in the gloom of the gaslight. His behaviour would now be termed stalking.

One evening in the autumn of 1875, Barnett once more took up that unsettling sentinel position on the Southgate Road, looking at the home of Nelly and her mother. He observed Nelly Power going out, and catching a hansom cab; some hours later, as he remained motionless, he watched as another cab drew up Southgate Road. Out of it emerged his wife and the man he had so frequently seen. This was Frederick George Hobson, later described by the excited newspapers as a 'betting man' and member of the Raleigh Club. He was also, as the excitable newspapers noted, an 'avowed admirer' of Nelly Power.

In the course of the violent scuffle that followed, the husband Barnett came off worse with a bloody nose. The next stage was the courts; and a case that readers devoured eagerly.

Anyone who imagined that Nelly Power might be reluctant to attend for fear of the damage it might do her reputation had misjudged her self-confidence. As Barnett tried to lay the accusation of assault against Hobson, he glared at Nelly Power and told the jury that 'the lady sitting beside you is my wife and I wish I had never seen her'.[3]

But Nelly Power had her own statement to make. She took the stand and told the court: 'Since I married this man, my jewellery and everything have been swept away.' The court was also informed that Hobson had suggested that '£1000 would square him'. The case brought by Barnett was now being turned against him. Nelly Power won a divorce in which her future earnings were 'protected'. And most importantly, the newspaper coverage was suggestive of a popular sympathy with the young woman in the matter. The fascinated public, in the form of ever-larger theatre audiences for her roles in 'Jack The Giant Killer', and 'The Merchant of Venice' gave their approval too. There was no suggestion of her own sexual morality being judged.

Nelly Power's life was tragically short; she died of pleurisy only a few years later at the age of 32. Her funeral was in Abney Park cemetery in the north London suburb of Stoke Newington; thousands of people lined the streets to bid farewell. All through her career, she had been a wildly popular figure.

And most crucially, she and so many other actresses – from Nellie Moon to Lillie Langtry – will have been alluring role models to countless young woman across the land. They held out the inspiring possibility of a world in which a woman could find fulfilment not in domesticity, but the achievement of a hugely successful career – if only one could find the opportunities.

After a few weeks back in Bideford, Hannah Dobbs was ready for a new attempt on London. She had contacted a 'servants' advertising agent'; he had written back to tell her that he had several potential vacancies for her. Once again, her she embarked upon that train journey; but this time, instead of taking lodgings in the murk of Rotherhithe, she instead found herself a room in Lamb's Conduit Street, Holborn.

The street itself, with its creaking architecture, was frowsy. But it lay close to the territory that Hannah wished to be in. She went out looking for situations herself.

Not half-a-mile away from her lodgings were some of the grandest and most elegant squares in Bloomsbury: Russell, Gordon and Torrington. At number 42, Torrington Square lived a landlady, Mrs Pearce, who rented rooms to a number of lodgers, and who needed several maids to deal with the workload. Hannah Dobbs was quickly taken on as a cook, with a salary of £12 a year.

It was this position, in the heart of Bloomsbury, that was going to alter the course of her life, and make another kind of life seem possible. Hannah and her colleagues certainly worked hard but here was also an extraordinary vantage point from which to view the fine ladies, the sumptuousness of fashion; it was also from here that the maids would have been keenly aware of the different sorts of young men – from the soldiers, the bright aggressive scarlet of their tunics blazing outside the public houses, to the men of property, coats dark but waistcoats and neckties silken and shimmering with finely woven patterns.

It was there in Torrington Square – Hannah Dobbs would later lethally claim – that she first met Severin Bastendorff. It was from that point onwards that she would find herself on that trajectory to her own dark form of celebrity.

And so it was, a few weeks after her release from prison in August 1879, following the murder trial, that Hannah Dobbs was to acquire rather greater fame and notoriety. She had a story to tell. And one that a newspaper publisher called George Purkess was extremely eager to pay handsomely for, to publish and send across the world.

Yet this was also a story that – in all its sexual seediness and horror – was going to smash at the foundations of the Bastendorff household.

Vue générale de la ville d'Echternach, dans le grand-duché de Luxembourg.

The landlord of 4, Euston Square and his brothers – who were among those about to be drawn into a vortex of luridly gothic allegations – hailed from the countryside near Echternach in Luxembourg. It was then a remote rural region, but rich in religious history and steeped in colourful folk tales.

No. 2587

(A.)

NATURALIZATION ACTS, 1870.

Certificate of Naturalization to an Alien.

HOME OFFICE, LONDON.

WHEREAS Severin Bastendorff an Alien, now residing at 4 Euston Square, in the County of Middlesex has presented to me, the Right Honourable Richard Assheton Cross one of Her Majesty's Principal Secretaries of State, a Memorial, praying for a Certificate of Naturalization, and alleging that he is a native of Bordorf in the Grand Duchy of Luxemburg – of the age of thirty one years – Fancy Cabinet Maker – is married, and has four children under age, residing with him, viz,

Christine Bastendorff, aged 5 years,
Peter Bastendorff, aged 3 years,
Severin William Bastendorff aged 2 years,
Rose Bastendorff, aged 4 months,

And

Landlord Severin Bastendorff, who ran a successful furniture business, was naturalised as a British subject in 1878; this records book, now in the National Archives, and filled with French, German and Italian names, is a fascinating testament to the fluidity of continental immigration in the 19th century.

One of the most popular celebrities of the 1870s, singer Nelly Power was a powerful role model for young working class and servant women everywhere. Apart from her music hall work, the public were gripped by her public divorce and finance battles and her fierce spirit of independence.

Matilda Hacker, one of the tenants at number 4, Euston Square, had always attracted jovial local notoriety for her eccentricity. She and her sister, both of a certain age, used to promenade in Canterbury and Brighton dressed as young girls.

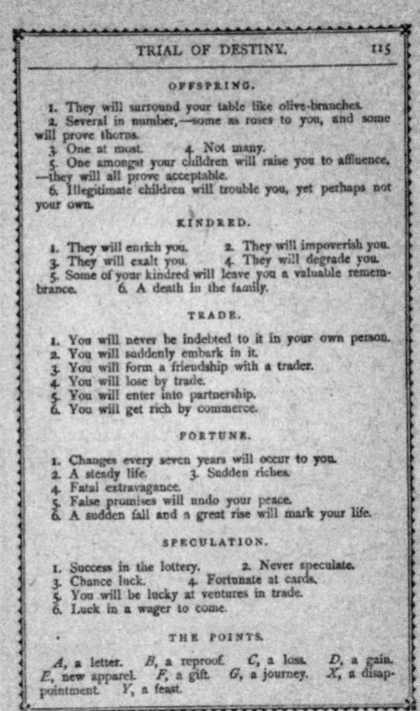

TRIAL OF DESTINY. 115

OFFSPRING.

1. They will surround your table like olive-branches.
2. Several in number,—some as roses to you, and some will prove thorns.
3. One at most. 4. Not many.
5. One amongst your children will raise you to affluence,—they will all prove acceptable.
6. Illegitimate children will trouble you, yet perhaps not your own.

KINDRED.

1. They will enrich you. 2. They will impoverish you.
3. They will exalt you. 4. They will degrade you.
5. Some of your kindred will leave you a valuable remembrance. 6. A death in the family.

TRADE.

1. You will never be indebted to it in your own person.
2. You will suddenly embark in it.
3. You will form a friendship with a trader.
4. You will lose by trade.
5. You will enter into partnership.
6. You will get rich by commerce.

FORTUNE.

1. Changes every seven years will occur to you.
2. A steady life. 3. Sudden riches.
4. Fatal extravagance.
5. False promises will undo your peace.
6. A sudden fall and a great rise will mark your life.

SPECULATION.

1. Success in the lottery. 2. Never speculate.
3. Chance luck. 4. Fortunate at cards.
5. You will be lucky at ventures in trade.
6. Luck in a wager to come.

THE POINTS.

A, a letter. *B*, a reproof. *C*, a loss. *D*, a gain. *E*, new apparel. *F*, a gift. *G*, a journey. *X*, a disappointment. *Y*, a feast.

Matilda Hacker was addicted to what she called 'the Book of Dreams'; this was published in various forms and under various titles and purported to be filled with mystical prognostications.

The house maid and the tenant; these portraits of Hannah Dobbs and Matilda Hacker can't convey the curious claustrophobic closeness of some servant/resident relationships within respectable boarding houses.

Hannah Dobbs came from Bideford, in north Devon. The arrival of the railway in the 1850s transformed this deeply rural area and also the imaginations and desires of its young people, who could now travel and move to cities such as London with ease.

"POLICE NEWS" EDITION.

THE EUSTON SQUARE MYSTERY.

EXTRAORDINARY STATEMENT MADE BY

HANNAH DOBBS

CONTAINING

HER LIFE AND EARLY CAREER — HISTORY OF MISS HACKER WHILE IN EUSTON SQUARE—HARROWING DETAILS—STORY OF THE MURDER, &c., &c.

PORTRAIT OF HANNAH DOBBS

PRICE ONE PENNY.

G. PURKESS, 286, STRAND, LONDON, W.C.

Harnessing the new power of mass readership, the proprietor of the 'Illustrated Police News' issued this pamphlet, purportedly by the housemaid Hannah Dobbs, containing wildly sensational (and libellous) allegations about life at 4, Euston Square, of which murder seemed among the least shocking.

For the journalists of popular weekly sensation paper 'The Illustrated Police News', the 'Euston Square Murder' was the perfect story to keep their readers hooked: a middle-class family, the discovery of a slain corpse, and the revelations in court of scandalous sexual relationships.

Imprisonment in the Clerkenwell House of Detention not only brought the fearful prospect of hard labour – oakum picking, the treadwheel – but also a range of humiliations that middle-class convicts, such as the resident from Euston Square, found essentially annihilated their old identities.

This rare photograph of Euston Square was taken in the 1930s – by then, the area had gone rather to seed. But it is possible to imagine how much brighter and smarter the terrace was in 1879 as the Bastendorffs presided over their eminently genteel boarding house, with its professional tenants and neighbours.

The Colney Hatch asylum, in north London, on the fringes of the open countryside, was regarded by many with terror: what if one were to be committed for the rest of one's life? Yet in the Victorian age, this institution did much to try and help and understand its patients: including the tormented inmate from Euston Square.

19

'The Expected Child'

On that day in September 1879, did Severin and Mary Bastendorff have any inkling of the further catastrophe that was about to strike? Possibly it was the case that they had awoken every morning with a sense of dread ever since the discovery of Matilda Hacker's corpse. With Hannah Dobbs' acquittal, there had been no sense of catharsis of closure; the murder was still a hideous mystery and it hung heavy over 4, Euston Square; no potential lodgers came calling. The house was shunned.

On top of this, following the searing sexual allegations in court about Severin's relationship with Hannah Dobbs – which he denied – it is difficult to know how the couple dealt with one another. On the face of it, the marriage held firm; but how united could they continue to stand?

In the meantime, efforts had been made between the Home Office and Scotland Yard to find some way of rekindling the case. There were letters passing back and forth attempting to explain why the trial collapsed, and why a killer was still free. A cash reward of £100 was now offered to anyone who could vouchsafe helpful information; and soon, a hitherto-unheard lady pawnbroker from near Camden Town volunteered herself to Inspector Hagen; she had some clothing that Hannah Dobbs had pawned. The clothing was confirmed as having belonged to Matilda Hacker.

This development had left some Scotland Yard figures wondering whether pursuing Hannah Dobbs on a charge of 'larceny' involving the old lady's property might be the way to bringing all the chief figures in this story back into the witness box, and thus under fresh pressure to finally confess the truth.[1]

But as the departments quietly corresponded with one another, an even more opportune possibility for bringing the mystery back before the courts was approaching.

It came one morning in September when Severin Bastendorff had been out on business and returned to read his morning newspaper; his eye was transfixed by a headline that promised 'Hannah Dobbs – Further Revelations'.

This was a news article that had been syndicated by the Central News Agency to every paper. It told of a forthcoming publication – a short autobiography – written by the recently freed maid herself; and it promised that this publication would be filled with the most sensational allegations.

Among these were Hannah Dobbs' assertion that there had not been just one murder in 4, Euston Square, but two others; and that the complicity in the shocking crimes was shared by the entire household. This work promised readers tales of brutal child murder, and even the torture of a live dog. The home of the Bastendorffs was to be portrayed as a gothic charnel house.

This teasing news story alone was enough to bring the crowds back to Euston Square that morning; and Severin, Mary and the family had to suffer the 'nuisance' of people outside the door, staring at the house, talking and pointing. It must have been nerve-stretching.

In the days that followed, with the dark promise of the publication of this special pamphlet (in appearance like a small very closely printed magazine) looming, Bastendorff sought legal advice; he was desperate to take out an injunction that would prevent publication. He even took himself to the Strand office from which the publisher George Purkess operated. And it was here that he was able to obtain an advance copy. He was later to describe the seismic effect of sitting down to read it.

On the cover of this pamphlet was an engraving of Hannah Dobbs. Her name was featured prominently as the title. Beneath was the subtitle: 'Her life and early career – History of Miss Hacker while in Euston Square – Harrowing details – Story of the Murder.'

Hannah – or more particularly her ghostwriters – had started by relaying the story of her upbringing, her early career in Devon, and indeed the early signs of her own moral failings and weaknesses, when it came both to fashion and sex.

This section was headlined: 'My Confession.'

She then relayed how she came to work for a Mrs Pearce at Torrington Square as a cook in 1875; and now she wanted to reveal how she really first met Bastendorff.

It was, according to her, on the pavement outside that house. (Bastendorff by that time had been married four years, with four children.) He was walking along, she alleged; and she instantly caught his eye.

'One morning, when the housemaid and I were cleaning the dining room windows, he passed and the remark that he made was whether we wanted help,' wrote Hannah (or the journalist who had transcribed and moulded her words). 'I answered "yes" and we remained talking some little time. He passed again at seven in the evening. I could not go out walking in the evening, as we were not allowed out so late.'[2]

The sexual subtext of Mrs Pearce's domestic stricture was quite clear to Hannah; and she intended to find a way around it. 'I was told servants often went out after eleven o'clock when their families had gone to bed, no-one knowing anything about it.' And so it was – according to her own account – that Hannah made a promise to Severin Bastendorff that she would be in a position to quietly leave the house at 11.30p.m. for an assignation.

This did not go quite as it should, she wrote; for she and her fellow servants, who all slept in one large bed downstairs, went for a nap at 11p.m. and fell asleep – so Hannah missed her appointment. They were woken by two policemen who had investigated the back door, which had been left open.

After this mishap, the following evening went a little more smoothly for Hannah. She managed to effect a solo exit from Torrington Square, and met Bastendorff at a pre-arranged spot. Hannah did not go back home, she said, 'until half-past two o'clock'.

Hannah related how she then went on to see Mr Bastendorff 'several times' in Torrington Square; and she continued to see him when she decided to leave Mrs Pearce's service and go to work nearby for a Mrs Cripps in Russell Square, who was offering a little more money. It was while she was adjusting to this new job when Hannah learned that Bastendorff was a married man. She seemed not to have been deterred.

'I learned that his wife would soon be in want of a servant,' she wrote, 'and that the wages were but £11 a year and that the difference might be made up in another way to me.' According to Hannah, Bastendorff told her that his wife Mary was shortly to advertise the position. 'I went to 4, Euston Square on 17th June, 1876.' In fact, there was another servant starting there too: a younger girl called Ellen Peek. She was to stay seven months; Hannah was there, as she recalled with striking precision, 'two years, two months and three days'.

The house then was a bustling establishment. The most important tenants were a Mr and Mrs Brookes, who retained their own servant. They had 'the dining and drawing rooms, the small top front room and the back kitchen'. The Brookes servant left just a few days after Hannah arrived; and Mary Bastendorff and Mrs Brookes agreed that Hannah Dobbs should begin working for them, as well as attending to everyone else in the house. Hannah noted of this that her 'wages were not increased' accordingly. Indeed, she also alleged that she only received her first wages an extraordinary four months after she started working there; making that summer of 1876 a period of unpaid labour. Hannah did not reveal in this memoir quite why she didn't leave; she would have had no difficulty finding non-exploitative work elsewhere.

It was also in the first few months that possessions belonging to Mary Bastendorff started finding their way to local pawn shops. 'Her ear-rings and brooch were pawned,' wrote Hannah, 'one in Hampstead-road and the other in Euston-road.' On top of this, 'a ring of Mr Bastendorff's and the family Bible were also pawned, but not by me'. Then by whom? Hannah Dobbs chose not to say, although she then went on to relate how the Brookes' were being systematically swindled. 'There were no coals to speak of then in the cellar where THE BODY OF MISS HACKER was found,' wrote Hannah, teasing her readers with the horror that was yet to come. 'In fact at this time I used Mr Brookes's coals for Mr Bastendorff's fires.'

It was at this stage that Hannah's account started to darken.

'Mr and Mrs Bastendorff then slept in the large front bedroom at the top of the house and I slept in the large back one with the children,' she wrote.

'He used to come in between twelve and one o'clock when his wife and children were asleep.

'In January 1877 I was afraid that I was with child,' she continued. 'I was told by the father that I need not fear, as I should not be allowed to want for anything. Also that I was to write home, telling my parents I was married, and when the time for my confinement approached, to go home on the pretext that I wished to be taken ill [sic] there, my husband being abroad.

'It was on the day that the Brookes' left – in December 1876 – that Peter Bastendorff . . . first sought to engage himself to me,' she continued. 'By an arrangement, Peter was to be imputed the paternity of the expected child and a key of the street door was furnished him so that he could let himself into the house at night to see me. That part worked as desired.

'I wrote to my mother telling her I was married and she never knew to the contrary until the discovery of the dead body at Euston Square. But I never became a mother. An illness prevented that.'[3]

In a few short paragraphs, Hannah's account had depicted a house of shame; of adultery and casual sex, of brothers complicit in sordid transactions, and worse: a house in which such acts took place near where children were sleeping. The publisher George Purkess (later to achieve stratospheric circulation of his torrid *Illustrated Police News* when Jack the Ripper struck in 1888) knew the laws of libel; but clearly his hard-eyed desire to cause sensation and maximise sales must have over-ridden any cautiousness about the outrageousness of these printed allegations.

Hannah wrote of some of the lodgers who came and went at number 4, and their sometimes equally immoral arrangements. There was the arrival in January 1877 of a Miss Griffith. She took 'the drawing room second floor and three rooms at the top of the house as well as the back kitchen and outside coal cellar'. And moving in with her, it seemed, was the strange salesman, Mr Findlay. Implicit was the suggestion that Mr and Mrs Bastendorff were fully aware of all the liaisons of their lodgers. Rather than being the guarantors of genteel behaviour, as most live-in landlords were presumed to be, they were, by Hannah Dobb's account, encouraging licentiousness.

After several months, wrote Hannah, 'Miss Griffiths' left and for a time, Mr Findlay went with her. But then he came back. 'Mr Findlay seemed to be a very mysterious personage,' she wrote. 'He had lots of money, got I know not how, but where he and his money have gone to, I am only permitted to suspect.

'The police have been too stupid to guess,' she added, 'their officers too imbecile even to accept a broad and STARTLING CLUE. Dogberry and Noodledum – no matter, that is public business now.' But what did she mean by this (apart from taking the opportunity to hit out at Inspector Hagen?) 'One day,' she wrote, 'I found a loaded revolver in Mr Findlay's bed. At my request, Mr Bastendorff went up and took it downstairs. Before I had finished the room, Mr Findlay came back for it, saying he had forgotten to put it in his pocket. Mr Findlay went away at length to Liverpool.'

After this cryptic passage, Hannah outlined a period of calm at 4, Euston Square, before the salesman's return. She described the arrival of the respectable sugar merchant Mr Riggenbach, who brought his own furniture with him. Then came a Mr and Mrs Loeffler who 'took the two rooms on the second floor.' When Mr Findlay came back, he 'took the large top front room'.

According to Hannah, Findlay and Severin Bastendorff became close during this period; and 'went out together'. She took a period of leave from the house in August 1877 'as the letters prove'; and when she came back 'I was told he (Findlay) had gone.' Added to this, soon afterwards, 'I had a gold watch and chain given me' (she declined to say by whom). 'It was a large keyless watch with a white dial, the chain was of gold with large links and now,' she added, 'when I recall the facts, it strikes me they were just like the watch and chain that Mr Findlay used to wear. Mr P. Bastendorff corroborates this. I returned the watch and chain before I received Miss Hacker's watch. What has become of Mr Findlay? That was the question which was asked at the trial but never answered.'

The woman who stood in for Hannah during her absence, Mrs Hobson, told the maid that she had not seen Mr Findlay leave; and more, 'that more than ordinarily liberal man had only left a shilling on the mantel-shelf for her.'

Yet Hannah Dobbs seemed to be throwing out ambiguities of her own; the suggestion here was that Mr Findlay had somehow fallen victim to Severin Bastendorff; and had been murdered. The next section of the pamphlet was intended to pull Bastendorff deeper into this mire, while also suggesting that the younger brother Peter was being dragged down too.

This curious side-plot started with Peter Bastendorff and Hannah Dobbs at Waterloo railway station in August 1877; he was under the impression that she was going home to Bideford for extended leave. But in fact, according to her own account, she was not. She took a train 'to Box Hill only', about an hour's journey away; then took the next train back. She met Severin Bastendorff at Victoria station and, she wrote, 'we went to Redhill together'.

It seems there was an illicit tryst at a Redhill inn. They returned to London the following day; and their aim, implied in the text, was to avoid being seen either by Mary Bastendorff or by brother Peter. 'Next night, a room was taken in the Edgware Road,' she wrote, 'and there I passed the night alone.' Hannah moved from rented room to rented room all over; from Kew to King's Cross. But then she alleged that she became a secret nocturnal visitor to Euston Square.

'The rest of the time I was ostensibly away in the country,' she wrote, 'I slept at 4, Euston Square every night, being let secretly into the house at night and slipping away unobserved in the morning, spending the day walking in Hyde Park and elsewhere.'

Here, Hannah seemed to become tangled in her own narrative web: she related that while she was supposedly away, she sent Peter a letter telling him that she would soon be returning from Devon, catching the train from Exeter to Waterloo, and asking him to meet her on the date she gave.

Yet Peter was apparently no fool; he noticed that the post-mark on the letter bore a 'London' stamp. He knew that Hannah had not been in Bideford at all. He declined to go and meet her as she supposedly 'arrived' at Waterloo; his brother Anthony Bastendorff – known to the family as 'Toon' – was sent to fetch her instead. Peter and Anthony, as Hannah related, had formerly worked with their brother Severin but had lately started up their own breakaway furniture concern in Francis Street, just off the Tottenham Court Road.

Hannah told the jealous Peter she was staying at her former place of employ at 42 Torrington Square; and when Peter returned from a business trip in the country and caught up with her, she maintained a charade of allowing him to walk her to the gates of Torrington

Square (many Bloomsbury squares were gated at that time). When away from Peter's gaze, and under the cover of darkness, Hannah – by her own account – would steal back to 4, Euston Square.

Her claim to have slept there every night throughout that period stretches credulity; surely Mrs Bastendorff would have had some sort of inkling? And yet the idea evokes the image of the unlit house at night, and the stealthy movements on the stairs of one who is familiar with every creak and groan. A midnight interloper: the confessions of extra-marital sex were one thing, but Hannah Dobbs was maximising this outrage by portraying herself as a sexual intruder, the husband's betrayal of his wife taking place under his very own roof as his family slept oblivious.

One day in the midst of this sinister arrangement, Hannah Dobbs – she claimed – chose an afternoon to go and see Mary Bastendorff; Hannah pretended that she had just returned from Devon. It was at this point that Hannah's stand-in, Mrs Hobson, was working there; but it seemed she was unsatisfactory. Mrs Bastendorff asked Hannah if she wished to return 'to her employ'; Hannah told her she would 'think about it.' But as well as her night-time visits, Hannah often went back during the daylight hours, by her own account, sometimes to take the children out to the Square gardens or 'for a walk'.

But it seemed Peter Bastendorff was getting more jealous, and suspicious. He 'charged' her with 'secretly meeting Severin' which she 'denied'. 'One evening, Peter, after saying 'good night' to me at the Torrington gates, went around the square,' wrote Hannah, 'and as I passed round on my way to Euston Square we met face to face and then he knew that I did not go into the house at 42, Torrington Square.' But Hannah was ready with a riposte to him: 'I told him I had come around just because I knew he remained to watch where I went to.' Peter apparently accepted this; the two of them walked a little further, towards his furniture workshop in Francis Street; the two of them bade farewell again; and Hannah by her own account 'then went out and met one of his brothers'. That brother being Severin.

There was one weekend when Mrs Bastendorff, seeing Hannah in the daylight, told her that she and Severin and the children were going to the country for several days; would she care to stay at Euston Square with the (inadequate) Mrs Hobson to help run the establishment in their absence? Hannah assented. Mrs Hobson was very shortly to leave; and Hannah moved back into Euston Square openly, now once more employed full-time.

It was a little after this that Matilda Hacker came asking about rooms. 'I showed her the rooms we had to spare on the second-floor front and the rooms at the top,' wrote Dobbs. 'She did not want to give 12 shillings a week for the second floor – that was the price asked. I then went and asked Mrs Bastendorff about letting Miss Hacker have the second-floor back, while Mrs Bastendorff took the second-floor front for her bedroom. Miss Hacker waited while I went to ask. Mrs Bastendorff said she was willing to change rooms but Miss Hacker, on seeing the back room, did not like it, because it had such a dull view, overlooking the mews. She then agreed to take the front room at 12 shillings a week and said she would come in the afternoon the next day.'

Apart from the minutiae of boarding house life, Dobbs might also have been slyly commenting on the state of the Bastendorff marriage; earlier she had stated that Severin and Mary slept at the top of the house; she now seemed to be suggesting that they were occupying separate rooms. She also emphasised the fact that she – and not Mrs Bastendorff – was running the establishment: that Mrs Bastendorff, sitting in the kitchen, had not even glimpsed this new lodger, and that it was left to Hannah to describe her as a 'grand old lady' who wore 'a blue silk dress, a black dichu, and white hat with a lot of white feathers'. The one concession Mrs Bastendorff made for her new guest was to go out that day and buy a new lamp for the room.

The next day, Miss Hacker 'came to the door in a cab with all her luggage, which consisted of a large trunk covered with American oilcloth, over which was a coarse wrapping, one or two small parasols, and an umbrella. She had on a black bonnet with blue feathers, the same blue silk dress, and a small black lace cape . . . The cabman helped me up with the luggage to her room, while Miss Hacker waited in the hall until the cabman came down, when she paid him. The trunk was very heavy . . . I did not see what Miss Hacker paid him but I think he wanted two-pence more for carrying the trunk upstairs and I think he did not get it.'

Hannah Dobbs was fascinating on the eccentricity of this new lodger. On that first day, the old lady went out to buy herself some food. She returned with 'a mutton chop, a loaf, and some butter'. Hannah 'cooked the chop for her and took it up to her with a kettle of boiling water with which she made tea'. Hannah showed Miss Hacker to a cupboard on the landing in which she could store 'eatables' as well as clothes.

Hannah went upstairs to clear away the plate for the mutton and the tea things; a little later, as the evening drew on, she went up again to 'tidy up' the room. She asked Miss Hacker what she would like for her supper; the lady explained that she did not 'take anything more than a glass of ale'. She did a little later give Hannah six pence to go out to the pub and fetch for her 'half a pint of stout'. As the day drew to a close at midnight, Hannah knocked and asked her if there was anything else that she required. Miss Hacker told her no, and Hannah noted that she 'was not in bed at that time'. She also noted that Mrs Bastendorff had still not introduced herself – or had even seen – her new lodger.

Matilda Hacker was not an early riser; she rang the maid's bell for her breakfast at 9a.m. 'She asked me to go out and get her a rasher of bacon,' wrote Hannah. The maid was reluctant to trouble the butcher for such a singular purchase; and Mrs Bastendorff authorised her instead to by 'half a pound' which she would use herself. Miss Hacker's rasher was cooked in the kitchen; Hannah took it up to her second-floor room. 'She was not pleased with the bacon,' wrote Hannah, 'saying she was glad she did not send for more than a single rasher as no-one could please her.'[4]

And so the rhythms of Matilda Hacker's remaining days – those days at Euston Square – were established. After breakfast, and at some point in the mid-morning, she would go out (Hannah knew not where) and she would take her lunch at other premises. Miss Hacker returned for tea; and at around 6p.m., Hannah would take a kettle of boiling water up to that room looking out over the gardens and the square. At 9p.m., Miss Hacker rang down with her request from the local public house; she had not been pleased with the stout so this time she requested that Hannah fetch her a 'half-pint of "four-ale"'. And this again satisfied all of the old lady's needs for that day; Hannah checking with her about midnight that she had everything required.

And the maid got a clearer sense of this new lodger; not merely her quirks but also the secluded nature of her life. The old lady always took her lunch elsewhere; but in the afternoon, she was back and either she would be writing a number of letters, or she would be consulting what Hannah called her 'dream-book'. There was an image of Matilda Hacker sitting at the table near the window, either thoroughly absorbed in the pages of this astrological almanack; or dealing Tarot cards to herself.

Hannah also caught a note of vulnerability; there was one day when Matilda Hacker had to turn aside from *The Book of Dreams*, with her head held back. The maid asked if she was quite well, and the old lady told her that she had a headache; that it was possibly a cold. Hannah asked her if there was anything she could fetch that would help: the answer was 'gruel with a little rum in it'. Hannah accordingly went out to buy some oatmeal; she then mixed it with half a pint of milk and a 'quartern of rum'. She heated it all up and took it to the old lady who drank it gratefully, declaring that it was 'very nice'. A little later that evening, Hannah looked in on her again and asked if perhaps she might like some of her habitual 'supper beer'; the old lady declined this but did said that if Hannah brought some boiling water upstairs, she would instead happily have hot rum. This she did.

Here, perhaps artfully, is a portrayal of the ideal boarding house relationship; the paying guest being looked after by a genuinely concerned servant. One of the contemporary concerns about such houses was their atomised quality; the absence of family leading to a soulless home filled with random souls who could form no connection. Instead, here, Hannah Dobbs was suggesting that there was not only a connection but also warmth. Even a wilful eccentric such as Matilda Hacker would not be left completely isolated.

Yet Hannah also seemed alive to the less attractive traits of this unusual lady. Her fussiness over the type of beer fetched from the public house seemed soon to become something of a nightly nuisance; so much so that the teenaged lad Frank who worked in the furniture workshop at the back was deputed to go for it instead. Hannah was also intrigued as the old lady gradually divulged something of the nature of her own property interests.

'When I took her tea up at six o'clock,' wrote Hannah, 'she asked if the house did not run to a very high rent. I said it did. She said, 'Yes, I know they do because I have houses of my own. They cost a great deal of money to keep in repair.' She also said, 'I used to keep a pretty little house for myself when my sister was living but when she died I gave it up, as I preferred to travel about.'

'People may ask,' wrote Hannah in an aside, 'why do I remember all these small details, but the fearful trial in which my life was placed in such jeopardy constrained me to rack my memory to recall every incident connected with the unfortunate Miss Hacker and my experience at the Bastendorff's, so that my counsel could give me the truest, ablest and best defence.' She wrote that since then, she had frequently lain awake at night thinking through those experiences. She was saving the darkest allegations until last.

The old lady continued to settle into the house; but no-one apparently had any more concrete idea of who she was or where she had come from. 'On Saturday, Miss Hacker had her breakfast as usual,' wrote Hannah. At the time when Mary Bastendorff was climbing the stairs to go to her own room, she apparently met her new lodger for the first time, and they talked.

On the following day, 'Miss Hacker went to church'. She asked Hannah to ask Mrs Bastendorff if she might borrow the copy of the church service book that she had seen in the house. Hannah fetched it; and on Matilda Hacker's return, it was time to cook the Sunday lunch that the old lady had bought for herself: a mutton chop. Matilda Hacker asked Hannah if she might have it with a few of Mrs Bastendorff's potatoes; she indicated that she would pay for these. Hannah procured them, cooked the old lady's dinner, and gave it to her.

What then followed was a fascinating – and again – artful outbreak of ambiguity. Hannah's narrative leaped forward two days. On the Tuesday, she wrote, 'Mrs Bastendorff made out Miss Hacker's bill, and I took it up'. 'It amounted to 12 shillings, 4 and a half d (pence). Miss Hacker looked at the bill and asked what the 4 and a half d was for.' It was for the potatoes. 'I never had more than one and a half d or 2d worth altogether,' the old lady apparently told Hannah. Hannah looked at the bill, turned to get it corrected – but then realised what was causing the misunderstanding.

'In a minute more, I said, "it is all right. There is one and a half d for the potatoes and 3d for the cruet, for pepper, salt, mustard and vinegar." The old lady asked if she would be expected to pay this every time for the cruet; she was told no, not unless she used it all. And with this, Hannah wrote, 'she gave me a £5 note and I think I went and got it changed'.

She wrote that she obtained the change and got the rent bill 'receipted' by Mrs Bastendorff; but she took it back upstairs to the old lady because it had not been possible to put a name on it. She said that the old lady had not given a name. And it was at this point, according to Hannah, that the old lady first told her that her real name was Matilda Hacker. 'She never was called Miss Uish,' wrote Hannah. This, she said, had been a name given by the Bastendorffs.

And so she came to Matilda Hacker's increasing integration into the house; a sense that the old lady was starting to feel at home. And her account seemed to overturn the chronology that had been heard in court. On one Saturday night, at twelve, Hannah went upstairs and saw a light under Matilda Hacker's door. She knocked, and went in, and asked if there was anything further that she should like. The old lady was on the sofa 'between the two windows' and had the table drawn up close to her. Upon the table 'lay her blue silk dress, white petticoat, lace cap and her bonnet.' She explained to the maid that she was preparing her things for church the next morning – and this included her gold watch in chain which she said she only ever wore for church as she 'did not trust' flaunting them in London otherwise.

She needed nothing more; and she said: 'Good night, Hannah.' Across the landing, Mary Bastendorff was also preparing for bed, with her door slightly ajar; there was a short exchange between her and Hannah and then 'Mr Bastendorff came in' and Hannah went up to her own bed. On the Sunday morning, Matilda Hacker went to church and when she came back, she asked Hannah if she might have the key to the gate that led to the gardens in the centre of Euston Square. It was her intention – if Mrs Bastendorff was agreeable – to take the little children Christina and Peter out to play there.

And indeed out they went, with the children seeming to have a jolly time with this youthful seeming old lady. When they eventually came back in, Matilda Hacker went upstairs to change; Hannah noted that whenever she did so, the old lady would fold up her things and either lock them in her trunk or lock them in the landing cupboard; the chests of drawers in her room remained empty. Via Hannah, Miss Hacker sent down a request that little Christina and Peter join her upstairs in her room. She had a treat for them: a selection of nuts and ginger nuts that she had bought earlier.

So the children went up for their little tea party; and Matilda Hacker beguiled the time, possibly by means of *The Book of Dreams* and the extraordinary stories around it; and Hannah went up at seven to tell Christina and Peter that it was now time for bed. She also carried a request from an apparently grateful Mrs Bastendorff: would she care to go down that evening to the dining room to while away some hours with the lady of the house?

Miss Hacker was reluctant; she declared that she had nothing suitable to wear. But Mrs Bastendorff sent Hannah with word that they were not expecting any visitors that evening; and so the arrangement would be perfectly informal. And at this, according to Hannah, Matilda Hacker relented. The maid was sent out to secure several bottles of lemonade. Mary Bastendorff's favoured refreshment for herself and her guests was lemonade and brandy.

It seemed the evening was a success, according to Hannah (and this was a direct contradiction of Mary Bastendorff's evidence at the trial in which she swore she had no dealings with the old lady); at one stage, Matilda Hacker withdrew briefly to go and fetch her 'photographic album'; she then showed her hostess 'her sister's and others' likenesses'. Indeed, she also handed over a likeness of herself for Mrs Bastendorff to appraise. In this account, the ladies remained in that dining room until 11p.m.

The photograph of Matilda Hacker remained on the property, according to Hannah. First, the children apparently had it; then it made its way to the Bastendorff furniture workshop out at the back of the house, when little Peter took it to show his uncle Anthony ('Toon'). 'Toon stuck the likeness on the wall beside the bench where he was working, where it remained for some time,' wrote Hannah. Indeed, one day, in a spirit of high jocularity, Toon called her 'to come and see his sweetheart's likeness'. 'I went,' she wrote, 'and the moment I saw it, I said, "Why that was our old lodger." I said it was a shame to put it there and I went and pulled it down. Peter and Toon Bastendorff then tried to get it from me; there was a struggle for it that ended with the likeness being torn up.'

This was some time after Matilda Hacker's disappearance; Hannah at this point almost off-handedly mentioned that she was 'given' (with no hint by whom) a gold bracelet that had been found in the second-floor cupboard that had been used by the old lady. The idea was that she was to pawn it; and she took it to a nearby shop in the Hampstead Road – 'and as far as I know, the bracelet is lying in that shop still,' she wrote. 'It was a rather large bracelet of plain plaited gold.'

Hannah returned to the old lady's period of residency, and some curious circumstances. One night, the maid 'heard something go smash'. At the time, Hannah was in her own room, changing her dress; by her own account, she ran downstairs and into Matilda Hacker's room. The old lady had had a mishap while trying to light the lamp; and its glass globe had shattered on the hearth. 'I picked the pieces up,' wrote Hannah, 'and in picking them up I ran a piece of glass into my finger.'

At that moment, Peter Bastendorff had knocked at the front door; Hannah went downstairs, wrapping a handkerchief around her finger. Peter was most attentive towards her injury; the landlady, on the other hand, when learning of the accident, seemed more concerned about the cost of the lamp. Miss Hacker was aware that she owed an extra two shillings for the breakage.

The ordinariness of life, the perfectly undramatic details, served to give a sense of gathering and motiveless menace; what was happening in that house that would then lead to such murderous violence? Yet there were unsettlingly odd undercurrents, at least according to Hannah. One day, she was approached by Mary Bastendorff who told the maid that her sister and mother were coming to visit, and she wanted the girl to go to the pawn shop to pawn a ring for her. Hannah wrote that she offered her employer a loan of a few shillings; but Mrs Bastendorff refused. If she pawned the ring, Mrs Bastendorff could get her sister to buy it later.

Her account came to the mysterious final hours of Matilda Hacker. She had been fully settled for a few weeks in her second-floor room. One morning, Severin Bastendorff interrupted Hannah as she was cleaning windows (an echo of the alleged first encounter three years previously) and told her to fetch the rent from the old lady. While it was certainly due that day, Hannah wondered at the peremptoriness of demanding it so briskly, and not even in person. The maid found Miss Hacker at her table, writing; she apologised for 'troubling her' and the lodger told the girl that at that moment, she didn't have any change.

This was the most crucial part of Hannah's defence; the encounter that she and no-one else could testify to. The old lady told her that she would be going out after she had finished writing her letters, and then she could 'obtain change'. Hannah offered to go and fetch it instead: and at this, she said, Matilda Hacker said 'very well then'.

According to Hannah, Miss Hacker got up, 'and turning towards the sofa lifted her skirt and took a five-pound note from her flannel petticoat'. Indeed, she apparently took out several notes, also concealed within a flannel arrangement which was fastened with ribbon.

'She smiled, and told me to look and see what a good plan she had got, and how nice it was to keep money for anyone who was travelling for no-one would think of looking in such a place as that for money,' wrote Hannah. 'This was the first occasion on which Miss Hacker showed that she had a considerable sum of money in her possession.'

Hannah related how she took the five-pound note downstairs and as well as telling Severin Bastendorff that she would obtain the change for it, she claimed that she also remarked to him that Miss Hacker 'had a roll' of such notes. 'A remark was made that it was desirable that she should drop her petticoat and let someone pick it up.'[5]

And now the outlines of motive for murder, so carefully seeded by Hannah and her ghostwriter, were beginning to become apparent. Crucially, there was also a studied vagueness about the days; in court, it was held that the murder had taken place at the weekend and that the house had been empty. Hannah Dobbs' pamphlet muddied this certainty.

Matilda Hacker, in this account, went out to post her letters; and returned at lunchtime. By this stage, according to Hannah, the maid was preparing to take the children up to Hampstead. They set out, she and Christina and Peter and the small baby, taking the horse-drawn omnibus that ran up the Hampstead Road, through Camden and up towards the heights of the Heath. There, she said, she had the children photographed (this, like donkey rides at Whitestone Pond, was one of the side attractions). The photographer, she averred, was 'a very fair man with a little moustache'. Then, she wrote, the weather turned. Hannah wrote that she took the children home and 'we got out of the 'bus at the top of Drummond Street and I sent the two children into the house through the (furniture work) shop'. She herself walked round the front with the baby, as the rain fell on Euston Square.

Mrs Bastendorff was in the front dining room, drinking tea. Hannah put the Hampstead photograph in the toddler's hand and told the child to take it to 'mama'. Mrs Bastendorff first told Hannah: 'The very idea of you having this taken. But don't the baby look pretty?'

And, Hannah added, 'it was that night that I was told that the old lady had gone away'.

20

'Oh God! What a Sight Met My Gaze!'

Up until this point, readers of Hannah's pamphlet would have been brooding not only about her quiet hints concerning what had really happened to the old lady; but also whether they were being told the entire truth. The selling point of the pamphlet was no more and no less ghoulish fascination; and the style in which it was ghostwritten left some fascinating ambiguities about Hannah Dobbs and her own behaviour.

But having set this occasionally seamy domestic scene – Hannah still in a romance with Peter Bastendorff while, readers were to presume, still engaging in sexual relations with her employer – the maid was now ready to turn the account into one of the starkest and most lurid gothic horror.

She – or more especially her ghostwriter – built the suspense stealthily. Hannah recounted her puzzlement at Matilda Hacker's departure; and Mary Bastendorff's comment that 'yes, she has gone into the country for a few days. She fancied she wanted a change and if the room is not let when she comes back, she will take it again.'

And so Hannah, after having put the children to bed, went into Miss Hacker's former room, puzzling (as she wrote) over her startlingly swift departure. 'Her heavy trunk was gone,' she wrote, 'and the room appeared to be cleared of everything belonging to her.' As Hannah went to pull down the window blinds, she noticed something curious: one of the panes was broken.

On going downstairs, she told Mrs Bastendorff and asked how it had happened. She was told that it had been an accident caused in the course of lowering those window blinds.

Hannah wrote that Peter Bastendorff came round that evening to see her; that she had wanted to show him the photograph of the children taken on Hampstead Heath, but it was already in the doting possession of Mrs Bastendorff's mother Mary Pearce. She also wrote about the disposition of the coal cellar at this time; that for the house fires, she fetched coal upstairs by the shovel – and so did Mrs Bastendorff. Hannah was also certain that there were very few coals in the cellar at that time. The implication was that Matilda Hacker – or her remains – had been taken somewhere else first.

The following morning, Mrs Bastendorff called to Hannah from Matilda Hacker's room. 'Whatever have you been doing to the carpet?' she allegedly asked. Hannah asked her what she meant and Mrs Bastendorff pointed to the stain on the carpet, telling the maid that she was a 'very tiresome girl not to have said anything about it'. And yet, Hannah wrote, this was the first time that she had seen it; she had not noticed it when she had been in the empty room the previous day.

'Mrs Bastendorff seemed very cross' and declared that she would rather be without lodgers if things got damaged this way; and that if Miss Hacker came back, 'she should pay for the damage'. Hannah claimed that she told Mrs Bastendorff that she herself 'should have looked out for it' when Miss Hacker 'went away'. And at this, she wrote, the conversation ended.

Hannah set about remaking the bed in the room after this; and she once more checked the drawers. But now, according to the pamphlet, she did find something: Matilda Hacker's beloved *The Book of Dreams*. She took it downstairs to Mrs Bastendorff and 'remarked' that Matilda Hacker would be certain to return, if only to retrieve this treasured possession.

That week, a new lodger, Mr Ross – 'an elderly gentleman of about fifty years' – took the second-floor room. Hannah's acquisitive eye had immediately fixed upon his two rings, 'one a signet, the other a diamond ring'. This tenant only stayed one week. But in the course of that week, there was 'a most remarkable incident'. 'Mr Ross called me to his room,' wrote Hannah, 'and asked if we had any mad people in the house.'

Why did he ask such a thing? He had apparently just found 'a revolver' which had been 'lying on the small shelf in the water closet on the second floor, the same floor on which Miss Hacker's room was'. The agitated Mr Ross told Hannah to go and fetch Mr Bastendorff; and presently, the landlord went up the stairs. The two men spoke for about ten minutes; and then Mr Bastendorff came downstairs again, holding the gun, which was apparently not loaded. He asked Hannah if she 'had put it there'. She denied it. And now, in the pamphlet, she asked why Mr Ross had not been tracked down as a witness.

Then there was a further curious twist in the alleged story of Hannah's sexual arrangements. She claimed that Severin Bastendorff gave her a box, containing a gold watch and chain; the face of the watch was broken. He claimed he had bought it in a sale, and that he would have it fixed for her. The watch came back, repaired and cleaned – the watch, Hannah claimed, that only later in court would be proved to belong to Miss Hacker. Severin Bastendorff attached one condition to this gift, Hannah claimed: that she not say a word about where she got it from. Hannah told him that if anyone asked, she would claim it was from an uncle who had died. The first to hear this lie was her lover Peter Bastendorff.

At around this time, she wrote, Severin Bastendorff was planning a business trip to Paris; and rather than go all alone, he wanted Hannah to go with him too. By her account, Hannah pertly demurred, claiming instead that she had plans to go and visit her family in Bideford.

She also told Peter that she was going home; but he was angry and apparently jealous. He told her directly that he had heard about the proposed Paris trip; and that he believed she was lying and that she was going with his brother. It was not until the following night – after he had spent some time with Severin 'at the public house' – that Peter found that Severin had cancelled his journey. Hannah pushed on to Bideford, taking the child Peter with her.

After several days, they returned and she was told that Mr Riggenbach's room had not been cleaned as he had recently acquired 'a black dog' and everyone else in the house was too afraid to go in.

She was also asked by Severin, she claimed, for a loan of some money; Hannah told him she did not have the amount that he wanted. He suggested pawning the gold watch and chain, with the promise that he would soon buy her a new one, which was less 'old-fashioned'. Thus it was that Hannah Dobbs sought to move the focus on the old lady's pawned possessions on to a landlord who seemed always to be in some kind of cash-flow difficulty.

But it was the following Sunday that – Hannah wrote – she made the most horrifying discovery. 'I went out into the back yard to get some shavings (kindling) to make my fire burn up,' she wrote. 'In the yard there is a flight of steps leading up to the work-room.' And under this was a cramped storage area filled with timber and wood shavings. 'I put my hand in to get these,' wrote Hannah, 'when I felt something move.'

In fright, she wrote, she ran back to the house and announced what had happened. 'They all ran out,' wrote Hannah, avoiding saying precisely who 'they' were. 'They' peered into the wood-store darkness and 'we saw a small boy – very ragged'. The frightened boy tried to wriggle deeper into the wood and had to be poked out 'with a long bamboo'. 'The child cried a little,' wrote Hannah, 'but at last ran out and endeavoured to make his escape.' And this is when – by her account – the horror descended.

'One of the party (how I shudder as I write it!) struck the little fellow on the head two or three crushing blows with a poker. I screamed and was going to run for the doctor but I was stopped and told to wait awhile. I helped undress the little fellow and put him in a bath and then he was wrapped in a blanket and laid under the bench in the workshop. Then, in a little while, they told me he was dead. Would to God they had laid me there too.'

What could be more horrible than the murder of a small and defenceless street child? 'He was very pale and slim,' wrote Hannah, 'his hair was light and his clothes though ragged had evidently been patched at times. I don't think he could have been more than ten years old. All his clothes were gathered together and burned at the workshop fire.'[1]

Again, she was remarkably discreet when it came to naming those in on the conspiracy. Presumably Severin, yes, but Peter? Toon? Mary Bastendorff? And what of any inquisitive neighbours who would surely have been drawn to their back windows to see what all the noise was about in the yard below? But Hannah's catalogue of horrors was by no means finished. Eliding the question of why she chose to stay in such a nightmarish house, rather than running straight to the police, and then seeking sanctuary at home, she and 'they' apparently carried on as though nothing had happened.

There is in fact some wholly unintentional black humour in the continued account, as well as further horrors. 'On Saturday afternoon, about three weeks after the little child was killed, I was sent to Meeking's to buy some brown Holland for childrens' pinafores,' Hannah wrote, as if it were perfectly natural for her to assent to life carrying on as normal. 'When I returned, both staircase windows were thrown open; but notwithstanding all this, a fearful smell pervaded the whole house. I asked what was the matter, and was told it was some rubbish in the (furniture work) shop. I tried the workshop doors and found them both fastened.'

At this stage in her account, Hannah became a form of gothic heroine. 'I rattled one, and said I wanted to come in,' she wrote. 'They told me I could not, and upon my asking what they were doing, I was told they were boiling some grease. Then I went up on the leads and opened one of the wooden slides and looked down into the workroom. I saw a bundle wrapped round with a blue counterpane. The boiler was standing on the stove. I called down and asked what was being done, when the reply was 'nothing in particular' and at this moment I was called away by Mrs Bastendorff.

'Two days after I had seen the bundle in the workroom, I went into the (front) area, and found the outer coal cellar door locked with a padlock,' Hannah continued. 'With a woman's curiosity, I determined to know what was inside, and I tried all the keys about the place until I found one to fit the padlock.

'I went into the cellar and found there a large bundle wrapped in a blue counterpane and tied round with new rope. I opened the bundle and there found some straw and on removing this – oh God! What a sight met my gaze! There were all that remained of our late lodger, Miss Hacker!

'How I got upstairs, I don't know; but I sat on my bed and cried until I thought my heart would break.'

And so what precisely stopped Hannah from running out into the street and summoning the police into this house of slaughter? Her explanation was that 'they' – she could only have meant the Bastendorffs – had entrapped her. 'They said if I spoke about it, I should be implicated too, as I had pawned the old lady's things,' she wrote. 'I was horrified and knew not what to do. I wanted to leave. I wanted to speak, but threats and persuasion overcame me, and I became a partner in the dreadful secret. Other feelings weighed with me. I had been a bad woman, but I had some of a woman's feelings. Scores of times I thought I would go and drown myself and now I am possessed with the same feeling.'

And so now, according to her account, Hannah was in some senses a prisoner in Euston Square. 'I grew nervous and frightened after this,' she wrote. 'I dared not go into the cellar without a light. I kept candle and matches beside me when in bed and night after night I have lain awake, thinking over all the dreadful things that had come into my knowledge. Once or twice I made up my mind to run away to my home and actually made preparations to do so but then the knowledge of that fearful crime paralysed my actions and I stayed on in the house, enduring the torments of hell.'

We have to imagine Severin Bastendorff reading all this that morning in September 1879, and in a giddy daze, taking it back to Euston Square and to wife Mary. We also have to imagine the many thousands of Londoners who were reading this at the same time; and the increasing murmur, heard from the back kitchen of 4, Euston Square, of people gathering outside the front of the house, discussing these sensational revelations. The Bastendorffs must have been in terror of a mob.

'One day,' Hannah's account continued, 'it must have been in February 1878, as it was after Mrs Bastendorff's confinement (which means she would have been heavily pregnant at the time of the horrors Hannah described) and while the nurse girl Lydia Barnett was in the house, I went into the cellar to get some coke.

'At that time, there had been a lot of coal in, and then some coke, and after, some coal again. I wanted to make an ironing fire and shovelled the coals aside to get round to the coke. I saw something sticking out of the coals. I could not make out what it was, but I felt frightened, and ran into the house.'

Given that she had already taken in the sight of the decaying Matilda Hacker, and yet managed to overcome this to shovel coals, what then was this nightmarish new discovery? 'They told me it was the body of the little boy who was killed by a blow from a poker after being pulled out from under the workshop,' she wrote. But there was a further hideous twist she had to impart: 'The remainder of the body was said to have been given to Mr Riggenbach's dog to eat,' she wrote. 'The cup of horrors never seemed full and I often wished I had been dead rather than keep such dreadful secrets locked up in my breast.'

She addressed the question of how it was that such dreadful secrets might be kept in a house where lodgers and tradesmen were constantly present. 'The remains were again carefully covered with coals,' she wrote, 'but the workmen were continually coming in to get coal for the workroom fire and it was not many weeks after that that one of the workmen in getting some coal came across the human leg the same way I had done. "Whatever is this Hannah? It looks like the leg of an old man." At this moment Mrs Bastendorff called me to bring some coals and I took the light from his hand and ran into the kitchen. I never saw anything of the body in the cellar after that time.'

In the meantime, the murky financial business conducted under that roof continued, according to Hannah's account. 'In March 1878, I pawned, by request, Mrs Bastendorff's necklet,' she wrote, 'but a few days afterwards I was asked to redeem this pledge, as it was found Mrs Bastendorff would miss it.' Hannah's silence over who precisely has asked her to carry out this theft none the less shifted the focus on to Severin Bastendorff. 'The pawnbroker lent £8 on the necklet,' she continued, 'and I was told that I might buy myself a small watch out of the money. This I did at the same place where the necklet was pawned, Mr Gill's in the Hampstead-Road, giving £2 10 shillings for it. To redeem the necklet I was only given £5 10 shillings and I was asked to pawn my watch to make up the amount required for taking it out of pledge. I was obliged, however, to put my own locket and chain with the watch to raise the requisite sum. I was promised that my things which I had pawned should be taken out soon.'

First murder; now the financial exploitation of the poor maid. The unnamed Severin Bastendorff's villainy seemed to know no limits. Yet the readers of this sensational work were to discover yet one more dimension of depravity to which he was apparently able to sink.

'So far as I have spoken in this book, I have been obliged to suppress the name of the principal actors in this awful tragedy,' wrote Hannah and her amanuensis who must surely have been aware that this omission would scarcely help them in a libel case. 'But there is one scene that occurred in my presence and which was witnessed by so many people that I can detail all the facts and, if necessary, bring forward witnesses to prove them. Joseph Bastendorff is the foreman in his brother Severin's workshop, and has been for some considerable time. Joseph had a little dog given to him.

'He took it home, and after that he brought it to the workshop with him and here it was fed on Mr Riggenbach's dog's biscuits. It was a pretty little creature, very affectionate, and always seemed so pleased to be noticed. One day about a fortnight after Joseph had the dog I was standing on the step leading down into the workroom, holding Mrs Bastendorff's baby in my arms, when I saw them tying the little dog up with cord.' Again, the 'them' went nameless.

'I asked what they were going to do and they said laughingly they were going to kill the dog,' she wrote. 'He was tied to the workman's bench and then someone fired at the poor little thing. It howled piteously and looked so plaintively up to its murderers that I cried out and begged them to desist, but they only laughed, and again and again the pistol was fired at the poor little creature.'

And one of these 'murderers'? Hannah named the dog's owner, Joseph. 'At last Joseph struck it over the head,' she wrote, 'and then carried the carcass into the gilder's gallery over the shop. They had only been there a few minutes when the most pitiful moaning and then fearful howling filled the whole place. They had *commenced skinning the animal before it was dead!*

'The horrible scene,' she added with wholly unintentional bathos, 'filled me with a tenfold longing to leave the dreadful place. The thought of the other dreadful secrets completely unnerved me and yielding to solicitations I still remained in the house.' But the barbarity did not end there. 'The cruel murder of this little inoffensive animal met with a fitting sequel in the disposal of its remains. Joseph took it home and had it cooked and some of the members of the family ate it! Amongst those who witnessed this horrible cruelty were Anthony Bastendorff, Bullisch, Wm Hanwell, Severin Bastendorff, a boy named

Frank and Joseph's little boy Charlie and three of these I have named ate a portion of the dog. This occurred in July 1878.'

And yet for all of this darkness, Hannah Dobbs did still manage to take trips home, where she somehow managed to maintain her silence. 'In August 1878, I went to . . . north Devon for a fortnight, and took Christina Bastendorff with me, and also little Freddy Pearce (a nephew of Mary Bastendorff).' Yet even on this innocent holiday, she managed to fall foul of malignant fate. 'I lost my purse and railway tickets on the journey,' she wrote (doubtless the story given to the station master) 'and wrote to Peter Bastendorff to lend me £3, which he duly sent. He sent me a letter a few days afterwards stating that Mr Riggenbach had come home and found some of his clothes gone.' (Riggenbach, as a sugar merchant, would have made frequent trips overseas to the continent.) 'When I went back to London I spoke to Mrs Bastendorff the first evening about the missing things.

'She said I was a fool to have taken any notice of (Peter's) interfering letter and that I could not make things better by returning before the time. I asked her what was lost, but she would not say, and although she endeavoured to dissuade me, I went upstairs and asked Mr Riggenbach about the robbery.

'He replied, "I don't know anything about it, no more than when I came home and found my things gone."' But clearly he had taken action. 'The same evening, the police officers came, but Mrs Bastendorff saw them. I asked her again about the things and she replied "what have I to say about them? You ought to know how you left the rooms and his things." I said, "So I do know. I left everything all right."

'There was a deal more said on both sides and it ended by my declaring I would leave, and next day I gave a month's notice and then she gave me the balance of my wages and said I might go as soon as I liked. I, however, stopped out my month, and then took a lodging at Mr Wright's, 67 George Street.'

Again, here was unintentional bathos: the idea that after having witnessed murder and depravity, Hannah Dobbs would have her domestic situation ended because of an accusation of pilfering from a man whose dog feasted upon the body of a murdered boy; and none the less saw out her month's notice. Yet Hannah was steering her story back to sexual scandal. 'When I left 4, Euston Square, Mr Bastendorff was in Luxembourg,' she wrote. 'But after he came back he called in at 67 George Street and asked to see me. Mr Wright allowed me on that occasion to take him into the drawing room.

'I frequently met Mr Bastendorff after this,' she continued, 'but he never called again at 67 George Street while I was there. I was led at this time to believe that I should be set up in a public house and by direction I called at Mr—, house broker, in the Euston-road, to get a list of public houses in the market. The broker told me I could not purchase a house myself, and on giving this message, it was suggested that I should take Peter Bastendorff with me. I did so, also being promised money, but beyond one pound, which I paid Mr Wright for lodgings, and a few shillings at a time, I had no means of living except by pawning my things.'

And it was here perhaps that another sort of story began to emerge with greater clarity: the economic dependence of a young working-class woman on men of property. This was a world where an unmarried woman was forbidden to embark upon any business transactions involving large loans; and Hannah was suggesting that the only remaining options were either finding another domestic situation; or becoming a paid mistress.

'I was asked if I would like to go to Paris,' she wrote, not saying which brother – Severin or Peter – had made the offer. 'But I replied I would not but that I would try for another situation.'

And she was now in financial difficulties. 'I had no money to pay (landlord) Mr Wright, and I was told to go and live with Mrs Crigger in Melton Street. She was a friend of Mr Bastendorff's. I only stayed there a week when I wrote home, asking my mother to send money, so that I might come to Devonshire.'

Again, if this was the case, then the perpetrators of the atrocities in Euston Square seemed strikingly relaxed about her movements. But in the pamphlet, Hannah was attempting to sketch out motivation. 'I was fearfully miserable at this time,' she wrote. 'The sight of what I had seen in the coal cellar at 4, Euston Square, the threats that if I spoke I should be implicated with the rest quite unnerved me and this, coupled with the desertion of those who should have been so true to me, almost drove me mad.

'I went home to Bideford, and said my husband was coming down to see me,' (indeed, keeping track of Hannah Dobbs' multiple narratives – the stories she told her readers and the stories she told her family – is occasionally dizzying). 'But I had a letter afterwards which suggested that I should telegraph (Peter), asking him to come down, and he did so, staying two nights.' So while Peter posed as her husband, had the original intention been to pass Severin off in this role? 'We then returned to London together and I took a lodging in Hunter Street. A whole week passed and I saw no-one. I was short of money – absolutely in want.

'I was tempted, and I took a dress and jacket which did not belong to me and carried then to the pawnshop. It was very wrong – that I well know. But at this time, I was fairly beside myself with trouble.' And here, she vouchsafed an insight that would have struck a nerve with suspicious householders everywhere. 'My apprenticeship as a lodging house servant,' she wrote, 'had not tended to develop any careful distinctions as to what belonged to myself and what was the property of the people.'

Hannah and her ghostwriter were also well aware that for this narrative to be truly satisfactory, justice had to be seen closing in. 'I had at this time made up my mind to have nothing more to do with the Bastendorffs,' she wrote. 'I removed lodgings to Burton Street and then applied for and obtained a situation which I was going to on the Friday evening when I was apprehended by the police for the theft I had committed. I told them the truth, pleaded guilty, and was sentenced to eight month's imprisonment, which I richly deserved.'

The brief homilies on prison and religion that were to follow will have been greeted by many readers with cackles of cynicism; by the late

1870s, in many parts of London, church-going was chiefly a matter for fervent evangelists. Agnostics had other uses for their Sundays. None the less, Hannah's bid for redemption was an important element in any sensationalist story.

'My life in prison differed, I suppose, in no respect from that of other prisoners,' she wrote. 'I behaved well, and was treated with some kindness and consideration. I saw the chaplain on the morning following that on which I was admitted. I dare not tell him all I should have liked, but I felt very very wretched and confessed to him what a miserable evil-doer I had been. I had not been confined there many days before I made my mind up to lead quite a new life and never see prison again.

'I was not sorry I was placed in prison,' she added, 'as I felt it was all for my own good. After I had been there six weeks I was set to work and then the time passed very much quicker but still I had such a load of guilt on my mind that I often longed to relieve myself of the whole burden. Then the old threats would recur to me and I was frightened to speak . . . I felt as though I must change my life. I prayed as I have never prayed since I was a child and I afterwards told the chaplain I should like to prepare for confirmation.

'[The chaplain] spoke so kindly to me and I joined the preparation class and was afterwards confirmed on April 29th. That day was not to me as it should have been, for my heart was sick with the secrets of others which I had kept locked up in my breast.'

Hannah Dobbs and her co-writer were now venturing on to slightly trickier ground. 'Inspector Hagen came to the prison in the beginning of May,' she wrote. 'I answered all his questions but still I volunteered no additional information which I might have given. I had made a solemn promise to keep what I had seen and heard a secret and I tried to conceal certain matters which would have thrown suspicion on the guilty parties. From what he told me I concluded the remains were of Miss Hacker and I was exceedingly surprised to hear where they were found as I was told the body had been interred in the Square.'

This was a fresh detail almost bordering on the whimsical: Euston Square was constantly busy with the traffic to and from the railway station. Even in the depths of the night, the digging of a grave under the gaslight – and the dumping of a body therein – would have attracted some curiosity. None the less, she said, she told the inspector that the remains were certainly those of Miss Hacker.

'On the second occasion when Inspector Hagen came,' she wrote, 'I was taken to the mortuary. He asked me several questions, all of which I answered truthfully, but I volunteered no information farther than what was being asked . . .'

And then came what Hannah claimed was an unexpectedly cruel twist. 'A few days after I went to the mortuary, I was surprised to find that I was to be confined to my cell,' she wrote. 'My clothes were taken from me each night, and a warder stationed at the door. I could not understand when I was taken in a cab to Bow Street but until I was placed in the dock I had not the slightest idea that I was going to be charged with the murder of Miss Hacker.

'I was dumbfounded, and knew not what to say,' Hannah continued. 'But the thought of my own innocence, so far as the commission of this crime was concerned, enabled me to bear up; in fact all through my examination and trial I was confident I could not be made to suffer for a crime which I never committed.' This composure, she said, endured even as she was committed for trial at the Old Bailey. 'I had such confidence in those whose vile actions had placed me in that position that I felt sure that they would not let me suffer for their crimes.'

Not, she said, that she felt desperate to save herself from execution: 'I had been a wicked wretch and death had no great terrors for me at that moment,' she wrote. As her trial was adjourned, and she was taken to the prisoners' area below, Hannah wrote that she met Kate Webster, even then better known as The Richmond Murderer; she too was awaiting her verdict and, she told Hannah, had no idea what the result would be. 'She seemed cheerful' though; and after she was called up to hear of her fate – a guilty verdict and a date for execution – Hannah wrote that she never saw her again.

She also related that her composure remained as the jury returned in her trial; the verdict of 'not guilty' was pronounced. Yet she looked around the court and 'no friendly eyes' met her gaze.

Hannah had to complete her term for theft; and she related that two days after the murder trial, a frustrated Inspector Hagen came to visit her once more. He asked 'to know if I could throw any light upon the affair'. Hannah wrote that she 'at once complied and commenced to tell' all she knew. But Hagen 'sneeringly stopped' her by 'throwing doubt on (her) truthfulness'. She went on, she wrote, to tell more, until 'he remarked harshly: "we don't want any of your lies." 'Why should he call me a liar then?' Hannah wrote. 'I was ready at that moment to have spoken fully and freely to anyone who would have listened to my story, but though Inspector Hagen said he would come again in three or four days time, I saw no more of him.'

She was released from jail 'on the 8th of August' and upon leaving, someone handed her a copy of a book called *The Great White Thorn*. 'I was much touched that anyone should have thought it worthwhile to remember such an abandoned wretch as me,' she wrote. 'The consolation I have derived from (its) perusal is more than I can tell.' The book – a reprint of a popular eighteenth-century work concerning Joseph of Arimathea coming to England and preaching about Jesus by the great thorn at Glastonbury – was 'a comfort when all else seemed to have forsaken me'. And, wrote Hannah, may it 'long continue to be a source of comfort to me and may Heaven guide my steps aright for the future!'

Again, this was almost demanded by the convention of popular literature and drama; the wicked woman who finds redemption. Yet some sort of concluding note was needed: after all, both Hannah and the Bastendorff family had somehow to continue their lives. She also had to say something about the possible impact of this pamphlet.

'And now one word as to the dreadful secret which was imparted to me,' wrote Hannah. 'Inspector Hagen has expressed a theory, so I am told, as to this case.' (This was extremely improbable, at least in the form Hannah was about to outline.)

'That the old lady had missed her property. That she made a noise about it. That she threatened to go for the police and then the murder was committed. His theory is correct. *And the one who suggested it to him was the one that committed the deed.* Let the authorities ask the men in the workshop if they remember the bell being violently rung on the day I was at Hampstead with the children.

'The men remember the day, as they joked me when I came back about donkey riding. Let the police ask if they remember the bell being rung a second time and then one of their number being asked to go upstairs. And also let them be asked whether they heard pistol shots, screams for police, and the smash of glass.

'Have the police tried to find the glazier who mended that window? If he can speak to the date, he will declare it was before Sunday October 14th. Have they tried to find Mr Ross, the lodger, who took Miss Hacker's room the day after I went to Hampstead and was living in that room on October 14th (the day on which it was alleged I had committed the murder)? The lodger, it will be remembered, discovered a pistol in the water closet on the day following his arrival in the house.'

There was also an explanation for the rope around the neck of the corpse of Miss Hacker. Once she had been murdered, Hannah averred, her body had first been dragged by this rope through an opening into the garret of the house; and there it remained until it was transferred to the coal cellar.

'In my statement, which has been forwarded to the Home Office,' she wrote in conclusion, 'I have mentioned other matters and given such definite information that if the police act on the suggestions thrown out, and work on the facts of the case instead of their own theories, the murder of Miss Hacker will no longer be known as the Euston Square Mystery.'

There was a reproduction of a handwritten addendum: 'I have read this through and declare it to be my own story and correct in every particular.' And there was her signature, dated 18 September 1879. Below was an advertisement for other 'books' that readers might enjoy: among them were the mystic, fortune-telling works that Matilda Hacker loved: *The Egyptian Dream Book*, *Napoleon's Oraculum: or the Book of Fate*, *The Egyptian Circle; or Ancient Wheel of Fortune* and *Raphael's Chart of Destiny*.[2]

Ever since he had first heard of the forthcoming publication of this pamphlet, Severin Bastendorff had been seeking legal means to have it stopped. But publisher George Purkess seemed happy to risk any court case; he knew that he could make a vast amount of money very swiftly from getting this pamphlet out on to the newsstands. It had a kind of terrible gravity; and in his frantic efforts to have all his denials heard, Bastendorff was going to find that he was dancing on the edge of absolute ruin. Rather than bring a sense of closure over the murder of Matilda Hacker, a further moral chasm was opened.

21
She Had No Character

There would have been no consolation for the Bastendorff household in the cynically amused response of some newspapers to the pamphlet. One wrote that 'Hannah Dobbs of Euston Square celebrity has been "exploited" as the French would say by some sensational writer for Penny Dreadfuls'. The reporter also acknowledged that this 'volume of startling disclosures' would be like 'red pepper in gin' for 'the readers of police news'.[1]

Given that he, his wife and his family were being accused of complicity in multiple murders, including that of a small child, Severin Bastendorff's immediate response on 27 September had the curious flavour of the soon-to-be invented comic character Mr Pooter. Perhaps he received advice telling him to stay calm in order to show the world that the maid's story was insane. But his initial statement, given out to newspapers, read very oddly. This was perhaps also a result of English not being his first language; how difficult it must have been, in terms of tone, for him to defend himself in his second tongue.

Bastendorff declared: 'I have read carefully what has appeared of (Hannah Dobbs') statements, and they are a wilful perversion of certain circumstances which have taken place, so artfully strung together by her as to make them appear to really bear on the death of Miss Hacker. All the things she relates have reference to other dates and other facts which occurred long prior to Miss Hacker coming to our house at all.

'As regards her story about a little boy, about ten years of age, being killed one night, and his flesh being given to Mr Riggenbach's dog. I never heard of it before and know nothing at all about it.' Given the luridness of the allegation, Bastendorff's phrasing here seemed exquisitely polite.

'With respect to her other allegations,' continued Bastendorff. 'I can only say that so far as I am concerned, they are not true. I know nothing at all about them and for all I know, Mr Findlay, the American, who did live at my house, is alive now.'[2]

Yet Hannah was also at hand with an immediate reply to this. 'I have written this book in order that justice may overtake the perpetrators of certain horrible crimes,' she said in a statement given out by the Central News Agency, 'to clear myself of the suspicion attaching to me as the author of one of those fearful deeds, and to make public that which the police, by prematurely charging me with the murder, prevented my making [sic] before the Coroner, and which by vulgar abuse they stopped me from saying after my acquittal.'[3]

The Bastendorffs could obviously not allow any of this to stand. 'A special application was made yesterday afternoon to Mr Justice Bowen,' reported the newspapers 'for an injunction to restrain Mr George Purkess, publisher, of 286 Strand, from publishing a certain pamphlet entitled 'The Euston Square Mystery' . . . on the ground that the said pamphlet contained libels on the plaintiff Mr Severin Bastendorff.

'Mr J.J. Sims, barrister, appeared for the plaintiff and Mr Edmund Thomas for the defendant. The plaintiff in his affidavit stated that . . . he had purchased and read the pamphlet in question.'

Here were the sworn denials of the facts as set out. 'He (Bastendorff) never saw Hannah Dobbs before his wife engaged her as a servant. He had nothing to do with her engagement (for the job), nor had he anything to do with the engagement of any female servant since he was married. He had always been greatly occupied in his business and had always left the management of his household affairs to his wife.'

Then there was the slander on his marriage that he wanted refuted. 'He and his wife had always since their marriage in 1872 lived on terms of the greatest affection,' the affidavit continued. 'He believed the charges in the pamphlet referring to the pawning of various articles of jewellery to be wholly untrue. The gold necklet mentioned Mrs Bastendorff now has in her possession, and there is no entry of it having been pawned with Mr Gill of Hampstead Road. He believes that the false statements contained in the said pamphlet respecting the pawning of articles belonging to himself and his wife are calculated to do him injury in his credit and business.'

There were the other rather more serious matters: 'The allegations respecting Mr Findlay, who was stated to have disappeared from 4, Euston Square, are wholly untrue. The whole of the statements in the pamphlet to the effect that he was concerned in the murder of Miss Hacker are wholly untrue. The allegation that he was a witness to a disgusting act of cruelty on a little dog, is wholly untrue. The publication of the said pamphlet and the libels therein are calculated to damage his character, property and trade.'

The newspapers also reported that Bastendorff had been 'greatly annoyed by crowds outside his house' and that he had 'commenced an action for libel against the defendant'.[4] With the affidavit read, the case was adjourned for a few days – with George Purkess required to give an undertaking that no further copies of the pamphlet would be sold in that time.

This was a crisis that reached rather wider than number 4, Euston Square and Severin Bastendorff; the distinctive family name was, after all, attached to a high quality furniture business; and indeed the brothers Joseph, Pierre and Anthony had been named in the pamphlet too, not only as witnesses to the murder of a small child, but also (possibly even more damning in the eyes of a sentimental public) the torture of a small dog.

It would be difficult to imagine, in fact, anything that could be more damaging to a business that required the name 'Bastendorff' to be synonymous with taste, grace, and a fine sensibility.

Hannah Dobbs' pamphlet also had the most tremendous impact on Severin's wife, Mary. She was depicted both as complicit in hideous crimes and their concealment, and also as a stupid, indolent woman who could not detect the sexual betrayals taking place within her own house.

She, too, swore an affidavit; and this too was solemnly reported by newspapers across the land (presumably happily, since it afforded an opportunity to remind readers of the most intensely gothic details). Added to this was a sense that her voice was being heard properly at last, following her faltering performance at the trial of Hannah Dobbs a few weeks previously.

As reported, Mary Bastendorff's affidavit – which seemed rather more strongly worded than her husband's – ran as follows: 'She says she . . . has read the pamphlet written by Hannah Dobbs. She selected Hannah Dobbs from several young women who called in answer to her advertisement in the *Clerkenwell News* in June 1876. She had never heard her name or known that there was such a person in existence before, nor was there any conversation between Mr Bastendorff and herself before she engaged Dobbs.'

And what then of Hannah's claims of a sexual relationship with her husband? This drew a sharply concise response. 'She [Mary Bastendorff] never saw any appearance of Dobbs being pregnant.' What then of Hannah's claim that Bastendorff left the marital bed and crept into her room late at night? 'I say positively,' went Mrs Bastendorff's affidavit, 'that I always made a practice of sitting up for my husband until he came home when he had gone out during the evening and I never went to bed until he came home.' And the idea that Severin's brother, Peter, effected entry into the house late at night?

'Peter Bastendorff was not allowed the privilege of a key of the street door, and no such key was furnished to him with her knowledge.'

And there was an intriguing element of ambiguity about two other named lodgers. 'Miss Griffiths, a middle-aged woman, came to lodge at number 4, Euston Square in January 1877. Mr Findlay came to lodge with Miss Griffiths. So far as she (Mrs Bastendorff) knew, there was no improper or immoral connection between them, and she never heard any suggestions of the kind on the part of Dobbs, or anyone else, before she saw the pamphlet.'

The wording of the affidavit might have been at fault; the suggestion possibly was that Findlay and Miss Griffiths had begun lodging there at the same time, rather than 'with' one another. And yet Mary Bastendorff also stated that when: 'Miss Griffiths left, Mr Findlay left also, to take a room in Miss Griffiths's new house, but not liking the apartments, he came back to 4, Euston Square.'

There was, she deposed, no mystery about his departure as the pamphlet had stated. 'She recollected Mr Findlay leaving when he went for the last time. She shook hands with him in the dining room and saw him walk away with his travelling bag. She has not seen or heard from him since.'

How did she respond to the allegations concerning the seemingly ceaseless pawning of garments? 'She never sold clothes, nor ordered any to be sold at any time, and she believed the statement with reference to such sales to be wholly unfounded.'

There had been Hannah's claim that while supposedly on holiday, she had crept back into Euston Square (to continue her relationship with Severin). 'She remembered Dobbs going away in August for a month. Dobbs never slept in the house to her knowledge during the time she was on her holiday.'

Then there was the minor – yet seemingly important – claim that the arrival of Matilda Hacker warranted a change of rooms. 'It was untrue that when Miss Hacker came there was any question of changing bedrooms,' continued the reported affidavit. Added to this, she 'knew Miss Hacker as Miss Uish and never heard the name of Hacker until it was mentioned by the police.

'The story of Miss Hacker's interview with herself and her husband in the dining room was wholly untrue, as also was the statement with regard to the pawning of a bracelet. The only money she received from Miss Uish was one payment for three weeks, which was on Monday October 15th, 1877. Dobbs said Uish was going presently, and an hour afterwards she said she was gone.'

This was clearly intended to place Hannah Dobbs back into the position of the person who had apparently last seen Matilda Hacker alive. Mary Bastendorff's affidavit, as reported, concluded with several other refutations. 'The only time Dobbs took the children to Hampstead was long before Miss Hacker came to 4, Euston Square, to lodge . . . she never employed Dobbs to sell anything or to pawn anything whatever.

'Dobbs was a most efficient servant, and she found her so useful in looking after the house that she gave her the entire control over the lodgers. Mrs Bastendorff's health at that time was such that she was incapable of much exertion. She declared many other statements in the pamphlet to be wholly untrue.'[5] The document had been signed 'Mary Snelson Bastendorff'.

And quite where did Scotland Yard stand on this extraordinary new flurry of claim and counter-claim? Inspector Hagen was presumably maddened with frustration. 'The Detective Department of Scotland-yard, acting under the direction of the Crown authorities, have within the last few days been making enquiries,' reported the newspapers, 'which are still proceeding into the truth or falsehood of Hannah Dobbs' allegations.

'Efforts are being made by various parties, in view of the pending actions-in-law (the forthcoming libel case), to ascertain the whereabouts of Mr Findlay, the former lodger at 4, Euston Square, who is supposed to have been a wealthy gentleman from America and whose present residence, if he is alive, is up to the present entirely unknown.

'It is alleged that he had in his possession a considerable amount of property, including railway shares and bonds. He lodged on several occasions at Bastendorff's house and is described as between forty and fifty years of age, tall, thin, with a stoop, very fair hair and beard. It is, we understand, intended to send notices to some of the chief American papers to see if any relatives of Mr Findlay can be found.'[6]

The forthcoming libel case brought by Bastendorff against Dobbs and her publisher, George Purkess, would once more require all parties to be sworn in on oath. It was reported that 'at the request of the Home Office authorities, Hannah Dobbs was directed to reduce her statement (the pamphlet) to writing for the consideration of the Crown legal advisers'. They understandably demanded more particulars about the little boy who was apparently murdered; and Dobbs obliged, telling them in a written statement that he was 'about ten years old', 'dirty and ragged' with clothes that had been patched. 'His hair was flaxen and his eyes were blue.' She also stated that she had 'started to get a doctor' to attend to him; though there was no indication of what stopped her.

In short, the authorities most certainly had to investigate these nauseating accusations; but this in turn might have been a broader stratagem to catch either Dobbs or the Bastendorffs out over the murder of Matilda Hacker; it was highly damaging to have such a widely publicised crime go unsolved, and its perpetrator unpunished.

Indeed, within days, the police issued their own statement with regard to the alleged child murder; that it was little more than a 'tissue of lies'. And once more Hannah Dobbs was in danger; this might have been construed as perjury, since she had made her sworn statement to the Home Office.

Yet the implacability of Dobbs, and to an extent her fearlessness, had sparked another layer of conflict; that between Bastendorff and the publisher George Purkess, himself also apparently quite without fear.

For when it came to circulation of the pamphlet, the court found – strikingly – that it was not its responsibility to restrain publication.

The portrait of Hannah Dobbs could continue to be seen staring out from the nation's bookstands. The sale of it could only be prevented, legally, by Severin Bastendorff winning a case of libel.

But Purkess had been arming himself against this possibility. He had obtained a copy of Bastendorff's sworn affidavit, and had examined it with a pitiless scrutiny; and he could see a vulnerability. To prove that vulnerability in a court would require the co-operation of many witnesses, but then it was worth it for the sake of his own reputation as publisher of the hugely popular *Illustrated Police News*.

In particular, there was one part of Hannah Dobbs' story that could be exploited and turned against Bastendorff; a key element that Purkess was willing to wager on. And to this end, he was in continued contact with both Hannah Dobbs and her solicitor.

It is not difficult to imagine the darkened rooms of 4, Euston Square in the thick nights of the gathering autumn; the young children having much greater freedom to run around and play in a house that was quite free of any paying lodgers. Equally, it is not difficult to imagine Mary Bastendorff, crushed with anxiety, trying to keep her home looking respectable and fresh, always ready to take in new guests, and her husband, whose drinking never seemed to have been moderate, spending more time in the pubs of Bloomsbury and St Pancras.

So when the summons was brought to the door, it must have been an even worse shock than the publication of the pamphlet. Bastendorff found himself accused by the Crown Prosecutors of perjury in his sworn statements. He himself would now be required to stand trial.

22

'I Have Disgraced You Before all the Country'

If Severin Bastendorff felt a prickling sixth sense of paranoia in the weeks before his trial, it was perfectly justified; the publisher George Purkess and Hannah Dobbs were preparing for the forthcoming court case with deadly seriousness, and with methods that were devious. Bastendorff had denied any sexual relationship with Hannah; the journalists from the Central News Agency were employing a range of furtive tactics to prove otherwise.

On one Saturday afternoon in September 1879, it was Severin Bastendorff who, having just returned home, went to answer the persistent knocking on the front door of 4, Euston Square. Standing on the step was a young woman, simply dressed. He did not recognise her; and she did not give her name.

Her request was curious: she very much needed to get to an address on the Caledonian Road, she told him. Could he oblige her by giving directions?

A little bewildered, Severin Bastendorff did so; he told her to go back to the Euston Road, turn left, walk on for a little past St Pancras and Kings Cross stations, and she would find Caledonian Road branching off to the left.

The young woman told him she was grateful; and with that, she turned and left.

Given the pervasive anxieties that he and his wife faced, Bastendorff may not have given any further thought to this curious encounter. The meaning of it, however, would become clear in court some weeks later.

He was not being entirely passive himself though: part of Hannah Dobbs' pamphlet had alleged that she and Bastendorff had gone to Redhill for an illicit weekend; and he and his lawyer understood that it was now important to reach the landlady of the inn that Hannah had named. It transpired that this landlady, Mrs Anne Carpenter, had recently moved a few miles away to Reigate, Surrey, to manage another tavern and hotel called The Beehive.

It is not known whether Bastendorff or his lawyer first had the inspiration; but when summonsing Mrs Carpenter as a possible witness in the forthcoming trial, the idea was to suggest to her that it was not Severin Bastendorff she had seen with Hannah Dobbs – but his brother, Peter.

Both Bastendorff and his lawyer caught the train down to Reigate; and a horse-drawn cab took them to The Beehive. But they were too late.

Mrs Carpenter had already been summonsed: by journalists and a lawyer employed by George Purkess. Beside the large roaring fire of that comforting inn, they had outlined to her the parameters of the coming case, and the importance of remembering that it had definitely been Severin Bastendorff she had seen in Redhill two years previously.

Other witnesses were gathered by the defendant; friends of Bastendorff, many from the German community, all hard-working and respectable and articulate. They would be there first to attest to his fine nature and his happy marriage; and also to account for his movements on certain key dates. These were men with whom he enjoyed shooting and fishing.

During this pre-trial period, the strain must have told on Hannah Dobbs too; it must have felt as though she and Bastendorff were now locked in a lethal duel. She and the lawyers were acutely aware of the new hazards that cross-examination in such a case would bring; the way that Inspector Hagen and associates in Scotland Yard would be poring over every word of testimony, alert to any inconsistency.

She was specifically tutored how to respond to any questions concerning her story about the murder of the small boy, and about the child's flesh being fed to Riggenbach's dog. Hannah was told to say: 'I decline to answer.'

Aside from avoiding pitfalls, George Purkess and his lawyer wanted the limelight kept very firmly on the relationship between Hannah Dobbs and Severin Bastendorff.

During this period, Hannah had either bought for herself – or more likely had Purkess and his journalists pay for – some new and ever more elegant clothing. The time for penitential display was past: the new clothes – which would lead to newspaper reporters describing her as 'showily-dressed' – were clearly intended to emphasise that she was not a common serving girl, but rather a lady who commanded respect.

And so, in the well-lit court at Bow Street, at the end of October 1879, there was a pre-trial hearing before the magistrate Mr Flowers.

At this, Hannah took the stand as the central witness; and immediately, under questioning, she was insistent that she and Bastendorff had first met when she was cleaning windows at Torrington Square in 1875; and she was very much more explicit now about the intimacy of their relationship. She even detailed occasions at Torrington Square and elsewhere when such intimacies took place.

In applying for an injunction to have Hannah's pamphlet withdrawn, Bastendorff's solicitor Mr Sims had declared that it 'had seriously injured his client in business, by destroying his credit'.[1] But this court seemed not interested in Bastendorff's legal grievance; there was only time for his alleged perjury.

And indeed, the court was told, that intimacy continued after Severin had arranged for Hannah to get the position as maid-of-all-work at 4, Euston Square in June 1876. Very shortly after this, Bastendorff had arranged to take her away for the weekend to the town of Redhill in Surrey. She 'had occupied a room with him from Saturday to Monday' at the Red Lion Inn.

Hannah told the court that Bastendorff's appearance had changed a little over the years; for that weekend, he 'wore a long beard and a light suit of clothes'.

Mr Poland stepped up to cross-examine her. She told him that before Bastendorff, she 'had never been in the habit of going out with gentlemen' though she added that she was 'not a chaste woman'.

So what then of her relationship with Severin's younger brother Peter? She told Mr Poland she had made the younger man's 'acquaintance' and 'had been guilty of immorality with him'. She added that 'he had a key of 4, Euston Square and was in the habit of letting himself into the house at night and leaving before the family was up in the morning'. She added that Severin was 'well aware of this' as she herself 'used to tell him'; conversely, Hannah did not tell Peter 'what had occurred' between herself and Severin.

Here was a world of illicit nocturnal assignations, according to Hannah Dobbs, who seemed to experience no awkwardness or embarrassment in relating these adventures to the court.

Mr Poland focused on the final paragraph of Hannah Dobbs' pamphlet: her sworn statement to the truth of everything within it. On the back page of the pamphlet, this was accompanied with a reproduction of what was apparently her signature. 'This, I see, purports to be a facsimile of your writing,' said Mr Poland. 'Is it so?'

Hannah Dobbs said: 'I decline to answer.'

The unspoken subtext of his question was: who was the real perjuror here? Mr Poland took her through the list of her previous offences, even though this made the magistrate Mr Flowers uneasy: 'Surely,' he said, 'we need not go into that matter?' But for Mr Poland, this was about establishing character. And for her own part, Hannah Dobbs was happy to answer him defiantly, despite her defence counsel Mr Montagu Williams objecting to this trawl through 'the whole of the pamphlet' when Bastendorff's alleged perjury only featured in one paragraph.

Mr Poland asked Hannah about her statements concerning Mr Findlay being murdered; about apparently being given his watch; about the possessions of Matilda Hacker that she acquired; and about her account of the murder of Matilda Hacker, and how she herself came to leave 4, Euston Square. In her responses, Hannah Dobbs adhered broadly to the published text.

Then there was the molten core of Dobbs' astonishing pamphlet: the mystery over the murder of Miss Hacker was one thing. The sensational allegation concerning the frenzied killing of a small boy was another.

'You speak of having seen a boy murdered,' said Mr Poland, 'so of course you were present?'

Hannah Dobbs hesitated, and then said: 'I decline to answer.'

'Then' said Mr Poland, 'you decline to say whether that story is true or not?'

Hannah remained silent. Poland then found the relevant passage, and he read it out to the court in full, including the 'crushing blows' of the poker, and ending with the little boy's clothes being destroyed 'at the workshop fire'.

'After this,' said Mr Poland, 'you go on to say that you smelled a strong odour like the boiling of grease and other matter, and you say you are 'obliged to suppress all names'. Do you refuse to give us any particulars about this boy?'

'Yes,' said Hannah, 'I do.'

'Was he employed at Mr Bastendorff's?'

'I decline to answer.'

'Do you mean to insinuate that Mr Bastendorff, your master, murdered him?'

'I decline to answer the question.'

'And you won't even say whether the boy was in his employ?'

'No, he was not,' said Dobbs. 'I decline to answer anything.'

'How long was this,' persisted Mr Poland, 'after the murder of Miss Hacker?'

'I decline to answer,' said Dobbs, adding sharply: 'It has nothing to do with this case.'

The magistrate Mr Flowers 'remarked that this was no doubt the fact – but if the object was to test the credibility of the witness, the learned counsel might infer that she was not a credible witness.' Mr Poland said that 'he was satisfied with that intimation'. Yet there was little comfort to be drawn from this by the Bastendorffs.

For there were other witnesses: Hannah Dobbs's former colleague Selina Knight was called. She declared 'to the best of her belief' that four years ago she saw Severin in Torrington Square and that he and Hannah first met then. But Mr Poland forced her to admit that journalists from the Central News Agency had recently persuaded her to ring the bell of 4, Euston Square to see once more the face of Severin Bastendorff. She was the woman who had randomly asked Bastendorff for directions to the Caledonian Road. It was obvious this was to ensure that she would corroborate the pamphlet.

When probed a little further about the reliability of her memory, she said: 'I recognised his voice from the German accent . . . I believed when I first saw him that he was the man who courted Hannah Dobbs and I believe so still.'

Also called was Mrs Carpenter, former landlady of the Red Lion Inn in Redhill, Surrey. She remembered in August 1877 that Hannah Dobbs came to stay there and 'she had a gentleman with her'. She added: 'I have seen him today. I have learned since that it was Severin Bastendorff.'

They had, said Mrs Carpenter, arrived on the Saturday evening and they stayed until the Monday morning. 'They occupied the same room,' she said, to ensure there could be no doubt on this matter.

When they arrived, 'I carried their black bag and parcel upstairs. He was dressed in rather a light suit. They sat in the smoking room before going to bed.' He had a glass of ale; they shared a plate of biscuits. The recollections were strikingly acute.

Was there any chance, the defence counsel asked, that she might have played host to Peter, rather than Severin? She insisted not, adding that Severin might have had 'a longer beard' back then.

The beard was important to the defence; for Mr Poland was still hopeful of proving that the older brother might in fact have been mistaken for the younger. But in fact it was going to cause further confusion. The next witness, John Aldolphus Dicke, a 'cabinet maker' in Charlotte Street, told the court that he knew both Peter and Severin Bastendorff. He 'knew the former [Peter] in 1875, when he could hardly speak English to be understood, and had no beard. He was,' said Dicke, 'little more than a boy at the time.'

At this, a photograph of Peter, taken around 1875, was produced by the prosecution. It showed him as 'a beardless boy' and Dicke agreed that it was very 'like him'. Dicke 'knew Severin a year before' he knew Peter. 'He had a fine beard always,' he told the court, 'and longer . . . than it appeared to be at present.'

This might have seemed the most absurdly trivial point; but given the defence's line that Hannah's pamphlet had deliberately misled by naming the wrong Bastendorff brother, and that this was a sinister case of swapped identities, it actually seemed to have become central. Prosecutor Mr Williams lost patience: and he angrily demanded 'the committal of the defendant'. This would have placed Severin Bastendorff in jail, awaiting a main trial.

Responding with a fiery tone, Mr Poland in turn took the magistrate back into the twisted roots of the conflict; the original charge of murder – and the opportunism of an amoral press.

'Two gentlemen connected with what is called The Central News Agency invited the cooperation of this abandoned woman,' he declared, 'and with Mr Purkess, the plaintiff in this case, induced her to reveal the secrets, real and imaginary, of her polluted life, and paid her money for "revelations" which they should, in the interests of society and even of the woman herself, have done all in their power to discourage.' These 'revelations', he insisted, including being the 'accomplice of at least three murders', had not been mentioned at her trial.

He then pleaded that there was no other evidence and 'asked the Court to pause before it branded the defendant and his wife with the infamy imputed to them by this abandoned woman, encouraged by men who ought to have known better and ought rather to have advised her to remain in obscurity for the remainder of her tainted life'.[2]

After this powerful plea, there then followed some legal bickering with the magistrate Mr Flowers becoming tangled in Severin Bastendorff's action for libel against the Central News Agency and Hannah Dobbs; before there could be any proceedings for perjury, surely he ought to wait until the result of that libel case was known?

Yet Mr Williams the prosecutor somehow managed to suggest that 'the alleged perjury had no relation whatever to the (libel) action.'

And caught up in these legal thickets, the seemingly ineffectual Mr Flowers made his decision. As there had been 'four witnesses to the alleged perjury' he was therefore 'bound to send the case for trial'.

The case would be heard at the Central Criminal Court, Old Bailey.

Mr Flowers asked Severin Bastendorff if he had anything to say. All he could think to reply was that Hannah Dobbs' story was 'a pack of lies'.[3]

He was required to give the court £5, in the meantime, as a surety that he would appear at the trial, which was set for a few days hence.

23

'I Depend Upon My Character'

In her single-minded struggle for survival, Hannah Dobbs was now prepared to put herself, as well as Severin Bastendorff, through every fire of shame. The persona she seemed to be inhabiting was complex: part sophisticated sexual adventuress, part repentant and bewildered country girl. She and the men of the Central News Agency were laboriously steering the narrative towards the suggestion that she had been pulled into Bastendorff's immoral vortex: that he himself was wearing a mask, that of a civilised London man of property. And that beneath this mask lay unspeakable depravity.

Added to this was a possibility that the most luridly shocking allegations in the pamphlet – child murder, dog eating – seemed designed to appeal to a rather gothic prejudice against the Germanic people; deep in those forests, the pamphlet seemed to be suggesting, who knew how these people lived?

Was this the reason why the judge at the Old Bailey seemed perfectly content to have a trial based around the character and morals of Severin Bastendorff? Equally, was there, for the police and the legal system, a frustrated sense that the murderer of Matilda Hacker might be detected under the stress of a largely concocted offence? Could it be that Bastendorff might stand revealed?

Those gathered in the gaunt space of the Central Criminal Court in that dark December would perhaps have felt their hearts beat faster; the proximity to the feared Newgate jail, which stood next door, would have added a sharpness to the swearing of oaths and the consequences of lying. The first witness to be called to the stand was an ever more poised Hannah Dobbs.

It is possible she thought this would be her final opportunity to transfer any suspicion of murder from herself; whatever the case, she was now willing to step beyond all boundaries of accepted decorum.

As well as repeating all the stories of illicit sexual encounters with both Severin and Peter, she was now prepared to go into ever more acute detail on the sordid mechanics of those nights; the language she now used seemed to have an extraordinarily modern quality of unflinching candour. Her words must have been akin to a razor tearing Bastendorff's skin.

She now recounted how, on the second night that they met in 1875, he first took her to a coffee house, and then to 'a room' in a house in a street that she could not now recall. 'I think it was on the second floor, I am not certain,' she told the court. 'We went to bed and he had connection with me there.

'We remained there for about an hour or an hour and half,' Dobbs added, 'it might have been two hours. We then got up and dressed ourselves and went back to Torrington Square.' This was the night on which Hannah got back at 2a.m. only to find that she had inadvertently held on to the servants' bedroom key – and Selina Knight and Clara Green had been waiting up furiously for her to return.

Hannah then told the court of another occasion when Severin paid a visit to Torrington Square on a Sunday afternoon, when the landlords were out. Hannah invited him in; presently, her fellow servants went out too. Hannah and Severin were left in the kitchen but, Hannah told the court, they swiftly made their way to the servants' bedroom where 'he had connection with me'.[1]

The assignations continued, with the pair generally meeting by St Pancras church, Hannah said. At the time, Bastendorff's beard was 'very long'. She recounted the story of how he had engineered for her the job at 4, Euston Square; and how 'there was intercourse between us from time to time'.

The defending counsels were interested to learn how such manoeuvrings might be possible within a house of many souls; and following on from this, how murder might be committed in such circumstances. Hannah was asked to take the court through all the lodgers that stayed there in her time – from Mr and Mrs Brookes to Miss Willoughby to the mysterious Mr Findlay to the tragic Matilda Hacker. She detailed how lodgers either used the downstairs drawing room as a common sitting room or else paid for two rooms so that they might lead rather more hermetic lives. Matilda Hacker was unusual in using the one room as a bedroom and a sitting room.

And it was there, late in 1876, and new to her position, that Hannah first met Severin's brother, Peter, who, she recalled, 'had very little beard' at the time. By her own account, Peter was instantly struck by her; and, indeed, she said, it was not long before he was asking her for a front door key 'so that he might come in in the night and sleep with me'.

She provided him the key; and according to her, his nocturnal visits, deep into the small hours, began. 'I had intercourse with him. It commenced at the end of January 1877,' she told the court. But just before that, she alleged, there was an intimation of catastrophe.

'I had reason to believe there was something the matter with me,' said Hannah. 'I told the defendant [Severin] that I thought I was with child.' She also told him how his younger brother had been pursuing her, how Peter had expressed his desire to 'keep company' with her, and of how she had obliged by passing him a street door key. According to her, it was Severin who came up with a plan to explain her pregnancy. She and Peter should sleep with one another again and she should 'put the child on him'. Yet 'Peter had not asked me to marry him' but only to keep company with her.

And in all the time in 4, Euston Square, she told the court, 'the connection between me and the defendant' continued.

Hannah Dobbs was also more explicit about the weekend away to Redhill; how she and Severin arrived at the inn on Saturday evening, he 'took a glass of ale' and then they retired to bed at around 9p.m. 'The defendant and I slept together that night,' she said. The next day they went for long walks across 'the commons' and 'we went straight up to bed directly we got back'. Under closer questioning, Hannah wanted there to be no doubt. 'We had intercourse there.'

There then followed a succession, for Hannah, of temporary rooms, after she briefly left 4, Euston Square; she told the court how Severin came to see her, for instance, at the 'Railway Hotel, Argyle Street, King's Cross'; of how 'the defendant was there with me for about two hours. He went to bed with me and connection took place there.' He then returned to Euston Square and she spent the night there. The impression given to the jury could not have been more atrocious; but at the centre of this, Hannah Dobbs' shocking candour clearly sounded to some like the honesty of pure confession.

In a previous court appearance, it had been put to her that she was not a chaste woman. Hannah was now most insistent that 'she had not been with any gentleman before' she met Bastendorff. 'I said at Bow Street I was not a chaste woman – but I did not know what it meant,' she told the court. 'The defendant was the first person with whom I had intercourse.'

It was put to her that in her pamphlet, she had mentioned how she had become 'intimate' with a footman in the service of Lady Buck in Bideford; Hannah brushed this off as another example of linguistic confusion, much as she claimed not to have understood 'chaste'.

The defence counsels, who had clearly been investigating every corner of Hannah's life, were attacking hard; long before Euston Square, what then of a gentleman friend she had briefly acquired when she had first moved to the south London district of Rotherhithe? He was a policeman, but he used to visit her 'in plain clothes'. She dismissed this impatiently; she simply 'kept company' with him but denied intimacy.

Mr Poland than focused on the short period in 1875 when she left London to work as a maid in Redhill, Surrey. He asked Hannah about the thefts that her employer had noticed, and what happened immediately afterwards. 'I stole £2 and 3 shillings from a box,' she told the court. Was she aware that this was a charitable collection? 'I don't know that it was a missionary box,' she said, adding with what must have seemed a certain brazenness, 'perhaps it would not have made much difference if I had known it.'

There was also the matter of some stolen silk; Hannah now admitted to the theft. 'My mother came up from Devonshire,' she told the court, 'and paid the money that was required, with reference to the box and the silk.'

So, in fact, it transpired that Hannah had had to be rescued by her mother before she returned to Bideford in the mid-1870s; 'I stayed there nearly twelve months, my mother and father maintaining me,' she now told the court.

And then she had been pulled once more back to the irresistible attractions of London, and the situation at 42, Torrington Square. Even there it seemed that Hannah's compulsion to steal was bordering on the kleptomaniac; there was 'dispute' over a sovereign that landlady Mrs Pearce had dispensed for the purchase of some butter.

Then, at 4, Euston Square: what would she say about the lodger Mr Riggenbach accusing her of stealing (and pawning) some of his clothes? Hannah Dobbs at first denied this, but then appeared to stumble over her own account. She told the court that 'there was a little dispute'; and that Severin Bastendorff had pawned many of his own items in the local pawn shops. But she then admitted that she had 'pawned the first lot' of Mr Riggenbach's apparently extensive wardrobe of jackets and waistcoats at 'Mr Clarke's' on the Hampstead

Road. And the reason, she said, was this: Bastendorff was trying to raise a little money so that they might go and spend the weekend together at Redhill.

So what then of the grave hints she dropped in the pamphlet of the mysterious lodger Mr Findlay being murdered? Some of the pamphlet was read back to her: including the passage about the 'imbecile' police and the officers 'Dogberry and Noodle-dum' missing startling clues. The defence counsel – realising that she did not know that the officer's names were a joke, Dogberry being a comically inept constable in *Much Ado About Nothing* – went in at this point for some sly and underhand teasing.

First, how could she stay in a house that was filled with such horrors? 'I did think he had been murdered,' said Hannah, 'and yet I remained in the situation.' And, said the wily Mr Poland, would she care to tell the court who exactly these police officers were? Hannah Dobbs faltered for a moment.

'I do not know who Dogberry is,' she said. 'I never heard of him until I read the pamphlet. I don't know where he lives. I don't know anything about it. I do not know who Noodle-dum is, or what he is, or where he lives.' Quite apart from inciting a laugh at Dobbs' ignorance, the larger point – that key points in this pamphlet were the work of journalists writing quite separately from the young woman – would surely have been made quite strongly.

She was not finished yet though. Under questioning, Dobbs seemed happy to expiate on the subject of the gold watch and chain and the eyeglass, all of which were the property of Matilda Hacker. In Hannah's account, she had simply somehow acquired these items a few days after the old woman was supposed to have left the house.

But now she became entangled in the chronology; and began to speak of when she knew the watch and chain had been Miss Hacker's when she 'saw the remains in the cellar'. So when precisely did she know that the remains were there, and that the old lady had been murdered? At this point, the prosecutor Montagu Williams jumped in with some urgency; he turned to Judge Hawkins and declared that even though Hannah Dobbs had been acquitted of murder, she was still 'liable to be indicted as an accessory after the fact'.

The judge, puzzlingly, agreed that Hannah Dobbs should decline to answer any questions that might in some way incriminate her.

Yet Hannah pressed on, at once claiming that she had seen the remains in the winter of 1877 (while remaining 'in service to Mr Bastendorff' for a year afterwards) while then finessing which part of the coal cellar the corpse was in and then declaring that 'I always understood from the defendant that the remains were buried in the square . . . that is, removed from the cellar.'

This seemed to be the closest that Hannah Dobbs had come to accusing Severin Bastendorff of the murder.

She was once more pressed on her claims to have seen a little boy killed; 'I said in the pamphlet that that was true but I decline to answer any of these questions,' she said.

The court heard more about her restless, peripatetic life after 4, Euston Square, which in a curious way, seemed to mirror that of Matilda Hacker; a constant moving about from lodging house to lodging house. And her relationship with Peter Bastendorff continued; she told the court, under questioning, of how she had gone to visit her parents in Bideford, and Peter followed her, staying at the family inn as Hannah's 'husband'. 'He slept with me at my father and mother's house,' she told the court.

The defence counsel wanted to know what the relationship was like now. 'Peter came to meet me at the prison gates . . . but I did not speak to him,' said Dobbs. 'I took a cab by myself, not with him. I spoke to him about a week after.' But was she claiming that the relationship was no longer so intense? 'It is true that since I came out of prison, I have had intercourse with him twice,' she said. 'I saw Peter last about three weeks ago, I think.'

The point that Mr Poland was edging towards was this: the extent to which Peter Bastendorff colluded with the preparation of the pamphlet. Was it still the case that there was enmity between Peter and his brother, Severin? 'He has not been on good terms with the defendant,' said Dobbs, 'but he is now, I suppose, because he told me he had made friends with his brother the last time I saw him when he came to see me [at her lodgings] in Southwark Bridge Road.'

And yet the pamphlet stated repeatedly that 'Peter Bastendorff corroborates this'. To what extent did he have a hand in the writing of it? Hannah conceded that Peter Bastendorff had been at the offices of the Central News Agency, and the text was 'read over in his presence or he read it over and said it was true'.

So to what extent had all of this been sparked by ferocious sibling rivalry? Prompted by questioning, Hannah Dobbs recalled how she made her home in 4, Euston Square; and she told the court that when it came to Peter entering her life, she had her own definition of the term 'engaged'; 'he never said anything about marriage' but 'people get engaged in hopes to get married some times' and she considered herself to be 'engaged to be married at some time'.

But then there was the darkness of the alleged sexual deceit: 'I was engaged to be married to Peter at the time I was in the family way by his brother,' she told the court. 'It was with the defendant's permission that I gave Peter the [front door] key . . . that he might come in in the night and have intercourse with me.'

Now she was preparing to go further than ever in imputing not one but several murders to Severin Bastendorff. During the period after she had first left 4, Euston Square for a time, moving from house to house, Hannah told the court that he gave her presents. First, there was a gift of a large watch and chain; she said she told Severin: 'It is like Mr Findlay's'. He reportedly said to her: 'How do you know it is like Mr Findlay's?' According to Hannah, he then said: 'It is not Mr Findlay's. I bought it at a sale . . . there are many watches alike.'

Hannah then told the court that she remarked that it was too big for her – it was a gentleman's watch. 'You can wear that,' Severin allegedly told her, 'until I get you a smaller one.'

Then, a few weeks later, Hannah said, Severin asked her to give back the large watch as he had a present for her. Inside a box was a smaller gold watch and chain, and an eyeglass. These, Hannah said, were the property of Matilda Hacker, though she did not know it. She told the court that Severin had said to her: 'You will say you had it given to you by your uncle, the same as you said you had the first one from.'

All the while, she told the court, any items of value from anywhere within 4, Euston Square were being pawned; Severin Bastendorff, she was alleging, was in constant and urgent need of money.

Hannah reported that he finally confessed what it was for (and here was a fresh new scandalous allegation): he had impregnated a young woman 'and he wanted to pay her off'.

'I don't remember the girl's name now,' Hannah told the court. 'She was a French girl. I remember seeing her at the house.'[2]

After some more questioning about the watch, Hannah was free to step down.

But the case was about perjury and deceit; and when Hannah Dobbs' former colleague, Selina Knight, was called, the defence counsels aggressively brought her own closely guarded secrets out before the wider world.

Knight was there to corroborate the Dobbs story that Severin and Hannah had met in Torrington Square in 1875; but in order to prove her fundamental untrustworthiness, the defence instead fixed her to the spot with questions about her own sexual history. Hideously, having sworn the oath, Knight was compelled to tell the story of the new domestic position she found herself, and how she – like Hannah Dobbs – had had a secret nocturnal visitor at North Audley Street in Mayfair. With extreme reluctance, Knight was forced to confess that these furtive encounters had resulted in pregnancy. Another later romance produced the same result. The babies were adopted by friends. What made these confessions so painful – and indeed they must have been difficult to listen to – was that Knight found herself forced to name the errant father of one of these children; a man called Richard Henry Jones. At one point, she seemed to make a plea to the court not to be pursued further on the matter.

'I have had the misfortune to have had two illegitimate children,' said Knight. 'I have tried as far as I could to conceal the fact. I am dependent on my character for getting a place as a servant.'[3]

Her 'fellow servant', Clara Green, was also called; her story seemed to match that of Selina Knight, suggesting a tutored quality which the defence was swift to pick up on. Central to the doubt was the idea that a man seen not more than three times, and even then not to any proper extent, could be recognised and sworn upon four years later. Green asserted that she 'should not want to see a man's face' more than once for it to become lodged in her memory. But she was repeatedly questioned about how certain she could really be about this.

She stated that Severin's beard was very 'much shorter' now than it was then. 'I say he is the man. I say so positively,' she declared. How then could she account for her unusually acute memory for faces, even though by her own admission she 'had not taken much notice of him' when he visited Hannah? Green made mention of his 'rather peculiar' face, rendered so by his 'unusually small eyes'. But like Selina Knight, she had had lengthy meetings beforehand with the team acting for the Central News Agency, which the defence lawyers made certain that the court heard about.

And so it was that Severin Bastendorff's friend and erstwhile colleague John Adolphus Dicke found himself in the witness stand being asked not about character or temperament but about his friend's beard, and the styles in which he had worn it since 1875. 'I have always known him with a fine beard, what I would call a full beard,' said Dicke. 'But I can't say whether it was before 1875 that he had a long beard. I never put anything of that kind down or take any particular notice – unless there is anything I ought to take particular notice of.

'I know once he had it cut out in the centre,' he added, 'what you would call a concave.'

Also being asked – possibly to his bemusement – about the style of Bastendorff's whiskers was another of his friends, Albert Kaw Derrell, a 'wholesale cabinet-maker' who lived and worked at nearby Argyle Square. He and Severin had, throughout 1875, been business partners. 'I think I saw him every day during that time, barring Sundays,' said Derrell. 'His beard was then very much longer than it is now, it nearly covered his shirt front.'

After the 'dissolution' of their business partnership, Derrell did not see Bastendorff so frequently but when prompted, did recall that in 1877 or 1878, on an occasion when they met, Bastendorff had changed his beard; he had 'shortened it' and also by shaving the hair off the chin – leaving the whiskers to run from the upper lip round to the cheeks – he was affecting a facial fashion popularly known as 'Piccadilly Weepers'. As with Dicke, this seemed to be all that the prosecution lawyers wished to hear from him.

Returning to court was Anne Carpenter, who had kept the Red Lion Inn in Redhill at which Hannah Dobbs had allegedly spent the weekend with Severin Bastendorff two years before. Even under quite searching questioning, nothing seemed to dim her belief that the defendant and her guest that weekend were the same man; even when it was put to her that he had a brother, and even when it was pointed out that she had, in fact, seen very little of the couple throughout the time that they were under her roof.

The last several witnesses must have produced some relief in the breast of Severin Bastendorff; for these people were to express scepticism about the claims made, and provide warming portraits of Bastendorff family life. Mrs Ellen Pearce, who had been the landlady of 42 Torrington Square when Hannah Dobbs worked there, was immediately keen to express her bewilderment about one small but crucial detail about the servants' accounts: they said that Severin had stopped initially as they were cleaning windows. But, the landlady said, 'a man was engaged to clean the windows'. More than this: 'Selina Knight distinctly stated when she took the situation that she would not clean windows . . . it was not the business of the servants to clean the windows, if they did, it was not in my presence.' The implication was that the window cleaning detail was wholly invented.

Mrs Pearce also cast puzzled doubt over the idea that a servant such as Hannah Dobbs might be able to let a man into the house surreptitiously at night, or sneak in and out at will in the small hours; the basement door used by the servants was locked after a certain time and the key, she said, was brought upstairs and was kept on the mantelshelf. This was, after all, a lodging house; and she had the security of her tenants to consider.

This in itself was not conclusive; but it appeared that Mrs Pearce had been one of the few witnesses who had not been tutored by either side before her appearance.

The really crucial element in this trial – curiously, given the unsolved murder and the allegations of further atrocities – was establishing the truth of that weekend in Redhill. Hannah and the inn landlady swore to it. But now the defence was bringing in several people who recalled seeing Severin in London on the weekend in question. The next lady to take the stand had recently lost her eyesight; but Margaret Hodson was happy to give evidence. She had been a maid servant, and she had been engaged at 4, Euston Square after Hannah had left for the first time. Her memories of the house were in sharp contrast to Dobb's sinister portrait; and she also distinctly recalled that Severin was present that weekend with his wife.

'He carried on his business there, he had a workshop at the back,' she said. 'Mrs Bastendorff was there that Saturday and in the evening, Mrs Bastendorff's mother came. Mr Bastendorff was there at dinnertime [this meant lunch] on that Saturday . . . I saw him after dinner.' Then he might have gone out; but he returned later. 'The last time I saw him on that Saturday was between 11[p.m.] and 12 when I went to bed. I saw Mr and Mrs Bastendorff and they wished me goodnight. They were in the back parlour, going to bed.'

There was another reason that particular weekend stuck out in her memory: two of the children, Christina and Peter, had measles, and were poorly. Mrs Hodson told the court that on the next day, the Sunday, 'Mr Bastendorff was in the house. I don't remember him going out at all.' His mother-in-law paid another visit; Mrs Hodson confirmed that Mary's mother was round at 4, Euston Square very frequently.

During her time working there, Margaret Hodson never saw any sign of Hannah Dobb's claim that the servant was being let into the house at night to continue her affair with Bastendorff. 'I never knew of her or anybody being let into the house,' she said. And she recalled that on the following weekends, Mr Bastendorff resumed his old routine of going shooting in Erith; taking the train down on Saturday evening and returning Monday morning. Occasionally, Mary Bastendorff took the train on Sunday to meet her husband on the Erith Marshes.

The prosecuting counsels tried to suggest to Mrs Hodson that she was getting her dates muddled; that she went to work for the Bastendorffs a little later on in the year than she thought. Mrs Hodson admitted that with the loss of her sight, it was quite difficult to be sure of much; but then she had spoken with Inspector Hagen earlier on in the Matilda Hacker investigation and the detective had found that her son kept a diary which appeared to confirm her recollection of the dates; and there was also a dated letter to her at Euston Square from a friend at Birchington On Sea.

And what of the second weekend she was there, when Severin Bastendorff was allegedly in Erith, she was asked? In reply, Mrs Hodson told the court that he 'brought back a rabbit'; the spoils of his shooting.

Now Bastendorff's mother-in-law, Elizabeth Pearce, swore her oath. She was adamant that he was there at Euston Square on the Saturday of that August Bank Holiday weekend, and not at Redhill; though he was not perhaps in the house all day. There was a chance he was absent in the afternoon. But, she told the court, he was certainly there all day on the Sunday, with the children being confined to the house with measles. Mrs Pearce, having been there on the Saturday, returned on the Sunday and was there until the late evening.

Indeed, she wanted to impress upon the court the regularity of domestic life at 4, Euston Square. 'I think I can say I have always been there on Saturdays and Sundays since they have been married,' Mrs Pearce told the court. And that particular weekend was also memorable because several days beforehand, on 2 August, it was 'the eldest boy's birthday'.

In terms of refuting the Redhill allegation, there was still that August Bank Holiday Monday afternoon to be fully accounted for: John Hackford, a 'gilder' from Weedington Street, Kentish Town, told the court that he had assembled a fishing party, comprised of Anthony Bastendorff, the defendant, Joseph Bastendorff and (as it turned out most unhelpfully for the defence) young Peter Bastendorff. The men took themselves into the hilly countryside that lay several miles north of Highbury and went fishing in a lake near Wood Green.

The memory was unhelpful because the defence had been trying to establish that Hannah had in fact spent that weekend with Severin's younger brother. 'We did not have any sport at the fishing,' said Mr Weedington. 'We only caught one fish.' This intelligence was of limited interest to the court.

Rather more cross than all the other witnesses to be standing once again before a judge was John Richards of Northumberland Heath, Erith, who had been the host for Severin Bastendorff's weekend shoots on the marshes in 1877. From August 11, Mr Richards insisted, the defendant never missed a weekend. On one of them, he was there with a couple of other German friends; on another, Mr Richards recalled, he brought along his eldest daughter Christina; and on another, Christina, his son, Peter, and wife, Mary all came.

Montagu Williams, for the prosecution, began to question Richards closely about the accuracy of his memory for dates; for at the trial of Hannah Dobbs, had he not stated that Bastendorff had come down to his house a little later in the year? Mr Richards bridled instantly at this.

'I have not been accustomed to be pulled about in a Court of Justice,' he said. 'And I don't like it. But I speak what I know to be correct. The 11th of August is fixed in my mind.' The reason was that he and his wife had been 'intending to have a holiday' but business was too good. In addition, he told the court, he could produce all sorts of bills and receipts – not only money paid to him by Bastendorff but, indeed, payments he had made to the Bastendorff furniture business for various items, which were also from that particular August.

Last to appear were two gentlemen who between them were suggestive of the strong community networks that were beginning to build in the fast expanding city. Pierre Gersthausen, a tailor then living in Gower Street, recalled that August Bank Holiday, and of how the Saturday evening was spent playing cards with a small party assembled at another friend, Mr Dicke; Severin Bastendorff, he said, joined the party at about 8p.m. and stayed until about midnight. 'It was a very wet night,' he said, 'and it rained very fast.' He concluded by stating: 'I have known the defendant four or five years,' he said, 'as a respectable, moral, truthful man.'

These sentiments were echoed by John Hoffman of Gerard Street, Soho, a messenger at the German Embassy. He, too, had joined that card party, since his wife and children had gone to the country. He paid a very similar tribute to Bastendorff: 'I have known Mr Bastendorff for about three years – he has always borne the character of a respectable, honest, truthful, decent man.'

Bastendorff might have been confident that these latter testimonies would have established the fact that he had not been in Redhill when Hannah Dobbs had claimed, and also that he was a sociable, popular man, leading a perfectly ordinary – even aspirational – family life. He might also have been impatient to press on with his own libel case in order that he may prove to the world that Hannah Dobbs' pamphlet was a nightmare of deceit.

There was an adjournment of a day or so; and it was time for 'evidence to be adduced for the defence'. The QC Mr J.J. Powell, addressed the court: he wanted the jury not only to consider what 'had occurred' at Torrington Square. But he also wanted to contend that by 'credible witnesses', he had 'disproved the statement of Hannah Dobbs' concerning Bastendorff being with her in that inn in Redhill. There were also 'discrepancies' between the evidence she gave in court and her statements in the pamphlet.

He wanted the jury to think on the accusation that 'for three weeks, the defendant had been in the habit of letting her into his house privately and after his wife and family had gone to bed, then had intercourse with her while his wife was asleep and finally turned her out before the family were up in the morning'. Such a story, said Powell, was 'utterly incredible'.

'And if it were false,' he went on, then what could have 'influenced her conduct?' The answer was in her pamphlet, he said: her confession of her inability to say no, and of her own 'moral cowardice'. Nothing had forced her to accept the 'blandishments of the gentleman connected with the Central News [Agency], backed by £30'.

The defendant, Powell continued, was a man 'against whom no charge had ever before been made, a man respected by many respectable persons . . . This was the man whom they were asked to convict of perjury, on the evidence of a person who from her own confession seemed to be the most abandoned woman that ever entered a criminal court.'

More, Severin Bastendorff had been seeking to defend himself against the publisher George Purkess, who had sold so many thousands of copies of the pamphlet. Did the jury think that Purkess cared for one moment about the 'public interest'? The man 'who collected into these publications, as into a common sewer, the literary garbage of the police cell, brothel, gaol and gallows and, seasoning it with details of the lives of criminals, poured it forth in streams most dangerous and fatal to the ignorant boys and girls who delighted to wallow in them . . . and hoped that they themselves some day might be distinguished like Hannah Dobbs by having their portraits exhibited in the shop windows of the *Police News*'.[4]

Montagu Williams rose to answer for the prosecution. It was, he said, equally 'incredible that any human ingenuity, if the story was based on deceit, could have invented all the details which had come out in Hannah Dobbs' evidence'. Those details included the comic misunderstandings surrounding Hannah Dobbs and Bastendorff's first meetings at Torrington Square; the 'unimpeachable' evidence given by the Redhill landlady; and the vanishing alibi: for if Severin Bastendorff had been out fishing on the day claimed, then the evidence given said that so too was his brother, Peter. Therefore, Peter could not have been at Redhill with Hannah.

Worse, the defendant's lawyers had victimised Selina Knight. She had 'tried to conceal the fact she had illegitimate children' but under ferocious questioning, 'this had come out' and 'now she was a ruined woman'.

There were, he said, many discrepancies over dates from those witnesses who said they had seen Bastendorff across those August weekends. The case, he said, was 'reduced to two questions'. Did the jury believe, as to Torrington Square, 'the testimony of the three girls'? If so, he said, defendant was guilty. 'Did the jury believe the evidence as to Reigate [Redhill]? If so, he was doubly guilty.'

In his summing up, the judge mused on what seemed to be Bastendorff's 'good character'; and he spoke of the 'sensational' nature of the pamphlet. But character alone, he told the jury, was not enough in a trial for perjury. Equally, even if the pamphlet had been written by 'several hands', as well as those of Hannah Dobbs, and even though she might be said to have an 'infamous character', that was no legal reason to presume that she was automatically telling untruths in this particular case. She had already been tried and acquitted for murder. And here the judge seemed to find the awkwardness, for she could not be tried again.

She had, he said, by her own admission, stayed at 4, Euston Square even after she knew about the body in the cellar; she even went about in the murdered woman's jewellery. To say the least, this placed her in a most 'unfavourable light'. None the less, no matter how 'infamous', the jury still had to focus on the alleged perjury concerning Bastendorff's denial of an affair with her. There was the word of the fellow servants at Torrington Square; and the defendant's friend who confirmed the detail of his beard length at the time.

The judge had one serious complaint, which to his mind complicated the entire matter: that Peter Bastendorff had 'not been called by either prosecution or defence'. He 'could have wished' that one or the other had done so as it 'would have possibly thrown some light on the case.'[5] This was masterly understatement; the entire relationship between Severin and his younger brother was almost wholly perplexing.

The jury was sent out. And it was two hours before they returned.

They declared to Mr Justice Hawkins that their verdict was 'guilty'. They found that Severin Bastendorff had in fact wilfully lied about his relationship with Hannah Dobbs.

Justice Hawkins declared that he found himself to be in agreement with the jury. And that Bastendorff's deceit under oath would merit a severe penalty.

For the moment, the court was adjourned; sentencing would be handed down the following week. Bastendorff was allowed to leave the court under very heavy bail conditions; two sureties of £500. It is easy to envisage him, and his defence counsels, in a trance of disbelief. There was no question that he would be facing jail; 'wilful perjury', he was warned, carried sentences of up to twelve years. But beyond that lay an even more frightening prospect: if he was supposed to have lied about the affair with the maid, then surely the wider public would believe every other allegation in the pamphlet, up to and including child murder?

24

'Such A Strange, Brotherly Part'

The furniture maker from Luxembourg was convinced that he had more than one kind of persecutor. This paranoia was soon to envelop many of his waking thoughts. The battle with Hannah Dobbs was one thing; but Severin Bastendorff was by now certain of the malevolence of the British legal establishment.

He was not alone in feeling that he had not been dealt with straightforwardly. The guilty verdict for perjury was being discussed all over London, and, indeed, throughout the country. *The Times* published an editorial reflecting this baffled perplexity, and it was re-printed with further comment added, in newspapers from Aberdeen to Kerry.

The frustration was clear: the trial should somehow have cut through the thickets of mystery surrounding the Euston Square Murder and produced something near to an answer to the enigma. But now, this conviction for perjury – Bastendorff was waiting to hear what punishment awaited – had increased the puzzlement.

'A British jury is not infallible,' stated *The Times*. The paper advised its readers to remember 'the narrow nature of the issue decided by the verdict'.

What could be made of Hannah Dobbs and her allegations? In the newspaper's view, 'if she did not explicitly acknowledge that she was an accessory after the fact to a couple of murders, she used language that admitted of no other interpretation. The truth or untruth of these suggestions was not, however, raised in the trial.'

The pamphlet 'purported to explain the whole circumstances of the murder of Miss Hacker and was in addition thereto a story of brutal vice' and 'a greedy public devoured it wholesale'. 'Whether the allegations of the story were true or false,' the leader continued, 'Bastendorff could not rest silent under them.'

The newspaper had no wish to quarrel with the jury; but it raised an interesting legal issue about the fact that 'Bastendorff himself could not be examined, even if he wished it'. That was the court procedure – defendants were not then permitted to speak for themselves. This in fact was soon to change; something *The Times* had been campaigning for. 'We are brought at once to feel how unsatisfactory the whole of this trial has been as an illustration of our jurisprudence.'[1]

The newspaper went on to describe Hannah Dobbs and her story as resembling 'that of Moll Flanders' in 'its absence of morality' and 'frequent deviations into crime'. And even though her pamphlet admitted that she had been aware of the murder, the law meant that she could not be placed on trial a second time.

The action for libel brought by Bastendorff would, the newspaper felt, have brought more light into the murk; and something should have been done 'to prevent the mischief of this trial on a partial issue' intervening to prevent it.

Hannah Dobbs' evidence 'was tainted with the odium of her own confessions that she was a thief, a strumpet, and an accessory after the fact to murder'. Meanwhile, the defendant's brother, Peter, 'who plays such a strange brotherly part in the narrative of Hannah Dobbs' was not called on either side.

The newspaper pressed for the judge to postpone his judgement; it is, the leader said, 'clearly desirable that Severin Bastendorff should prosecute his action without delay'.

But the desire to see the murder solved was not quite the same thing as sympathy for Severin Bastendorff; and a few days later this was to be made clear at the Central Criminal Court. On 17 December 1879, under the glow of gaslights illuminating the chamber in the thick winter gloom, Judge Hawkins and also Senior Judge Baron Pollock were presiding. Bastendorff was 'brought up for judgement'. Following the lead of *The Times*, his defence counsel Mr Poland began outlining a strenuous case for staying the sentencing.

Most pressing, Mr Poland told the court, 'judgement should be postponed until the trial of the action for libel brought by him against Mr Purkess had been disposed of.' The reason? 'The defendant could be examined and cross-examined and all the facts would be brought to light.' Added to this, he said, he had in his hand 'a statement signed by a number of respectable witnesses testifying to the good character of the prisoner'.

Moreover, the focus of the alleged perjury – Bastendorff's 'immoral' relations with Hannah Dobbs – was very far removed from Bastendorff trying to clear his name of the very much more atrocious allegations within the pamphlet.

What followed in that Old Bailey court, in the darkness of that cold December, was a stately legal dance. The lawyers and the judges bickered about the timings of appeals, and the proper time to make them.

Bastendorff was formally called into the dock to hear the sentencing. Justice Hawkins addressed him, saying 'perjury was a very serious offence, calling for severe punishment under any circumstances'. The reason was that justice 'could only be administered upon the veracity of an oath, and where wilful perjury was committed, it was calculated certainly to interfere with the administration of justice'.

Justice Hawkins thus pronounced sentence: 'that the defendant be imprisoned and kept to hard labour for the space of twelve months.'[2]

In the reports, there is no sense of how Severin Bastendorff reacted to this shattering prospect; but there was no pause. He would have been immediately led away from the dock, down some steps and deep into the passages that led to holding cells.

And the prospect of hard labour must have brought with it a sense of annihilation; not merely because of a sense of physical dread, but also the complete social humiliation.

Bastendorff's solicitor had forwarded to the judge a written statement from his client which was a plea for clemency: it began with a short account of Bastendorff's upbringing in Luxembourg, his emigration to England, the efforts to learn the language and find an economic foothold; his subsequent success, marriage and family.

'Wherever I have been,' Bastendorff wrote, 'I have always borne a good character and paid everyone.' And now this. 'After the discovery of Miss Hacker's remains,' Bastendorff wrote, 'my business fell off, owing to my being unable to attend to it, at Bow Street, at the trial, and elsewhere, and the general disturbance of the place.

'I have been entirely ruined,' he continued. 'The house is valueless and I cannot keep up my payments out of the business. I have had to borrow money to defend myself and they falsely accuse me of three murders and now they want to imprison me so that I shall not be able to defend myself any more. I have a wife and five children entirely depending on me for support.'[3]

The letter had made no impression; nor did the judge seem interested in that note of persecution – his enemies crowded under the simple 'they'. His situation did, indeed, seem desperate.

And what of his wife, Mary? She was pregnant again. How could his marriage possibly survive all that had been said in court? And as Bastendorff intimated, how was she to manage while he was in jail? There was at least the sense there that her mother and sister were close by; and also that Anton and Joseph Bastendorff – her brothers-in-law – might show a little support. But what sort of income could she hope to generate from letting out rooms in what was now one of the most notorious houses in the country?

Darker thoughts yet swarmed through Severin Bastendorff's mind about the devious nature of the British establishment; as would become clear later, the sense of injustice burnt like the most corrosive acid.

Some who had been through the Victorian prison system later wrote that the process of entering it could produce a form of disassociation, as if the cataclysm was not quite happening to oneself. For Bastendorff, there was the walk from the court through white-tiled passages to the waiting police cab outside, divided into cellular compartments; the obscured, dim, jigging ride through the streets of the city, crossing the bridge that lay across the underground lines at Farringdon – once the course of the river Fleet – and presently drawing up at a vast institution near the church of St James, Clerkenwell. It is possible Severin Bastendorff was in a daze as the cab reached the gate of the Clerkenwell House of Detention. If this was the case, the procedure for induction would have shocked him back into the present.

As an anonymous Captain, who had also been sentenced to be incarcerated there, wrote later:

> The reception we received in the Reception Room was far from a cordial; it was indeed as cold as the weather outside. The Reception Room is octagon shape with benches arranged over the entire floor; on these we were directed to sit down, about a yard apart. In front was a large desk and a high stool, on which a turnkey was perched, whose sole duty was to prevent the least intercourse between the prisoners. In fact the entire room and its fittings conveyed the impression of being connected with a charity school for mutes.[4]

Bastendorff would then have been required to step forward and surrender his personal property: his watch, handkerchief, any pen he might be carrying. These would be placed on a desk while they were meticulously catalogued in a Property Book.

Then, he would have been led through to another room where he would have been required to remove all his clothing. What lay ahead was the bath. All who came here were required first to scrub themselves. The same was true for the workhouses. The quality of such baths varied from institution to institution – there were some inmates, quite unused to such facilities, who thought them rather luxurious. Severin Bastendorff, on the other hand, might possibly have shuddered at the prospect. Some prison baths were described as having a coating of 'a curious slime'; others apparently had water with the consistency of 'mutton broth'.

In a broader sense, many prisoners later described this as the moment when they understood that their identities had been transformed. A former MP who had been convicted for fraud in the late nineteenth century observed: 'Even though I . . . was prepared for this experience, this breaking with the old life by the casting away of its garments proved a greater trial than I had anticipated.'[5]

As Bastendorff was immersed in this dark new world, he did have friends outside in Bloomsbury and Somers Town who were happy to let it be known that they were standing by him, and that they wanted to see the jail sentence greatly reduced, if not cancelled altogether.

'Last evening,' reported the *Daily Telegraph* on 20 December, 'a number of gentlemen interested in the case of Severin Bastendorff and 'who are desirous of seeing the Euston Square mystery fully investigated' met together at the Rising Sun tavern, Euston-road. Steps are being taken in respect to petitioning the Home Secretary for Bastendorff's release, or for a shorter term of imprisonment, as evidence has been obtained since the trial which will, it is alleged, throw discredit on the testimony of material witnesses for the prosecution.

'It was resolved by the meeting,' the report continued, 'to communicate with the German Club and other German societies, with the object of obtaining pecuniary assistance so that Bastendorff may be in a position to prosecute his action for libel against Mr George Purkess. In any event, that action will be persisted in. It is expected,' the newspaper added, 'that Peter Bastendorff will shortly make an important statement.'[6]

Perhaps another instance of the unpredictably strange relationship between the brothers; yet if any such statement were given, it was not publicly heard. Nor was there any sense that any appeal to the Home Office had even produced an official response, let alone a positive one.

And so for Bastendorff, the passing days would soon become a week, then more. He had a range of sometimes unexpected humiliations to face. The prison uniform was frequently less than uniform in the sense that it could comprise unmatched shirt and trousers, brown, blue, beige or dark red; nor was there any guarantee of underwear, or 'flannels'. Again, to a man such as Bastendorff, who had always dressed well, walking the London streets proudly, the process must have been lowering.

There had across the years been some local controversy to do with noise at the prison; the tall, gaunt eighteenth-century architecture, combined with the shape of the enclosed exercise yards, could amplify the shouts and bellows of the prisoners and turn them into a sometimes uncanny cacophony. Upon arrival, this weird echoing roar must have been terrifying. Perhaps the prospect of the cell locked might have seemed like sanctuary.

In many cases, the cells were of whitewashed brick, with black-painted doors, furnished with a hard bed, a scarcely less rigid mattress and pillow and indifferently laundered bedclothes. Even with a narrow window, the light would have been feeble. Yet here at least was the possibility of rest; one prisoner of another London prison wrote years later that even though the bed was as hard as a wooden barrel, he did, after about six months of his sentence, eventually become used to it. And, indeed, from that point, he declared, he had no difficulty sleeping on that or on any other uncomfortable surface. It was extraordinary, this former prisoner wrote, what one could always adjust to.

Bastendorff's sentence was for 'Hard Labour'; here in Clerkenwell, this had been turned into something of an art. Three immediate prospects awaited Bastendorff: in one part of the institution was a hall in which the prisoners would be gathered to sit and pick oakum. This was the process of taking old tarred and frayed ship's rope and – using fingernails and fingers – untwining it so that it was transformed into fine thread fibre, which could be used to create fresh lengths. The work was initially brutal on the hands and nails, leaving them bloody and blistered and blackened. 'The strands of the rope,' recalled one prisoner, 'had to be pulled apart until they were as fine as silk.'[7]

The rope provided for unpicking often 'in hardness and firmness, resemble[d] wire pit ropes more than anything of a hempy or flaxen nature'. At this task, the prisoner would be expected to spend anything upwards to twelve hours, and he would also be provided a target weight of unspun rope to reach. The pain and the sense of futility would have been intense at the start.

But after some time, there were those prisoners who somehow adapted; the work was a little easier on their toughened hands or they had developed the mental strength to go into a form of trance while engaged or indeed they had devised ingenious dodges to make the task a little easier: particularly prized were concealed iron nails which, while the wardens were not paying full attention, could be used to loosen up the most intransigent ropes.

In another large room, prisoners would be set to work sewing; as well as the large canvas sacks used by the Royal Mail, there were also sacks used for carrying coal; and like picking oakum, there was a physical intensity to this work that many found initially defeated them; the canvas material was too coarse, the needles provided insufficiently sharp. As well as the pain in the fingers, the frustration of continually failing to produce the required daily quota had its own cruelty.

Yet there were other forms of sewing that some prisoners came to find curiously congenial. An imprisoned Lord, William Nevell, wrote that he was set to sewing stockings, 'which almost anyone can learn in a few lessons and which after a while becomes rather absorbing'.[8] But he confessed that mistakes, such as dropping stitches, or failing to pay enough attention to the heels, could be disproportionately maddening.

And all of these above tasks would certainly have been preferable to the treadwheel; an element of hard labour that the authorities had made a particular science. First introduced to prisons earlier in the century – and occasionally a means of grinding corn – these vast wooden constructions, designed for many men (or sometimes women), standing in a row, inspired a certain species of horror. The prisoner, facing the dark wood of the wheel, would be required to 'climb' widely spaced steps as the construction turned beneath his feet. There were handrails above for steadying balance. And so, for many hours each day, with breaks at regulated intervals, the prisoner would move the wheel, his arms above him. Some who were new to it were led off at the end of the day crying.

It was not merely the utter futility; it was also the hallucinatory boredom. Even if the prison governor set a daily target of 'steps' – some suggested climbing the height of Ben Nevis, others the height of the Matterhorn, partly at least to give the prisoner a visual imaginative aid and a sense of challenge – the repetition could be deadening. By the end of a spell of the wheel, sweat would be cascading but the mind would be dulled.

This remained the case as the prisoner quickly became accustomed to the routine; even if, as in some cases, he now found that the wheel moved easily beneath him, and that he 'was walking on air', the Sisyphean element of being condemned to an eternally meaningless task would still have been psychologically harsh.

It is not known how often Severin's wife, Mary, or his brothers came to visit him; but it is reasonable to speculate that each separate visit would have constituted fresh agony for Bastendorff; a reminder that the ignominy that stained him had left that stain on them too.

Certainly, throughout the course of that year, Severin Bastendorff brooded heavily upon Hannah Dobbs and that pamphlet; and the need – as he saw it – to see justice properly done. He was at last released in the darkness of December 1880; Bastendorff was reunited with his suit, his watch, his tie, his shoes.

There is no record of whether anyone was there to meet him outside the prison gate. But it is possible he made the walk from there through the tight Clerkenwell alleys filled with watchmakers and barometer-makers to Farringdon, and thence north through Coram's Fields about a mile or so back to Euston Square; a chance to gaze in winter twilight on richly lit shops and busy streets. He might have needed some time to adjust and prepare. He was returning home to meet a new son, a baby just a few months old.

And remarkably, it was only a matter of several weeks before he was once more presenting his case to the courts, regardless of how such a course of action had resulted the last time. Severin Bastendorff burned to clear his name.

25
Disintegration

Above all else, Severin Bastendorff would appear to have owed it to his wife, Mary; over the course of the last eighteen months, she had been pulled by the wrist through a nightmare of murder and courts and scandal and prison, while pregnant and also attempting to keep an entire household economy running. She would have been piercingly aware of the swift glances that she was receiving while shopping for food; terrifically sensitive to the prospect of friends falling away, frightened by the darkness that seemed to surround her house and family.

On 26 January 1881, Mary Bastendorff suffered further strain as the Queen's Bench Division of the courts – together with a special jury, and all under the Lord Chief Justice – met to consider the original libel action against George Purkess for printing and distributing the Hannah Dobbs pamphlet.

Severin Bastendorff was present, and ready to be called as a witness. Perhaps his own state of mind does not require very much imagination to conjure.

He now had new defence counsels; and it was Mr Edward Clarke who opened the case. He explained to the court the circumstances of the discovery of the corpse; of Hannah Dobbs' trial for murder and her acquittal; and then the publication of the pamphlet. 'The plaintiff then brought his action for libel,' Clarke told the court, 'denying one of her statements imputing to him an intimacy with her.' This led to an indictment for perjury and Bastendorff's year in prison 'which he had suffered'.

Clarke told this new special jury that this libel case 'raised very grave and serious issues,' since the libel imputed to his client 'the guilt not merely of murder but of several murders'.

Just as the counsel began to go into further detail, he was halted by an interjection from the Chief Justice Lord Coleridge who said – with rather extraordinary and 'expressive' disdain – 'must this case go on?'

It took the prosecuting counsel Montagu Williams to tell him that yes, 'at present' he 'thought it must'.

'Then the mischief be done,' said Lord Coleridge. 'No doubt the parties have a right to take up the time of the Court.'[1]

There was no sense here at all of a judge who might have considered that Bastendorff had been atrociously wronged.

And the moment must have been vertiginous for Bastendorff. Yet he was clearly ferociously determined. 'Having heard the statements read from the pamphlet,' ran one report, 'he said there was no truth in the charges that it contained and the consequence of their publication had been to cause him serious injury.' Indeed, Bastendorff stated: 'I have suffered in my business and in my reputation.'[2] He did not mention prison; perhaps he had been counselled against doing so.

This time, judgement was swift – and surprising. 'A conference took place between counsel in the case,' ran the report, 'which ended in a settlement'. It was agreed; and in Severin Bastendorff's favour.

The verdict was 'for the plaintiff'. There was a 'withdrawal of the charges against the plaintiff'. And he was awarded £500 (roughly equivalent to £65,000 today, though such a sum would have gone a very great deal further; it was a fortune).

The prosecuting counsel Montagu Williams said that 'he agreed on the part of the defendant to that verdict'. That defendant, publisher George Purkess, 'also desired to express his regret that he should have published the statements, and to intimate that he withdrew them'.

Lord Coleridge, who might simply have been relieved to have been spared a lengthy case for which he had little interest, said that he 'rejoiced at the settlement of such a case, which would spare a great deal of public time that would otherwise have been taken up in the inquiry'.

There was no apology for the prison sentence; no hint that compensation for that judicial wrong might be forthcoming.

Severin Bastendorff was free to return to Euston Square and – somehow – resume his business interests and more importantly reintroduce himself to his young family. His victory was publicised in newspapers across the country.

But there was no sense that that would have been a help to him. The 'Euston Square Mystery' was still being regularly referred to in news reports as a case seemingly beyond solution. The odour and the squalor clung to his name.

The money awarded would have helped in the short term; his legal costs were also covered by the judgement, so the aim would have been to begin restoring the fortunes of his furniture business. But even in the initial relief of the win, something was broken within Bastendorff.

By this stage, Hannah Dobbs had relinquished her desire to be widely known; even if this pursuit had been less to do with the rejoicing in celebrity and more to do with a grim fight for survival and a terror of once more being accused of murder, it was clear from the hideous damage wrought by the pamphlet that discretion would now be the wiser course. There were suggestions that she and Peter Bastendorff were still romantically linked, and even that they were common-law husband and wife, in his Somers Town lodgings. But now they were very careful to avoid the press. Peter Bastendorff continued with his own furniture trade in the area. Indeed, in the years to come, this business would see some expansion.

At what point in the coming days and weeks and months did Severin Bastendorff begin exhibiting signs of frightening instability? And what triggered it? The 1881 census provided a list of the inhabitants of 4, Euston Square that summer. Severin was there, 'head' of the household, aged 34, with his occupation described as 'cabinet maker, employing 10 men and one boy'. There was wife Mary, aged 36. The children were listed: Christina, aged 8; Peter, aged 6; Severin, aged 4 (rather quaintly, the youngsters had, as their occupations, the term 'scholar'). The smallest children were Rosa, aged 3, and Richard, just one.

Interestingly, there were two lodgers: one, 26-year-old William Pierce, was also listed as a 'cabinet maker' and might have been working for Bastendorff. But there was also a 66-year-old widow called Elizabeth Powell. Had she heard of the house's bad name? Or were her circumstances such that she could not allow herself to be bothered?[3]

Clearly, with ten employees, Severin Bastendorff's business was thriving against the many bitter odds against it. His brothers, Joseph and Anton, appeared to be thriving too; the style for Chinese lacquer-work cabinets was now at a peak of fashion.

But there was a point at which Severin Bastendorff broke down; a day some time in the early 1880s, when he suddenly and blankly walked out of 4, Euston Square. What is known is that he made his way to the pleasant south London suburb of Camberwell. It had always been popular with the German community, and so it is possible that he had either friends or acquaintances there. But his ultimate destination was rather more desperate. By this stage, his behaviour was erratic enough to be noticed by the police. As would become clearer later, a large part of this involved Bastendorff having aural hallucinations and listening to voices that he said conveyed commands. He was taken off the street and conveyed to the Camberwell workhouse.

This institution, just off the Peckham Road, had been expanded in recent years, and it did not merely cater for the crisis-hit poor, or the elderly.

There was also a separate, special ward for what were termed 'lunatics'.

Some would have shuddered at the idea; it might have sounded like a recreation of the eighteenth-century 'Bedlam'. But the Camberwell architects had given some thought to a dedicated space that was – to some psychologically vulnerable inmates – a safe haven of solid brick and tall bright windows.

The ceilings were fourteen feet high, so there was no sense of claustrophobia. The floors were kept scrupulously clean, and there was a carpet in the middle of the ward. The lavatorial facilities were deemed by inspectors to be fine, and there were frequent opportunities for decent bathing too. The beds, quite close to one another, had mattresses of horse-hair but were judged to be reasonably comfortable.

And on top of this, at one end of the ward could be found skittles and games of backgammon; efforts to keep the inmates amused and happy. Like all such institutions of the time, the quality of the staff would have been variable; but for some with severe mental health problems, this special ward of the Camberwell workhouse might just have afforded valuable respite from the unfeeling clamour of the densely populated streets.

At some early stage, the authorities must have established who exactly he was; but the news of her husband's removal to such a place will have been a further horrific blow to Mary Bastendorff. Apart from anything else, she was now becoming increasingly reliant upon the kindness of Bastendorff's brothers; her own income, deriving from lodgers' rents, was minimal. Added to this, it is possible that Mary resented the close meshing of the family; and she may have resented it a great deal more when Anton Bastendorff and his wife, Elizabeth, moved into number 4, Euston Square.

In general terms, a workhouse was not a prison; the inmates were free to leave if they chose. The cruelty lay in whether or not they could afford to. But those who dwelled in the 'lunatic ward' were under much closer watch than the other workhouse inmates; granted, the attendants were not medically trained, but the vestrymen of the parish who were responsible for running the institution would have ensured that only the most temperamentally suitable people were selected for the job.

Severin Bastendorff spent some time here; the nature of his illness – listening to voices, whispering to himself – might have been growing more intense. Possibly he showed no sign of wishing to leave the ward. But gradually, after some weeks, he regained some of his old health. Eventually, someone in authority deemed him recovered enough to be discharged. But his marriage by this stage was essentially over.

It is difficult to know when Mary Bastendorff first tried to have her husband committed to the rather larger lunatic asylum at the fringes of north London in Friern Barnet. But it was clear that she no longer felt safe around him.

To have taken such a grave step, Mary Bastendorff would have involved the police; but it also involved a counter-signature on the requisite forms from one of his brothers.

So it was that the dark tragedy of Matilda Hacker's murder continued to reverberate throughout 4, Euston Square. Attendants from the lunatic asylum presented themselves at the house; Severin Bastendorff found himself being removed from the home that he had worked so hard for.

And from here he was escorted – closely guarded – to the nearby King's Cross station. A local train pushing northwards; within 15 minutes, Bastendorff's destination would be seen: a vast and elegant construction on top of a green hill. It had its own special railway sidings. He was being taken to the Colney Hatch asylum. It is possible that he found the first sight of it terrifying. Many Londoners did.

By the mid-1880s (while the records for his later spell in the asylum are complete, those for the first period there are no longer extant), the place had begun to acquire a seriously forbidding reputation. It had not begun that way. Indeed, Colney Hatch was intended as the physical expression of a renaissance in the care of the mentally vulnerable. It really was intended to offer both asylum and sanctuary.

The architecture was Italianate in flavour; there was a grand central tower with a dome. Stretching off from this were immensely long wards and dormitories, two and three storeys tall, rendered in brick. And around these buildings lay expansive gardens and fields. Colney Hatch, built and opened in the 1850s, had been conceived out of compassion; previously, those suffering from mental health problems were consigned to those special wards in workhouses, or if better-off, to the unregulated care of 'private madhouses'. Colney Hatch and its sister institution in Hanwell, to the west of the city, was the public and civic declaration that treatment and rehabilitation were possible.

Previously, mental illness had been dealt with in a manner that was almost medieval: close confinement, darkness, ignorance. Colney Hatch, by contrast, was staffed by 'physicians' and nursing staff who had an interest both in caring for and curing those who had once been regarded as incurable. To begin with, there were problems: the use of restraints, regarded by the supervising authorities as barbaric; sanitation and heating were primitive; and there was no comfort for distressed souls in the forbidding furnishings and décor.

The restraints were soon abandoned; and one of the institution's early chief movers, Dr Tyerman, brought a distinctive Victorian energy to the role. At Colney Hatch, the patients would not be idle but instead set – if they chose – to invigorating work. This, he insisted, was the opposite of exploitative.

'The great desideratum is to promote . . . uninterrupted, interesting, varying employment, which strongly claims the attention, and leaves the morbid idea no time to develop itself,' he wrote. 'A glance at the list of trades and occupations of those admitted . . . as of gas-fitters, plasterers, painters and grainers, engineers, carpenters – the resources of this immense Establishment afford opportunities . . . for developing latent and nascent intelligence.'[4]

He added that many inmates, who had previously worked in 'sedentary' occupations, greatly appreciated the chance to take up outdoors work. The fields around Colney Hatch were seeded with crops, which were harvested; the institution was self-sufficient in vegetables and corn.

There was also – as the institution evolved – a determination not to completely segregate male and female patients. There were chances to mix at mealtimes. There was cricket. Added to this, it was felt to be important that the inmates of Colney Hatch were not shut away completely from the wider world; both for their benefit, but also to ensure that the local villagers in Southgate, Barnet and Finchley did not regard the institution with fear. In the summer, there were fairs in the grounds: inmates and local people encouraged to mingle. There were concerts too, and dances. Again, these were occasions for inmates and visitors to meet; an opportunity on both sides to eradicate misconceptions and to dissipate dread on both sides.

In addition, given that the great sprawl of London built-up suburbia had not yet quite reached these hills, it was possible to take the patients out for country walks at the weekend, around Pym Brook and Bounds Green.

Yet for all of the idealism, by the 1880s, the institution had also developed, for many Londoners, an aspect of dread. Possibly one reason was that its prominent position on top of that hill, visible from miles around, was to many a constant reminder of the fragility of mental health; equally, for patients, the well-meant architecture proved oppressive in very particular ways.

There were shadowy corridors that stretched to a third of a mile; even in the brightest summer, they were dark. Patients in large dormitories were sometimes terrified of the people around them. The building was filled with echoes, in the halls, on the stairs; the noises of involuntary aggression or indeed fear would be amplified. The only element of effective soundproofing would be found in the cells that had been specially padded for emergency cases; a recent innovation.

There were never enough trained staff to give the many patients the individual care they needed. And of course, for many patients, there would have been the darkest fear: that this was now to be their permanent home. No matter how pleasing the grounds, no matter how engaged and sensitive the attendants, this was still an institution that was guarded, with a high wall. All individual agency was removed; whereas in prison, one might count out the days of one's sentence, in Colney Hatch, that sentence might be indefinite, and one might never understand why.

Was there the sense among the doctors and attendants and others who cared for Severin Bastendorff that this instability might have been an element in the fate of Matilda Hacker?

At one point, Bastendorff contrived to make an escape. This would not have been immensely difficult; there were plenty of opportunities when taking exercise to scale the wall and leave the grounds. Bastendorff would have faced a five mile walk back across the increasingly built-up hills of Hornsey and Haringey towards Euston Square; in other words, a journey of about an hour-and-a-half. For a man blazing with a sense of multiple injustices having been done to him – plus also the bewilderment of having fallen so far from the heights of successful craftsman to inmate of Colney Hatch – such a walk must have passed as in a dream.

Yet his attendants were not far behind. They caught up with him (it would not have been difficult for them to reason where he was going) and persuaded back to his new home. And indeed, there must have been an essential pacifism about Bastendorff's manner around his carers. Because a few months after that incident, he was deemed to have made sufficient progress to be discharged altogether from Colney Hatch; he was free to return home.

It might be that Bastendorff was once more lucid, and showing a keen interest in the business that he had laboured over the years to build up.

One of the elements that made Colney Hatch asylum relatively progressive in its outlook was its policy of not incarcerating patients for any longer than was deemed necessary for their own good; a man or woman might, in some cases, be discharged after only a few days.

Indeed, there were those who returned to the hospital years later not for re-admittance, but simply to convey their grateful thanks to the staff who had worked so hard to heal them.

In 1885, Bastendorff was again at liberty; and now he had returned to 4, Euston Square, reunited with his children and his wife even if – as it is reasonable to speculate – he and Mary now kept separate beds. This respite was not to last. None the less, he attempted to return to his old furniture-making work; it can only be assumed that in his absence, the other Bastendorff brothers had taken on his previous clients. Added to this, Peter Bastendorff was listing 4, Euston Square among his other business addresses, such as Hampstead Road.

There was a public flash of Severin Bastendorff's intense paranoia in the autumn of the year. It came in the form of an extraordinary newspaper advertisement that he took out in the *London Evening Standard*.

'In accordance with the law,' this advertisement ran, 'I hereby give notice that after this date, my wife Mary Snelson Bastendorff, is NOT to receive money as cashier in my business. Anyone paying money to her is liable to be called upon for the same. S. Bastendorff . . . 4, Euston Square Oct 3, 1885.'[5]

The marriage disintegrated further over the coming weeks; Bastendorff was forced to move out of Euston Square and take a room in the nearby Midland Hotel. Then there came a further crisis point as Severin returned to the house to confront Mary one morning in mid-November 1885.

He climbed the stairs to Mary's bedroom; and finding her within, he confronted her angrily 'about a £5 note' which he had 'missed'. With apparent anger, she replied that she had spent it on family 'maintenance'. He was carrying an umbrella; and at this, he raised it up and 'thrashed her with it about her shoulders'. 'She ran downstairs screaming into the kitchen where again he beat her.' The assault only ended when a young man in Bastendorff's employ, Walter Vortigan, came down to the kitchen and 'interposed'. He did so, he told the court, because he was aware of 'the other affair' that had occurred in the house and was worried that there may be another fatality.[6]

Yet Bastendorff considered himself the wronged party following this assault; and indeed waited in the kitchen as a policeman was fetched. As the constable arrived, Bastendorff made his position clear: he wanted his wife arrested. He was clearly convinced that the 'missing' £5 constituted theft.

Protesting, Mary went to the length of lowering her dressing gown to show the policeman 'the marks of violence about her'. Presumably satisfied that the assault was over, the policeman then left: no arrests, no charges. Although the courts at that time were filled with cases involving domestic violence – it is a misconception about that era that such cases were overlooked – the police were not often as assiduous as they might have been in such matters.

None the less, the incident was enough for Mary to take out a further 'summons' against her estranged husband. The aim was to have him taken back to the asylum.

Bastendorff was in no doubt that a monstrous injustice was being wrought against him. On a grim winter's day – just twenty-four hours before the summons was due to be delivered to him – he bided his time around the central garden of Euston Square and then approached his eldest children, Christine, Peter and Severin, as they returned from school. How would they like to come with him to Germany for a short holiday?

His daughter, Christine, and son, Peter, were happy to go. Somehow – extraordinarily – Mary Bastendorff was either content with this too or had felt compelled in some way to agree to this arrangement. The childrens' things were duly packed, and Bastendorff had his own small portmanteau. Mary even went with them to Liverpool Street station to see them off on the train.

As soon as he was out of the country, a warrant was issued. It seems certain that he stayed with family relatives on the borders of Luxembourg and Germany, with his daughter and son; but then he decided to return, strikingly leaving Christine and Peter behind. Upon his arrival at Euston Square, someone in the house or in the workshop alerted the police. The aim was to have Bastendorff returned to Colney Hatch and the children brought back from Germany.

But it proved a little more difficult to have Bastendorff removed this time. The case had to be heard before a magistrate and there was a delay of a few weeks. The Bastendorffs' marriage was irretrievable; Severin continued to rent a room in the nearby Midland Hotel. When the case for his assault on Mary with the umbrella was heard, the sadness of it all was once more relayed in newspapers right across the country.

Mary was called to testify against Severin; and she told the magistrate that he had 'used threats against her'. She also said that 'her children who were abroad were in a destitute condition'.

She was asked by the prosecutor: 'Have you put your husband away in an asylum?' 'Yes, I have,' she said. 'How many times?' 'Twice,' she said. 'Are you now taking proceedings against him in lunacy?' 'Yes,' she said.

The prosecutor then asked her: 'Is not your object by this prosecution to assist in the lunacy proceedings?' 'Yes,' she said. 'I applied to the relieving officer yesterday because I don't consider that he is in a fit state of mind to be around.'[7]

It emerged at this hearing that 'the prisoner's brother' (it was not stated which) 'signed the petition in lunacy on the first occasion'. But in this court in January 1886, the magistrate seemed reluctant to consign Bastendorff once more to the wards; and he ruled that he considered it unseemly that a court such as his should be used to make such a judgement upon a man's sanity. Presumably to the great dismay of Mary Bastendorff, Severin was merely bound over to keep the peace for six months.

Although there are no records, it is reasonable to assume that in the interim, one of the other Bastendorff brothers made their way to the old home in Echterdorf to fetch back Severin and Mary's children; what is certain is that in that period, Severin's mental health deteriorated further. He was exhibiting signs of what might have been seen as acute paranoia, or a sense of ceaseless persecution. Bastendorff had an increasingly agitated manner that was seen in public the following year.

He was back in the Bow Street court, eight years after Hannah Dobbs' pre-trial hearing: on 27 May 1887, Severin Bastendorff, now 45, was 'charged with being a lunatic not under proper control'. It was reported that when he was placed in the dock, he 'smiled vacantly'. Detective-Sergeant Brown told the magistrate how Bastendorff had come into the Whitehall Place police station earlier that morning and announced that he wished to make a statement.

Bastendorff had declared: 'I have been sent by Almighty God to claim £50,000. My brother Peter and his wife murdered Miss Hacker.'

'There was no doubt,' ran the report, 'that the prisoner was insane.'[8]

The quiet judgement was that he should be returned to the asylum. As Bastendorff was being led through the Bow Street corridors, he glanced up and saw a portrait of the late Mr Flowers – one of the judges who had committed him to face trial for perjury in 1879 – and he shouted: 'That man has no business there. The Lord told him to discharge me and he would not.'

And it was at this point, back in Colney Hatch, that Bastendorff's life became a subject of study by a number of interested doctors. 'Facts specified in Medical Certificate upon which Opinion of Insanity is founded' was the introductory line in Bastendorff's medical notes. 'He has the delusive idea that God speaks to him,' noted the anonymous doctor, 'that He speaks in English, French and German – that sometimes God's voice is audible close to him – sometimes it seems as if at a distance – that when I ask him a question – he listens – hears the voice of God which dictates the answer and then (Bastendorff) answers. He will not wear the Ward dress being as he says directed by God not to do so. He says God's voice is distinct like music, that God came on a cloud and he saw Him.' The verdict: 'mania'.[9]

Alfred Wilson, an 'attendant of the Insane' at the Camberwell workhouse where Bastendorff had previously been, added the observation that while he was there, Bastendorff had refused to wear the regulation trousers saying 'the Almighty had ordered him not to do so'. It is not difficult to hear the echo of Bastendorff's entry to prison in December 1879: the stripping away of the clothes that had been part of his identity, and the humiliation of being made to assume the identity of a common convict.

The receiving doctor at Colney Hatch also noted of his returned patient:

> A fairly nourished German, with a bushy, reddish beard, moustache and whiskers, a small, piercing, restless grey eye with which he winks and smirks in a silly, coquettish manner; poses and demonstrates his imaginary powers and skill by relating how he cures stones in the bladder, works miracles, coins money . . . he is egotistical and vain while relating how he has overcome false witnesses, how he has laid a claim against the government for £30,000 and obtained instead a million and a half. All this he proceeds to show is through the influence of voices from God. Pupils contracted, tongue protruded normally, speech unaffected, gait steady but somewhat constrained.

The diagnosis: 'Mania.'[10]

How might Bastendorff have been diagnosed today? Was this a breakdown, the result of the intolerable pressures of the past few years? Or was it a deeper underlying condition: manic depression, even paranoid schizophrenia? The brutal trauma of hard labour and the loss of his respectable reputation could have been a trigger; but additionally, it must be remembered that for many in those late Victorian years, having come to the vast city from rural areas, the relentless and cacophonous nature of this new urban life could eventually become overwhelming. On top of this, the records of the hospital from this time feature a striking number of European names: and it might reasonably be argued that any vulnerable immigrant, experiencing prejudice in a hundred quite different ways, might come to form a view of a society that was indeed set on persecution.

In the wards of Colney Hatch, the study of mental health was still a new science; psychology in its most basic terms was in its infancy. But there were some things that they took care to do right: at one point the colour scheme of the wards – until that point, bright whitewash – was changed to a more restful pale blue which the patients preferred. And different therapies were tried; excitable or distressed patients were allowed long hot baths and indeed spells in a specially installed Turkish Bath, which was found to aid sleep.

Added to this, the hospital expanded its facilities for different sorts of workshops, for those patients who were interested in filling their days with productive work. There were rooms for the weaving of baskets and mats; but additionally, given the large number of skilled craftsmen who were admitted as patients, there were also workshops in which furniture could be made and upholstered. In some instances, the furniture made was used in the hospital. There would have been an outlet for Bastendorff's talent in the construction of beautiful cabinets, although according to the hospital notes, he did not seem to be interested in returning to his craft: much of the time he remained 'unemployed'.

He would not have suffered any physical privations. Much work had also been done on improving the sanitary conditions and the lighting; by the 1880s, Colney Hatch had proper bathrooms, plentiful hot water and good lighting through gas. In the winter, no-one would be dirty or cold or shivering in the dark. Some patients who came here with temporarily disabling conditions – cases that might seem close nowadays to post-traumatic stress – found the asylum had actually been a terrific boon. Unlike their lives in the precarious London world outside, they had spent a lengthy period being looked after both mentally and physically, with good food and attentive warders seeing to any wounds or otherwise painful conditions.

For those detained there indefinitely, however, the flaws in the institution – which became more apparent in the late nineteenth century as numbers rose and funding became tighter – were all too visible. There were structural faults in the outwardly elegant structure on that north London hill; stonework that was already crumbling, forbidding lighting, missing hand-rails for stairs. And no matter how attentive the doctors and orderlies, no matter how strenuous the efforts to maintain hygiene and calm and to relieve the daily monotony with different activities, nothing could quite rid the place of its uncanny atmosphere; this was the fault of the architecture, which had created those seemingly illimitable echoing corridors.

In Bastendorff's records, the phrase most frequently used by doctors was 'no change'. Each year, he got a new, short (sometimes one line) summary on his patient notes. Yet there were changes. For a time, Bastendorff became agitated by the idea of telephones; that everything he said was being monitored by these machines; that there was a telephone 'perched' outside on the guttering. When he spoke to doctors, he would sometimes raise a sheet, or a length of fabric to cover his mouth, and he would speak in a half-whisper. He was adamant that he was being monitored by enemies.

Occasionally, he fell prey to the diseases that would sweep through the institution like fire; in the 1890s Bastendorff suffered a bad attack of pneumonia (though he evaded the outbreak of scarlet fever that came a little later). Food became a matter of disquiet for him; he became convinced that his foes were attempting to 'poison' him, and he could only be persuaded to eat with difficulty. One doctor noted how he had become 'much thinner'.[11]

By 1893 – six years on his ward – Bastendorff had 'delusions of grandness – that he is a king'. He was 'so feverish in his talk'. The possibilities of any future discharge were looking increasingly remote.

This was to be Severin Bastendorff's home for the rest of his life.

There were photographs taken of inmates in the late nineteenth century and the early years of the twentieth century: they are immeasurably haunting. Some of the patients – thin, sometimes mottled with the tokens of infectious diseases like scarlet fever – look at the camera directly. Others gaze elsewhere. There is no emotion in the eyes; but there is the sense behind them of the troubles that brought them to this place.

In 1899, a portrait was taken of Severin Bastendorff. He was photographed looking to the left. He was aged 52. His hair was still thick and full of colour – no discernible grey in that reddish thatch – and his whiskers were still long. His cheeks were hollow. The clothes he wore – a suit of plain material, with a high waistcoat and a patterned shirt – were some distance from the style he had been used to in his former life, but nor did he look shabby. As he looked away, what was he thinking?

Another photograph, taken later in the 1920s, showed a group of young male patients, dressed up in suits and smart clothes for a day out: some look down, some look away, some have a distinctive gait, a way of holding the shoulders, that is indicative of their condition. The clothes were intended as a means of showing those on the outside that the inmates of Colney Hatch were not 'Others' to be shunned, but all part of the same community.

Yet this was not what was portrayed in the growing popular culture of thriller novels and silent films. Increasingly, institutions like this were rendered as places of gothic menace; so many thrillers, such as *The Cat and The Canary* (1927), involve the alarms being sounded as an especially dangerous lunatic escapes; and even later, the characters around P.G. Wodehouse's Bertie Wooster can be found accusing him and others of insanity, and threatening them with incarceration in Colney Hatch.

This was the only world that Bastendorff knew for the remaining twenty-two years of his life. The hospital notes give no indication of whether – or how often – his wife and now grown-up children managed to visit him. Would he have even received them? Underneath that carapace of delusional behaviour was one strong recurring theme: that of a proud man who had been grievously wronged.

He lived until the spring of 1909 and died aged 62, of a heart complication.

When he was taken for burial, his sons and daughters would have been in early middle age. How much did they tell their own children about the father whose mind had been broken?

In the absence of Severin Bastendorff at Euston Square back in the 1880s, it seemed that the other brothers decided to take it on. They had their own troubles. In 1893, Anton Bastendorff was summoned to Clerkenwell magistrates, charged with 'neglecting to maintain' his wife, Caroline. Indeed, it seemed she had ended up in the St Pancras workhouse, and was now 'the responsibility' of the Guardians there (as the couple's five children remained at home). Anton Bastendorff 'denied that he failed to support his wife' and the reason for her present state was that she had fallen into 'intemperate habits'. He made arrangements to have her removed back to his address: 4, Euston Square.

Yet there were suggestions that both Anton and Caroline were heavy drinkers; and it appeared that she died not too long afterwards of what was described as 'quinsy' – a septic complication of tonsillitis against which there would have been little defence at that point.

By this stage, the Bastendorffs' sister Elizabeth was living in London (after some time in Paris) with her husband, Wilhelm Hoerr. And it appeared that also living with them was Peter Bastendorff. There was no official suggestion come the 1880s or 1890s that Hannah Dobbs was by his side; yet would it not have been possible that she had changed her name as she had before? The notoriety she had experienced had not brought any sort of gain; indeed, it would have made her utterly unemployable. Who would even consider having such a maid around their domestic establishment after her barrage of accusations, and her self-confessed kleptomania?

The bamboo furniture business, it seemed, continued to thrive for a time; after all the horrors of the body in the cellar, the family name was once more seen in regular advertisements across the city. Indeed, these featured in upmarket periodicals.

Yet Peter Bastendorff by the 1890s had taken a step to disassociate himself with any other memories of the family name: moving premises in north London, he began using the name 'James Roberts' for company business. And as the decade wore on, was Peter afflicted with some form of nostalgia for a city he had fleetingly known years back? Whatever the case, it would appear that he left London, sailed across to France, and made a new home in Paris. By this stage, he would have been about to turn 40 years of age. It is simply impossible to know: was Hannah with him? Would she perhaps have now lived with him under the name 'Hannah Roberts'?

Paris by this stage, suffused with the new light of electricity, had been reborn in elegance. It would have been a thrilling city in which to begin a new life, especially given the circumscribed possibilities of life back in London.

Yet this might be an assumption too far; Hannah Dobbs' own disappearance – or the vanishing of her old self at any rate – seems to have been too complete for anything to be stated with iron certainty.

According to one suggestion put forward in a genealogy discussion conducted a few years ago, Peter Bastendorff's move to Paris was his last: he was said to have died in January 1898. He was also said to have left the sum of £160 (now worth about £11,000) to his sister, Elizabeth. There was no hint of any other bequests; not a suggestion that a more constant companion had inherited more.

But the business notices in the national newspapers in London announced the winding up of his remaining commercial concerns; that the company James N. Roberts, 'trading as' Peter Bastendorff, a bamboo furniture maker, was now bankrupt.

And by this stage, 4, Euston Square seemed to have gained, rather than faded, in notoriety. Which each passing year, the dank mystery of Matilda Hacker seemed to become ever more tantalising to an ever-widening reading public. Indeed, the house was about to take on a most unwelcome new life.

26
A Length of Washing Line

The police and the Home Office had tried to think of different angles by which they might have attacked the investigation; re-arresting Hannah Dobbs on a charge of larceny had been one idea to once more bring all the concerned residents of 4, Euston Square to court in the hope that more light be let within. But then, in the wake of the perjury and libel trials, it seemed clear that anyone who might have had any confession to make was going to hold rigidly to their carefully crafted stories.

Certainly, there was nothing more that the Scotland Yard detective Charles Hagen could do; and in any case, there was a range of new cases to occupy him. At the time, increasing numbers of passionately angry and radicalised French and German émigrés were settling in the area around Fitzroy Square (where the Bastendorffs had begun their careers). Some had set up inflammatory anarchist and socialist newspapers and, in 1881, Hagen was forced to make several arrests, following the publication of one particularly seditious journal.

In April of that year, Hagen, with three colleagues, raided the offices of *Freiheit* (which means political freedom or liberty) and arrested the editor Johann Most, who was, as the reports said, 'deprived of his watch, money, bank book and letters'. The offices were said to be in 'a very dirty condition'; Most was described as 'a literary man';[1] he was rather more than that. An exile from Germany, he was one of the continent's most voluble anarchists, who believed fervently in the legitimacy of violence for political ends. The arrest was prompted by the paper's exultant reaction to the bloody assassination of the Russian Czar Alexander II. The charge, curiously, was 'libel'; the underlying concern was clearly about the contagion of revolutionary sentiment. This was already a time of Fenian dynamite bombings in London and around the country. Hagen and his Scotland Yard colleagues were clearly concerned about anarchic Europeans sparking more violence. Such bomb-throwing figures would later inspire Joseph Conrad's chilling novel *The Secret Agent*.

These were the sorts of émigrés that would have made the Bastendorff brothers flinch; they had come to London to participate in this blossoming bourgeois life, not to scorn it.

Charles Hagen won promotion again in the meantime, rising to become Chief Inspector of the Metropolitan Police. Although he was now less frequently out in the field, he still took a particular interest in cases that had a continental flavour. What cannot be known is if he ever had an itching sense of frustration about the Matilda Hacker case. It was upon his instincts that Hannah Dobbs had been charged; and there had never been any indication that he had been satisfied by her acquittal.

Did he occasionally sit back, late into an evening, and brood over other possible explanations, motives, killers? Who else might possibly have been in 4, Euston Square, and who might have had some murderous intention that escaped initial attention?

His interest might have been revivified by the news of Severin Bastendorff's removal to the asylum; reflexively nervous attitudes to mental health back then must have made Hagen wonder about the possibility. It is more difficult to see now. The assault upon his wife with an umbrella notwithstanding, Bastendorff was certainly delusional but he did not seem to be suffering from psychosis. Nor indeed among his later hospital notes was there the least indication of violent tendencies.

Yet should we pay more attention to Hannah Dobbs' pamphlet? If we were to do so, we would have to think of the Bastendorff that she and the journalists portrayed: a man seemingly perpetually in the tight grip of financial worries; a sexual adventurer with an apparent disregard for consequences. The police of course found – and Hannah Dobbs admitted – that the stories of a murdered Mr Findlay and a nameless little boy and indeed a dog were little more than fairy tales. But what of Matilda Hacker?

The exact date of her death was never established; so in one sense, Bastendorff's alibi about having spent the weekend shooting in Erith might have been disregarded. But what then could possibly have happened? We would have to envisage the eccentric lady returning from one of her promenades, or perhaps from a mission to her Lincoln's Inn solicitor, and letting herself into 4, Euston Square with her latchkey. Is there the chance that Bastendorff had picked up on the truth of her reasonably substantial wealth? Had he glimpsed the expensive-looking clothes and jewels and imagined that they betokened greater hidden riches? Had Hannah Dobbs mentioned the 'roll' of bank-notes that the old lady kept concealed within her clothes?

Miss Hacker had of late become a favourite with his young children; perhaps he had heard them excitedly discussing the grand old lady and *The Book of Dreams*. Perhaps the lady had woven some fantastical yarns about herself to the children.

But then a great leap is required; to picture the circumstances in which Severin Bastendorff might enter her room with the intention to rob her. Perhaps he has waited until she is out upon one of her errands. We would have to imagine him moving through that garden-facing second-floor room, searching the drawers of her writing desk, or examining the clothes that she always kept not in the wardrobe but in her hamper trunk, patting them down for money. A noise upon the stair, a movement of the door knob; Miss Hacker has returned unexpectedly to behold the scene. And she understands very quickly what it is about.

So we would have to imagine Severin's panic; his efforts to silence her instant, noisy outrage. Matilda Hacker was known to have a temper like molten lava; and a scene such as this would be sufficient for an eruption. And so it is that Bastendorff might grab hold of her, to stop her shouting to his wife; and perhaps the struggle grows more physical, more furious, and then in his panic, his hands move to her throat in an effort to muffle her noise. She struggles furiously; he tightens his grip; and now the only thing that matters is ensuring that she makes no noise at all. Soon, there is nothing; her eyes are wide but there is no breath.

Then the aftershock of horror; the blank fugue state as he waits to make sure the house is quiet and empty, then carries her body downstairs, out to the kitchen, and then swiftly out of the basement door, and across the narrow yard to the coal cellars, where he secrets her in the furthest corner. He finds a length of clothes line; perhaps he is frightened she is still alive. So a couple of minutes in that musty darkness, winding the line around the old lady's neck, and pulling it tight until he can be completely sure that there is no trace of breathing.

But none of this makes much sense, even in a case of psychosis. If the motive was primarily financial, why would Bastendorff have bestowed several highly identifiable items of value upon Hannah Dobbs? Surely he would have taken them himself to a pawn shop very far from the house, and then used the cash for whatever purpose he chose?

And again, even in a case of psychosis, it would require quite an extraordinary level of abstraction to give no further thought to a corpse in a cellar which was frequently used by servants, and regularly seen by delivery men. Surely his priority, if this had been the case, would have been to await the most opportune moment to remove the body, take it a long distance from the house, and perhaps dispose of it by night on the wild heathlands of Hampstead or Epping Forest?

There is another faint – and distinctly baroque – possibility that might have commanded the attention of Inspector Charles Hagen: that the murderer of Matilda Hacker was not a resident in the house at all. Hagen would have seen, one year after the trials, an intriguing news report concerning an alleged long-lost brother of Matilda Hacker called Edmund, who had been missing for some considerable number of years; and of how Edmund's children were now petitioning to be recognised in the wider Hacker family inheritance (which had been added to by Matilda Hacker's property interests).

For the purposes of the legal action, the children were asking the courts to accept that Edmund Hacker was dead. Anyone who had read the enormously popular Charles Dickens novel *Our Mutual Friend*, first published in 1864, might have immediately wondered to themselves if the wider family could really be so certain that he was in his grave. The contrivance in the Dickens story is of a wronged protagonist, thought to have been murdered, who moves among the streets of London under an assumed identity.

The fortunes of the Hacker family seemed strikingly eccentric as they were; was it beyond the realms of possibility that this brother, who appeared to have abandoned his wife and children, was not dead?

What if this brother had been among those in pursuit of Matilda Hacker, those aggrieved creditors? What if he had returned from wherever he had been, in need of some of that family inheritance of which she had now received such a grand share thanks to the death of their sister? She moved like a nervous sparrow from house to house; was it partly not merely to evade irritated builders and tenants but also a rather more shadowy figure from her earlier years?

But to imagine such a shadowy figure, perhaps following her back to Euston Square from the lawyer's office in Lincoln's Inn, is somehow too reminiscent of a Wilkie Collins novel: the long estranged brother biding his time outside Euston Square, effecting entrance, confronting Matilda Hacker in her room when he knows the house to be largely empty. It would not explain murder, nor quite why such a figure would risk discovery by spending time looking for a suitable hiding place in the cellar for the body.

And indeed the news story might not have been as firm as it first seemed; for there was no subsequent attempt to follow it up. This was not for lack of interest in the Euston Square Murder, which was to crop up frequently in the press for many years yet.

And so the strongest possibility is that Charles Hagen's instincts were right after all. If we look once more at Hannah Dobbs – even through the distorting glass of the ghostwritten memoir – we see interestingly that she, like her employer, might have been subject to a particular mental health condition.

Her kleptomania was perhaps a symptom of something wider. Even in her own words, she was fascinatingly blank about the endless compulsion to steal, and about her complete inability to regard the property of others as private. But she was also fascinatingly blank about much else. This was clear not merely in the pamphlet but also in her many appearances in court, which took on increasingly theatrical aspects. The lies simply grew larger and ever more baroque and then utterly grotesque. What then if this was not a desperate survival strategy but in fact the indicator of a deeper derangement?

Hannah Dobbs' mother had reported early on in the case that she feared that her daughter would bring disgrace. What if she meant a stigma rather darker?

In today's terms, we might understand Hannah Dobbs better as a sociopath: utterly lacking any empathy or remorse. This of course would not automatically make her a killer. But what if the relationship between herself and Matilda Hacker had been more complicated than the jury could guess?

In that 1887 court appearance before he was taken to Colney Hatch, Severin Bastendorff exclaimed that the old woman's death was the responsibility of his brother, Peter, 'and his wife', meaning Hannah. It is possible that he was closer to it than anyone. There clearly was a fervid atmosphere within 4, Euston Square in that autumn of 1877; and Matilda Hacker might have been sensitive to it as well.

We can imagine her having retired to bed for the night; her bedroom in darkness, the occasional noise of a passing horse-drawn cab outside. She might be aware of Mr Riggenbach downstairs preparing for bed. And then the house becoming still and quiet. But then we would also imagine how Matilda Hacker – in common with ladies of her age, a light sleeper – would then awake in the darkness of the small hours, fully alert. She would be acutely sensitive to the noise of furtive footsteps trying to find the places on the stairs that would not creak. The movement on the upper landing, the sound of doors being opened and closed quietly.

It would be on nights such as these when a lodger would understand that these houses could have an uncanny quality, putting them some distance from feeling like a family home. An unfamiliar tread on the stairs would heighten any sense of vulnerability; and there would also be the discomfort of sensing that the house is permeable, porous; that even when it was supposed to be locked up at night, strangers could still be creeping past your door.

And the response to being awoken and then lying in that state of tense speculation about who was abroad in the small hours would naturally be one of anger.

This is the time when lovers meet secretly; the maid and the young man who has his own latchkey. Matilda Hacker lies and listens to the forbidden assignation. Perhaps she has heard two or three times. Perhaps, as a result, she is becoming increasingly furious about life in number 4, Euston Square.

Then the scene of crisis: a Sunday afternoon on the cusp of autumn, as Matilda Hacker returns from one of her promenades in Hyde Park, she climbs the stairs to her room on the second floor. She opens the door and instantly she is suspicious. There is a sense of the furnishings and of her belongings having been disturbed. She has recently been watching the maid Hannah Dobbs, and has noted that she does not have the submissive eye of a servant; there is something too bold there. She suspects the girl might be a thief.

The house is quiet; Severin Bastendorff has gone down to Erith for more shooting; his wife has gone up the road to pay a visit on her mother; Mr Riggenbach is out on business. Out the back, the furniture workshop is closed for the sabbath. Perhaps Matilda Hacker has the house to herself.

The old lady looks into her hamper. Her belongings have certainly been moved about; though it does not look at first as if anything has been taken. None the less, there is something so brazen about the speculativeness of the rummage that Miss Hacker finds herself burning with rising indignation. She considers ringing for Hannah Dobbs; a tug of that length of material on the wall, the corresponding bell agitating in the kitchen. Yet even in her anger, she waits; for the smallest of creaks from up the stairs tells her that there will be a more opportune moment yet for furious confrontation.

And as Matilda Hacker sits motionless at her writing desk, staring out of the window at the cabs below, another creak, and another, then the sound of feet coming down the stairs, rouses her from her trance.

She moves to the door of her room and opens it at precisely the moment when those feet reach her landing. Matilda Hacker has surprised both Hannah Dobbs and Peter Bastendorff, who stand there in that semi-darkness. Perhaps there is a small smile of triumph on the older woman's face. Perhaps Hannah Dobbs silently and urgently beckons Peter Bastendorff back up the stairs. The maid is supposed to be in charge of the children; the eldest have been persuaded to play in the attic – the baby is asleep – while the two lovers have carried out their secret encounter. And as Peter nods and moves, Matilda Hacker tells the maid that she wants to know what she means by it.

Hannah Dobbs replies that she does not know what Miss Uish means. Again, there is a hard defiance in the maid's eye and something odd about the shape of her mouth – not a sneer, but not quite straight either. The old lady beckons her over the threshold of her room.

Both women hear the noise, from above, of Peter Bastendorff joining the children in the attic for their games while the baby sleeps.

With her anger sharpening, Matilda Hacker now accuses Hannah Dobbs of theft; the maid hotly denies it. The old woman shouts that her possessions have been disturbed, and that no-one had permission to rifle through her belongings; again, the maid denies it, her own temper rising.

It is then that Matilda Hacker, now almost in a trance of anger, tells Hannah Dobbs that she knows all about her dealings with Peter Bastendorff; how she has heard them through the night. Miss Hacker tells the maid she is resolved to speak to Mary Bastendorff about the squalid dealings taking place under her roof. A maid with no morals, and a young German tradesman slaking their lust in what should be a decent family home. Theft and fornication: these, declares Miss Hacker, are the foundations of 4, Euston Square.

From her time working on a dairy farm, Hannah Dobbs has long been physically strong; and when the old lady makes a move seemingly for the door, the maid moves to block her progress, going so far as to seize the old lady by the wrist. At first, in her flat voice, Hannah seeks to persuade the old lady that she is mistaken; that Peter Bastendorff is a particular friend, and that the only time she enters the lady's room is to clean it.

The two women are engaged in a clumsy dance; the old lady struggling to get free of Hannah Dobbs' grip, Hannah gradually pushing her back closer to the fireplace where some coal still glows from the morning fire. Matilda Hacker becomes ever angrier, and begins to use coarse language concerning the maid and her behaviour; and she is stronger than she looks too, for as the words come out in a near-growl, she is jerking back and forth, pulling the maid with her. Their struggle becomes more physical yet, with the maid attempting now to seize both the old lady's arms. Matilda Hacker's right arm comes free, and swings; a new glass gas lamp is knocked off the mantel-shelf, and it crunches into the green carpet.

Matilda Hacker, now trying to free herself from the maid's strong grip, shouts that she will let everyone know what sort of a girl she is; and Hannah now simply staring at the old lady, very suddenly lets her go; and equally suddenly shoves her hard towards the bed and the desk, so that she falls, catching the back of her head against the sharp edge of the table. Matilda Hacker screams.

Perhaps it is this that is unendurable to the maid; for now, she lowers herself, and sits heavily upon Matilda Hacker and jams her hands hard up against the old lady's mouth and nose to stop her making any more noise. The old lady's eyes continue to flicker with anger; nothing registers in the gaze of Hannah Dobbs. Matilda Hacker tries in vain to move her head, and her face now becomes redder; Hannah Dobbs simply increases the pressure. The old lady's anger turns completely to fear; but she is helpless.

The suffocation is slow; and in the meantime, the skin that was broken on the back of her head against that sharp table edge is bleeding with great profusion, as even the shallowest head-wounds do. The blood is seeping out across the green carpet as Hannah Dobbs, her expression perfectly featureless, does not let up the pressure from her hands on Matilda Hacker's nose and mouth until the old woman is unconscious.

All of this is a possibility if we see Hannah Dobbs' behaviour patterns as forming a portrait of sociopathy.

The curious pattern of self-sabotage in her career – thefts that she seemingly could not help committing, lies that she could not resist telling – spoke of a wider lack of empathy. When she was on trial for her life, the newspapers might have admired her composure, and her attention to appearance; similarly, they might have also noted her extraordinary lack of fear when facing the possibility of the death sentence. Certainly there were moments when she appeared under stress, as the verdict was brought in; but there was an innate showiness, even a flavour of inauthenticity, about this and her subsequent public appearances, either leaving prison or testifying against Severin Bastendorff.

Equally certainly, Hannah had been in a furious fight for survival; but this was a struggle in which any fellow feeling that she might have once had for the family she lived with was completely eliminated. The carnival of untruths she presented for the delighted ghost writers of that pamphlet went beyond simply ensuring her own safety, and instead spoke of an almost clinical destructiveness. Nor was it inspired by hate or rage; she very simply lied because she could not help herself. Her greatest need was for the world to accept the narrative that she herself was writing of her life.

So we might see that the prospect of Matilda Hacker revealing her squalid secrets would trigger in Hannah Dobbs not murderousness, exactly, but more an impulse to ensure that her version of the truth remained; the old woman literally had to be silenced. This was how.

So we must imagine that dark quiet house, the lamps as yet unlit, on that autumn afternoon in 1877; the suggestion of laughter from the rafters above as Peter encourages the children's games. Hannah now standing and gazing down at the old woman. Of course, there must be no possibility that anyone must know of this; Hannah Dobbs is going to pretend that Matilda Hacker has gone away.

And so it is that she quite methodically goes to the cellar to pick up a length of oilcloth; takes it back upstairs and lifts the fat old woman on to it. Perhaps Hannah Dobbs has noted that despite Matilda Hacker's unconsciousness, there seems to be fitful breathing. She knows she has to be quick.

The old lady and her bleeding head has now become simply a mass wrapped in oilcloth, which Hannah Dobbs is dragging through the door, and down the stairs. Again, anyone else doing this might have been quivering with fright at all the possibilities – people returning to the house, the old lady roaring back into life – but for a sociopath, all that would matter would be the objective: getting this mass out through the scullery and through to the coal cellar. The oilcloth has absorbed the blood from the head wound.

And, in the glittering darkness of that coal cellar, Hannah Dobbs would have known just how far over the line she was; and what she would now have to do. She remembers that spare length of washing line; hurries to fetch it.

The strangling does not seem to take long; the old lady has never recovered consciousness and so there is no resistance. Hannah Dobbs drags the body into the furthest corner of the cellar.

Then, the shovel; moving a pile of coals to make room for the body in the oilcloth; the body then moved into the space; then the coals moved back on top of it.

There, Hannah Dobbs might think to herself. She has gone away.

The effort to clear the blood and the broken glass from the old woman's room is more strenuous; and now, with the children distracted once more, Hannah must enlist the help of Peter. Is he too naïve to see in her eye what has happened? Is he the first person that she tells that the old lady has left?

Is there perhaps a hideous thrill for the young man that his lover has acted so decisively?

It is his job to pack some of Matilda Hacker's belongings in her wicker trunk; and to take that trunk to the attic. Perhaps Hannah has told him that the old lady has left in such a rage that she could not be bothered to take her goods.

And so it is that even when Francis Riggenbach returns later that afternoon from his calls on friends, there is nothing in the house that suggests that violence has taken place. The children have now been brought downstairs; and Peter Bastendorff has already, discreetly, left, to return to his own lodgings around the corner. Hannah Dobbs, in the meantime, is perfectly calm, as she lets the children try to pick out tunes on the piano in the front room.

27

The Stain That Would Not Go

Even back in 1879, after Hannah Dobbs' trial and acquittal, the residents of Euston Square had been horrified by the noisy attention that it was attracting; and by the time of Severin Bastendorff's trial for perjury, horror was mixed in with squalor; here was a story that suggested that the neighbourhood was low. The gawping public might imagine each of these houses filled with lodgers and servants, transients all, living lives of sexual promiscuity and betrayal. Worse though than the ghoul-tourists who were marching up and down the pavements, peering over the edge of the railings of number 4, Euston Square down into the front basement area, was the possibility that this lurid case might also affect the value of all the neighbouring properties.

Partly this was the concern of an association of Euston Square residents who petitioned the authorities (from the parish council onwards) to change the name of the square. The new suggestion was 'Endsleigh Gardens'. But they were not – immediately – to be granted that wish. They made representations to the St Pancras Vestry (the local council). The following year, on the south side of Euston Square, the name was changed. Endsleigh Gardens remains on the street signs to this day.

But the reputation of the house lingered. In 1906, newspapers were serialising a new fiction by best-selling novelist Charles Pearce called 'The Hidden Hand'. In one passage, two women are walking in the area:

> She walked by Angela's side keeping very close, disagreeably so, the girl thought. 'You'll excuse me my dear, but I always feel awfully creepy when I pass this spot.'
> [It was Euston Square.]
> 'Why?' asked Angela.
> 'There was a murder committed in that house,' said the woman, dropping her voice and pointing across Angela. 'The body of a woman was found in the coal cellar and it was never discovered who murdered her. She was lying there about two years. Her name was Matilda Hacker. Perhaps you've heard of her?'[1]

By the 1920s, the rumours that the house was horribly haunted began. These were picked up (and amplified greatly) by the great 'true' ghost story anthologist Eliot O'Donnell. This prolific author made the perfectly unverifiable claim, in the 1930s, that his aunt had known Matilda Hacker – hence his unusual interest in the terrifying things that were said to have happened in her room years after the murder.

For a start, it was said that the bloodstain that Mrs Bastendorff had found on the carpet had soaked through to the boards – and no matter how hard and how repeatedly they were scrubbed, nothing would make the stain go. Added to this, the bloodstain was one of the focuses of 'super-physical' manifestations.

'At around the same time every night,' O'Donnell wrote, 'the most awful sounds were heard proceeding from the room, the climax being reached when a piercing, blood-curdling scream, suggestive of untold terror and pain, rang out, followed by a heavy thud and sounds like the opening and shutting of the room and the dragging of some heavy body across the landing and down the staircase to the hall.'[2]

Other manifestations of haunting: people witnessing the door handle of Miss Hacker's room twisting violently on its own. There were also bad dreams: claims from those who slept in the room of troubled nights. The theme was always the same: the room's cupboard door creaking slowly open in the darkness and of something 'very uncanny' emerging.

In addition to all this, dogs refused to go into the room; and even passing it on the landing would make them cry piteously.

There came a point, in the 1920s and 1930s, when many such boarding houses around Euston and St Pancras and King's Cross sank into what seemed like irredeemable frowsiness: this was the seedy world depicted by novelist Patrick Hamilton in *Twenty Thousand Streets Under the Sky* and by Jean Rhys in *After Leaving Mr McKenzie*; yellowing lightbulbs, peeling wallpaper, and dreams of happiness or even simply security that would never come close to being fulfilled.

Because of University College London, and all its attendant departments, the large contingent of students in the area meant that it never sank quite as low as Agar Town, or Maiden Lane. But to seek out lodgings in the area of Euston Square come the middle of the twentieth century meant that perhaps not all of life's plans had come to fruition.

The heavy-handed vandalism of 1960s city planners and British Rail architects swept all memories and traces from the north end of Euston Square in 1960. The classical railway station – and the stone arch that framed its entrance – was obliterated. The replacement station concourse, a construction of concrete and glass, had the modern suggestion of an airport. Number 4, Euston Square, together with all the other houses in that terrace, which had escaped the attentions of the Luftwaffe in the Blitz (not so Endsleigh Gardens and Drummond Street) was flattened to make way for a swish new black-paned office development and a bus stand.

And the streets around – all those great lines of nineteenth-century boarding houses – became progressively seedier in the 1970s and the 1980s. One hundred years beforehand, there had been some concern about such houses proving fertile ground for immorality; by the second half of the twentieth century, the areas of north eastern Bloomsbury, Somers Town and Battle Bridge, were notorious for drugs and prostitution.

Yet in recent years, change has come once more; and the Bastendorffs, if they could see, might be intrigued by the renovated houses that now play host to eager travellers from the Continent, who have arrived at St Pancras on the Eurostar railway lines. The German Gymnasium is no longer a gymnasium – it is instead a thriving and very smart restaurant noted for its breakfasts. Meanwhile, the streets in which Mary Bastendorff's relatives lived, near St Pancras Old Church, gleam with fresh paint. But there is still a sense in the wider area around the railway stations – in all those estates and tenements – that it is a place where new arrivals try to gain a foothold, hoping to prosper in the impossibly rich city.

The horror and the tragedy that overwhelmed Severin and Mary Bastendorff and their children was, in part, a hideous collision of different people who had sought to mould new lives and identities for themselves in the streets of London. But those streets then – and now – also had a blankly pitiless quality.

It was also, in part, a fable of modern city life, which is precisely why it attracted so much attention on both sides of the Atlantic. Publications such as *The Spectator* may have jocularly dismissed any notions that people living in London's boarding houses should be alarmed; but it rather callously ignored the point that so many of these people were women, sometimes of a certain age, who felt vulnerable. This was a story not just about fear of crime, but also a certain economic fear too; that the only way one might afford to live in the city would be to live among strangers.

At a time when London's population is once more expanding enormously, it is an idea that finds a curiously modern currency; the city on first glance might appear to be a market of entirely self-enclosed houses and apartments, where bathrooms and kitchens are private.

Yet in many areas, this is very far from being the case; in suburbs from Kingsbury to Barking, so many houses are not merely 'multi-residency' with shared facilities but are in fact packed with tenants, sleeping in bunk-beds, on mattresses, in ill-ventilated basements.

To live in such a city, in such a way, requires a hundred daily negotiations and understandings. For the Bastendorffs, it meant having strangers in the family home; and for their tenants, it meant having trust that one's fellow residents were essentially benign.

Matilda Hacker has recently been commemorated in a rather unexpected way: becoming the subject of a play that was staged in her home city of Canterbury.[3] For the other remarkable aspect of her story, the one that still resonates today, is one woman's determination to live outside of all social conventions, blithely stepping away from any kind of responsibility. As well as the horror, there is also a curious element of liberation in her story.

For Hannah Dobbs, however, no such freedom was available; she might have imagined, as she gazed on pictures of London society and became hypnotised by the clothes and the jewellery, that it was possible for a woman with no means to attain such a life. London of the 1870s allowed for her sense of adventure but little else. What sort of a world did she and young Peter Bastendorff inhabit as they lay in bed side by side?

Meanwhile, Severin Bastendorff was ultimately devoured by the city; not merely the suspicion of murder, but the utterly remorseless cynicism that went into proving (or not quite proving) his affair with Hannah Dobbs. To have ended being cared for in an institution such as Colney Hatch suggests that Bastendorff may have had mental health problems all his life; it is certainly without question, whenever the first symptoms showed, that the chain of events following the discovery of the body were more than sufficient to destabilise his delicate balance.

Even today, the act of taking in lodgers is a remarkable act of trust in an otherwise wholly anonymous urban world. The lodger trusts that he or she will be safe and secure under the roof of the landlord to whom they are paying rent; and equally, the landlord will have to trust that he has not admitted into his household someone of anti-social or frightening tendencies.

Even more pressingly, though: there are prospective tenants from around the world who will be looking and hoping to find not atomised loneliness in such a home but instead the warmth of a surrogate family.

Back in the 1870s, what was never pointed out at the time of the Euston Square tragedy was that countless thousands upon thousands of newcomers to London had found exactly that.

Notes

Preface

1 – An 1876 lease for 6, Euston Square, in the same terrace, contains wonderfully evocative descriptions. The original document is held at the London Metropolitan Archives. Ref: 0/462/011

2 – The interview appeared on 5 January 1879. A reproduction of it can be found (among other places) at www.marxists.org/archive/marx/bio/media/marx/

Chapter 1

1 – Severin (sometimes spelled 'Sewerin') Bastendorff's naturalisation certificate is at the National Archives. Reference HO 334/8/2587

Chapter 2

1 – These and other minute details of the discovery in the cellar and the movements of all parties concerned emerged on the first day of the inquest two weeks later. All national (and, indeed, local) newspapers reported on the proceedings, with very slight variations of quotes. A report can be found in *The Times*, 22 May 1879.

2 – As above

3 – As above

4 – As above

5 – As above

6 – As above

7 – As above

8 – As above

9 – The account of the medical examination was reported in *The Times* on 22 May 1879

10 – As above

11 – As above

Chapter 3

1 – As reported in the *North London News*, 17 May 1873

2 – As reported in *Reynolds Paper*, 23 December 1877

3 – As above

Chapter 5

1 – Correspondents from a variety of newspapers across the country were sent to Bideford. There were pooled reports too. This featured in Dublin newspaper *The Advertiser* on 15 May 1879.

2 – As above

3 – Detail featured in the *Western Morning News*, 15 May 1879

4 – Details relayed by the Press Association to all newspapers, 16 May 1879
5 – Detail featured in *Birmingham Daily Post*, 16 May 1879
6 – Details relayed via telegram to all newspapers by the Press Association, 16 May 1879
7 – Report of inquest proceedings from *The Times*, 17 May 1879
8 – As above
9 – As above
10 – As above
11 – As above
12 – As above
13 – As above
14 – As above
15 – As above
16 – As above
17 – The further mortuary details as reported in *The Times*, 17 May 1879
18 – As above
19 – As reported in *Reynolds News*, 17 May 1879
20 – As above
21 – Severin Bastendorff, as relayed to a correspondent from the *Dundee Courier*, 17 May 1879
22 – As above
23 – As above

Chapter 6
1 – From 'The Adventures of Philip on His Way Through the World: Shewing Who Robbed Him, Who Helped Him and Who Passed Him By' by William Makepeace Thackeray, first published in serial form in *Cornhill* magazine, 1861–62
2 – *Paul Kelver* by Jerome K Jerome (Hutchinson and Co., 1902)
3 – *The Nether World* by George Gissing (Smith, Elder, 1889)

Chapter 7
1 – *The Morning Post*, 17 May 1879
2 – As above
3– *The Morning Post*, 19 May 1879

Chapter 8
1 – *London Evening Standard*, 19 May 1879
2 – As above
3 – 'Our Canterbury Correspondent Writes' in the *London Evening Standard*, 19 May 1879
4 – As above
5 – As above
6 – As above
7 – 'A Brighton correspondent says …' The intelligence sent via telegram and published in the *London Evening Standard*, 20 May 1879
8 – As above
9 – *London Evening Standard*, 21 May 1879

Chapter 9
1 – Sometimes known as *Napoleon's Oraculum* and *The Book of Dreams* or *Dream-Book*, this text, said by eager publishers to have been by Napoleon's side constantly, was first translated into English in 1822, and subsequently went through many reprints and inspired many fortune-telling rivals. The text itself featured hundreds of closely typed prognostications, many of which now have the distinct feel of fortune cookies.
2 – As above

Chapter 10
1 – As reported in the *London Evening Standard*, as well as other newspapers around the country, 24 May 1879
2 – As above
3 – As above
4 – As above
5 – As reported in the *Daily News*, 27 May 1879. In contrast to the Standard's reporter finding Hannah Dobbs stout, the *News* correspondent was adamant that she was 'tall, good-looking'.
6 – As above
7 – As above
8 – As above
9 – As reported in *The Times*, 21 June 1879

Chapter 11

1 – As compiled in *Luxembourg: Land of Legends* by W.J. Taylor Whitehead (Constable, 1951)

2 – From Severin Bastendorff's own written testimony, reproduced later by the *Daily Telegraph* on 20 December 1879

3 – As above

4 – In the 1870s, the front page of each day's edition of *The Times* carried not news or photographs, but hundreds of small classified advertisements arranged by area of interest. The furniture advertisements were profuse.

5 – As above

6 – Henry Mayhew writing for the *Morning Chronicle* and published in London *Labour and London Poor*, Vol. 3 (Giffin Bohn, 1861)

7 – As described in *Little Germany: Exile and Asylum in Victorian England* by Rosemary Ashton (Oxford University Press, 1986)

Chapter 13

1 – As reported in numerous newspapers, including the *London Evening Standard* on 4 June 1879, and the *Illustrated Police News*. As with previous court reports, there are some variations; this chapter presents a synthesis of these reports.

2 – As above

3 – As reported by the *Illustrated Police News*, a few days later, on 14 July 1879

Chapter 14

1 – Grand Guignol was a turn-of-the-century French theatre genre specialising in baroque depictions of murder and violence, from dismemberments to scalping

2 – Editorial from *The Spectator*, 12 July 1879

3 – As above

4 – *The Rise and Fall of the Victorian Servant* by Pamela Horn (Gill and Macmillan, 1975)

5 – As above

6 – *Victorian Women's Magazines – An Anthology*, edited by Margaret Beetham and Kay Boardman (Manchester University Press, 2001)

7 – As above

Chapter 15

1 – The trial was reported in numerous newspapers; this chapter draws chiefly on the account given in *The Times*, 3 July 1879

2 – As above

3 – As above

4 – As above

Chapter 16

1 – As with the previous day's proceedings, the case was comprehensively covered in a wide variety of publications; and again, this chapter draws chiefly on the account given in *The Times*, 4 July 1879

2 – As above

3 – As above

4 – As above

5 – As above

6 – As above

7 – As above

8 – As above

Chapter 17

1 – This detail, together with a brief account of her life in what was then called Devonshire, appeared in the opening section of 'Hannah Dobbs' – a pamphlet published by George Purkess in September 1879. The autobiographical pamphlet, for which Hannah Dobbs received payment, was ghostwritten and its true author or authors are not named. It is available to read at The British Newspaper Archive at the British Library Reading Rooms, St Pancras, and at Boston Spa.

2 – *Victorian Womens' Magazines*, as above

3 – *The Rise and Fall of the Victorian Servant*, as above

4 – The phrase is from *Tess of the D'Urbevilles* by Thomas Hardy

5 – From the pamphlet 'Hannah Dobbs', in the first section of which she sketched out her early life and career
6 – As above
7 – As above

Chapter 18
1 – Details from the pamphlet 'Hannah Dobbs', as above
2 – As above
3 – As reported in *The Era*, October 1875

Chapter 19
1 – There is a file in the National Archives on the case chiefly composed of correspondence between various police departments. It is under the reference HO 144/41/8411
2 – From the pamphlet 'Hannah Dobbs', which although relatively short, was split into several sections. This was from the second, headlined 'The History of Miss Hacker while in Euston Square'.
3 – As above. Throughout the course of the mystery, Hannah Dobbs never gave a consistent account of the miscarriage; at one point, it was darkly alleged in a hint that Severin Bastendorff was partly responsible – that he 'gave her something'.
4 – As above. The hyper-focused nature of her memories of Matilda Hacker and the details of ordinary domestic life are in fascinating contrast to the ambiguity that is to follow.
5 – As above

Chapter 20
1 – From the pamphlet 'Hannah Dobbs', as above. It was the point in the narrative which Scotland Yard knew would have to be investigated with some speed, despite Dobbs subsequently refusing to answer any straightforward questions on the matter.
2 – From the back page of the pamphlet 'Hannah Dobbs', placed directly beneath the reproduction of her signature

Chapter 21
1 – This delightfully cynical and true sentiment – voiced in the *Kerry Evening Post*, 1 October 1879
2 – As reported in *The Morning Chronicle*, 5 October 1879
3 – The response from Hannah Dobbs, issued through her solicitor based in Grays Inn Square, was reported on the same day
4 – *The Morning Chronicle*, 5 October 1879
5 – *The Morning Chronicle*, 5 October 1879
6 – *London Evening Standard*, 11 October 1879

Chapter 22
1 – *The Times* gave a full report of the hearing on 1 November 1879
2 – As above
3 – As above

Chapter 23
1 – As reported in *The Times*, 4 December 1879
2 – The unexpurgated transcript – *The Times* moderated much of Dobbs' sensational evidence, redacting and substituting much of her explicit language with the term 'improprieties' – is available at www.oldbaileyonline.org which has many historical trials
3 – As reported in *The Times*, 5 December 5, 1879
4 – As above
5 – As above. The legal wranglings concerning the need for Peter Bastendorff to be either present or absent from the court had previously proceeded at some length.

Chapter 24
1 – *The Times*' leader was interestingly reproduced by *The North Devon Journal* on 11 December 1879; the local interest was of course intense
2 – *London Evening Standard*, 18 December 1879
3 – *Daily Telegraph*, 20 December 1879

4 – *Victorian Prison Lives* by Philip Priestley (Methuen 1985)
5 – As above
6 – *Daily Telegraph*, 20 December 1879
7 – *Victorian Prison Lives*, as above
8 – As above
9 – Severin Bastendorff's records are held in the London Metropolitan Archives. It is necessary to visit the site to see them. Nor are they filed directly under his name; rather, the Archives hold files of ledgers from the former Colney Hatch hospital, handwritten and kept alphabetically by patient name, year by year.
10 – As above
11 – As above

Chapter 25
1 – Reported in the *Pall Mall Gazette*, 27 January 1881
2 – As above
3 – Census details to be found at the London Metropolitan Archives; they are also available via subscription to ancestry.co.uk
4 – Quoted in *Psychiatry for the Poor* by Richard Hunter and Ida MacAlpine (Dawsons of Pall Mall, 1974)
5 – As displayed in the *London Evening Standard* on 3 October 1885
6 – Reported at his court case by the *London Evening Standard*, 13 January 1886
7 – As above
8 – As reported, among other newspapers, by the *Yorkshire Gazette,* 28 May 1887

Chapter 26
1 – As reported in *Reynolds Newspaper*, 3 April 1881

Chapter 27
1 – First published in 1903, and serialised across the country for several years afterwards, in newspapers such as the *Derbyshire Courier*.
2 – *Rooms of Mystery* by Elliott O'Donnell (Philip Allan and Co., 1931)
3 – *The Canterbury Belles*, staged by The Really Promising Company in 2017

Picture credits

p.1 Above: © Mary Evans Picture Library, below: Courtesy of The National Archives, ref. HO334/8/2587;
p.2 Above: © Historic Images/Alamy Stock Photo, below: © Mary Evans Picture Library;
p.3 Above: © Mary Evans Picture Library, below: Newspaper image © The British Library Board. All rights reserved. With thanks to The British Newspaper Archive (www.britishnewspaperarchive.co.uk);
p.4 Above: © 19th era 2/Alamy Stock Photo, below: Courtesy, The Lilly Library, Indiana University, Bloomington, Indiana;
p.5 Newspaper image © The British Library Board. All rights reserved. With thanks to The British Newspaper Archive (www.britishnewspaperarchive.co.uk);
p.6-7 © Mary Evans Picture Library;
p.8 Above: © London Metropolitan Archives, City of London, below: © Antiqua Print Gallery/Alamy Stock Photo.

Afterword:

A Bloomsbury and Somers Town Walk

Number 4, Euston Square – and, indeed, half of the square itself – is long gone. In the 1960s, the northern half was redeveloped as offices and a bus station for the railway station. But it is still possible, in some nearby corners, to see the city that Hannah Dobbs, Severin Bastendorff and Matilda Hacker moved through daily.

Just a few streets south of the Euston Road and St Pancras station is Mecklenburgh Square. Although hit in the Blitz, it has two beautiful surviving Georgian terraces which look over a large garden square. The terraces are close in feel and style to those of Euston Square in 1879. The wide road, at the weekend, is broadly traffic free. And it is possible to stand here, gazing at the houses, and imagine what it would be like filled with horse-drawn vehicles.

Now, dart a few hundred yards north, over the Euston Road, up past the red brick wonder of St Pancras International station, and thence to the extraordinary graveyard of St Pancras Old Church: the Hardy Tree – with all the gravestones pressed and clamouring around it – is still there. And, if you step inside the church, dating back to the eleventh century, you feel thrillingly removed from time.

Then beyond to Camley Street, Goods Way and the renovated wonder of the gas works, canal and rail-marshalling yards: Victorian industrial architecture on a vast scale, now repurposed for the modern city. The Bloomsbury promenading enjoyed by young Victorians has been transposed here triumphantly – now couples stroll along a landscaped towpath, past dancing fountains, enjoying the restaurants, theatres, nature reserve.

And, more than anyone, Matilda Hacker, dressed in her blue silk dress and sash, would have absolutely adored this fashionable concourse.

Afterword Two:

Illustrated Murder and Mayhem! – The Victorian Press

For those who loathe the excesses of today's popular press, it will be no consolation to hear that it used to be very much worse. Throughout the latter years of the Victorian age, the reading public thrilled to the gaudy, gory reporting featured in the *Illustrated Police News*. This was a publication that danced weekly along the borders of extreme bad taste. It was the prototype for the modern tabloid.

Despite the title, the paper – published on Saturdays – had no official connection with Scotland Yard. This was the news as gleaned from the courts and inquests: and reported with all the juiciest details. Also thrown into the mix were disasters: horse-drawn coach crashes, people falling off roofs, accidental drownings.

Of course, the case of Severin and Mary Bastendorff, Hannah Dobbs and 'The Euston Square Mystery' was rich material for the paper in 1879; not just the murder, but the unfolding multiple scandals of sexual impropriety. And the paper's proprietor, George Purkess, bought Hannah Dobbs's exclusive and wildly libellous story for a spin-off publication. It brought ruin to the Bastendorffs, but it was all just business for Purkess. He had started the paper in 1864, casting his news wide on a weekly basis to catch all sorts of sensational stories: shootings, suicides, domestic violence, colonial massacres.

The front page of every Saturday carried a variety of engraved illustrations: the highlights of that week's menu of mayhem. '*Shocking Suicide on a Train*' had an image of a train conductor finding a young man slumped in his seat, bleeding from the temple, a revolver at his feet. Elsewhere, there was an '*Assault with a Flat Iron*', with a husband pictured in the act of raising the weapon to his wife.

Some of these lurid stories were a little more baroque: '*Attempted Assassination of Two Priests*' was illustrated with a gunfight in a large Catholic church. '*The Policeman and The Ghost*' had a wonderfully creepy night-time engraving of a constable in a graveyard in Bootle being startled by a staring, wide-eyed woman in white.

There were lighter items, too. Amid the assaults and stabbings were '*Monkey Chased Across Town*' and '*Fall from an Omnibus*', as well as an unlikely tale concerning a sailor on a tropical island being speared just as he found a chest of treasure.

The paper covered disasters as well: on 28 December 1879, during a violent storm in the Tay Estuary, the railway bridge to Dundee collapsed and a train was derailed and fell calamitously into the churning waters beneath. The *Illustrated Police News* depicted various scenes from the tragedy, including an engraving of divers under the water fishing corpses from the carriages. There was no sense of holding back. (Indeed, the paper was keenly aware of questions of class: one of its illustrated panels of the disaster involved the 'search for the First Class carriage'.)

Though always popular, it hit a giddy new height in the late summer of 1888. '*Revolting and Mysterious Murder of a Woman in Whitechapel*' ran the headline beneath an engraving of a female corpse in an East End alley. Jack the Ripper's dark career had begun. But it was a while before the killer was given this name. The *Illustrated Police News* was there to report that '*the Monster of Whitechapel*' had struck again. It started carrying drawings of suspects wearing butcher's aprons; little scenes with early speech balloons featuring men accosting women outside East End pubs and offering them drinks ('*will you?*'); and local women preparing to fight back: '*Ready for the Whitechapel Fiend: Women Secretly Armed*' came with an illustration of ladies in Commercial Street holding knives.

The Ripper struck five times; sales went into the stratosphere. And amid the illustration panels were captions involving 'a foreign-looking gentleman' – the publication had always had an undercurrent of xenophobia.

By the turn of the century, the *News* was focusing ever more strongly on immigration, playing on racist notions of violent foreigners: this was the poisoned atmosphere in which the first serious government effort to restrict immigration – the Aliens Act of 1905 – was brought in. By this time, Purkess was dead (he had passed away in 1892), but the *News* lived on; surprisingly, into the 1930s.

It is instructive to look back at issues from its earlier years: of course, fascination with crime and murder has been with us since Cain and Abel. But what we see in these late Victorian engravings is a distinct aesthetic: the frozen, captured moment of violence or terror, the captions written in a stylised, florid hand. It is real-life given the patina of drama or fiction: knowing and brashly entertaining. The front page illustrations for 'The Euston Square Mystery', featuring portraits of Mr and Mrs Bastendorff, Hannah Dobbs and the house itself, conveyed a sense of a tasteful middle-class world, juxtaposed with Gothic menace and seamy scandal. George Purkess, in commissioning these images, did much to create an idea of the Victorian age that we still hold today. And however much we may disapprove of such vulgar excess, it remains to us undeniably and shamefully alluring.

Selected Further Reading

When you find yourself looking at a nineteenth-century street map, or a similarly old street photograph or engraving, there is sometimes that strong yearning to physically enter the past: to see the people, the shops and the traffic, to summon the sights and flavours, the smells in the air. While researching this book, there were so many times – buried in various volumes and original Victorian documentation – when I found myself in a trance-like state. From the prospect of mules pulling blue-liveried trams along the Euston Road to the dense, clanking, nocturnal industry of the great rail terminals to the first widespread use of electric light and the fascinating tokens of immigration, the London of 1879 seemed, at once, a different world and incredibly close at hand. For those who want to know more, there are a few fascinating books focusing in on these and related areas.

Little Germany: Exile and Asylum in Victorian England by Rosemary Ashton (Oxford University Press, 1986). This is a gorgeously detailed overview of German immigration to Britain in the nineteenth century, focusing on the poets, philosophers, political radicals, the composers, the authors. It is excellent on the ideas and the innovations that came with them. Quite apart from the ideas of Marx and Engels, there was also the popular introduction of the kindergarten and of German beers and lagers to public houses. Given that there currently seems to be such an intense focus on Europe and its future cohesion, it is wonderfully instructive to find out more about an age which had genuine freedom of movement.

The Victorian Home by Jenni Calder (Batsford, 1977). Again, for me, one of the most fascinating aspects of the Bastendorff story was the character of the household and the day-to-day nature of domestic life. Calder's book is illuminating, not only on the history of interiors, but also on their meanings and the psychological impulses that could be detected in the way homes were made.

Psychiatry for the Poor by Richard Hunter and Ida Macalpine (Dawsons of Pall Mall, 1974). For the part of this story that ends in the Colney Hatch hospital, I confess I went in with heavily weighted preconceptions about the nature and quality of Victorian mental health care. This book is a corrective to that, tracing the development of the first properly medical institutions, with specific focus on Colney Hatch and the efforts made not only to cure, but also to treat patients with kindness and compassion.

A Magazine of Her Own? Domesticity and Desire in the Woman's Magazine 1800–1914 by Margaret Beetham (Routledge, 1996). I was very keen to understand about the growth of womens' magazines in the late nineteenth century and the sorts of features that appealed to readers then: this wonderful book contains many reproduced images and is of serious social historical fascination. One might imagine that it was a more innocent age: yet there appeared to be a sly, humorous knowingness about some magazine features.

Victorian Prison Lives by Philip Priestley (Methuen, 1985). Again, the Victorian prison system is one that we imagine we are at least partly familiar with; this book both confirms and confounds preconceptions of punishment and rehabilitation. Throughout the Victorian era, attitudes towards penal servitude swung like a pendulum: periods when liberal reformists came forward, demanding better opportunities for former convicts; and times when prison meant retribution through soul-crushingly futile labour and floggings for minor infractions.

The Rise and Fall of the Victorian Servant by Pamela Horn (Gill and Macmillan, 1975). There are so many layers to explore in stories of servants and employers; not just in terms of exploitation and low pay, but also in terms of how essential strangers sharing the same home in these circumstances negotiated means of living with one another.

The Nether World by George Gissing (Smith, Elder, 1889). Written in 1889, but set some ten years beforehand, Gissing's novel is a powerfully evocative piece of social realism. While in previous decades, even the poorest of Dickens's characters were animated with colour and eccentricity and energy, here are Londoners who are crushed under a sky that seems perpetually low and grey. Set in and around the streets of Clerkenwell, about a mile away from Euston Square, it also gives a valuable taste of the sharp contrasts between different districts and even streets; and also a sense of the lives that are lived behind doors that never usually get a second glance.

The Secret Agent by Joseph Conrad (Methuen, 1907). Though written (and set) some years after the Euston Square mystery, this profoundly unsettling story of anarchists and radicals and terrorists prowling the narrow London streets feels in some ways like the culmination of the real-life political fervour that had been building in the taverns around Fitzrovia and Euston Square – embodied, as we saw, in the case of Inspector Hagen arresting Johann Most in 1881. Here is a city seething with firebrand figures from Germany to Russia: from spies to bomb throwers. And, indeed, in real life, there is a fascinating and direct line from the socialists handing out revolutionary literature in the 1870s, and Stalin's sojourn in Whitechapel at the turn of the century.

In addition, there are some rather more obscure titles that can be found in the stacks of the London Library and the British Library. Among them are Charles Wittingham's *The Wilds of London* (Chatto and Windus, 1881) and *The Golden Guide to London* (Chiswick Press, 1879), roughly synchronous with the Euston Square mystery and quite simply captivating in their own right – peregrinations through the Victorian city, the writer gazing upon all the quite new marvels that it boasted. There is also the magisterial six-volume *Old and New London (Illustrated)* by Walter Thornberry (Cassell, Petter, Galpin, 1881), and taking us, district-by-district, through every corner of London with exquisite engravings. These volumes are a little more widely available and are worth seeking out as works of art in their own right. They are a glimpse of huge Victorian pride in the capital.

Also beguiling are works on the development of music hall (one such is DF Cheshire's *Music Hall In Britain* (David and Charles, 1974); and the story of Euston Station itself in Alison and Peter Smithson's *The Euston Arch and the Growth of the London, Midland and Scottish Railway* (Thames and Hudson, 1968), with a foreword by Nikolaus Pevsner himself. And indeed, for those who want a further taste of the rural world in which the Bastendorff family grew up, WJ Taylor Whitehead provides a charming insight in the very rare volume *Luxembourg: Land of Legends* (Constable, 1951).

Acknowledgements

First of all, I would like to draw attention to a quiet (and wonderful) institution called the London Metropolitan Archives, based in Clerkenwell, which proved beyond value in research. These archives contain so much beautifully preserved and catalogued historical material, from house leases to handwritten ledgers to vintage photographs. For further information, visit www.cityoflondon.gov.uk/things-to-do/london-metropolitan-archives.

There is another interesting archive with a range of material concerning Somers Town and St Pancras at the Holborn Library, 32–38 Theobalds Road, London WC1X, which all can visit (and which in itself is a terrific piece of architecture from 1960).

Huge gratitude to my brilliant agent Anna Power for wisdom and encouragement and enthusiasm, and to all at White Lion Press: Richard Green, Jennifer Barr, Kerry Enzor, Charlotte Frost, Julia Shone and Stacey Cleworth for pretty much the same. And particular thanks to Aruna Vasudevan at The Literary Shed for her sharp, insightful editing.

Sinclair McKay lives in the East End of London, in the shadow of Canary Wharf. He previously worked for the *Daily Telegraph* and the *Mail on Sunday.* His previous books – ranging from the stories of the Bletchley Park codebreakers to the history of rambling – have been linked by a focus on English social history. When not researching in archives, he is fascinated by the living history of London's streets: the traces and tokens left behind by different ages.